Preface

The 1996 Yearbook is designed for classroom teachers. It includes examples, resources, and success stories to assist educators in providing their students with the necessary skills to be successful at work and in life.

The Yearbook is divided into three parts:

Part I is entitled *Examining Business and Education Environments.* Business education has a strong history of providing education for and about business. The first six chapters address issues relating to the changing needs of business and provide multiple examples of successful education programs. Chapters discuss developing apprenticeship opportunities, creating business alliances, and modifying traditional class schedules.

Part II, *Teaching in Today's Classroom Environment,* addresses the ever expanding set of skills teachers need in secondary and postsecondary education. The first three chapters in Part II provide an overview of learning principles, a discussion on diversity, and an explanation of authentic assessment. The remaining chapters in Part II encourage educators to use technology and innovative teaching strategies to reach and challenge students.

Part III focuses on *Invigorating the Business Curriculum.* The SCANS report challenged educators to address a multitude of skills in the classroom. Part III provides a wealth of ideas, resources, and teaching strategies in such topics as dealing with change, international business, ethics, workplace readiness, applied academics, team building, and problem solving.

Classroom Strategies: The Methodology of Business Education is a refereed yearbook. Chapters were reviewed by at least three persons. Members of the editorial review board were:

Brenda Erickson, John A. Logan College
  Carterville, Illinois
Terry Frame, University of South Carolina
  Columbia, South Carolina
Elizabeth Goodrich, Central Michigan University
  Mount Pleasant, Michigan
Pat Graves, Eastern Illinois University
  Charleston, Illinois
Kenneth Horn, Southwest Missouri State University
  Springfield, Missouri
Arnola Ownby, Southwest Missouri State University
  Springfield, Missouri

Lena Cunningham Smith, Southwest Missouri State University
    Springfield, Missouri
Lynn Wasson, Southwest Missouri State University
    Springfield, Missouri
Bonnie White, Auburn University
    Auburn, Alabama

Heidi Perreault, Editor

Classroom Strategies: The Methodology of Business Education

NATIONAL BUSINESS EDUCATION YEARBOOK, NO. 34

1996

Editor:
HEIDI R. PERREAULT
Southwest Missouri State University
Springfield, Missouri

Published by:
National Business Education Association
1914 Association Drive
Reston, Virginia 22091

CLASSROOM STRATEGIES: THE METHODOLOGY OF BUSINESS EDUCATION

Copyright 1996

NATIONAL BUSINESS EDUCATION ASSOCIATION
1914 ASSOCIATION DRIVE
RESTON, VIRGINIA

$15

ISBN 0-933964-47-1

Contents

PART I
EXAMINING BUSINESS AND EDUCATION ENVIRONMENTS

PART I

EXAMINING BUSINESS AND EDUCATION ENVIRONMENTS

CHAPTER 1

Business and Industry Need Qualified Workers

WANDA L. STITT-GOHDES

The University of Georgia, Athens, Georgia

Businesses in the United States continue to have a difficult time recruiting and retaining a well-qualified workforce. As we rapidly approach the 21st century, the changing demographics and changing demands of the workforce require concomitant change to take place in our classrooms. What follows provides an overview of the workforce of today, the changing demands of the workforce for tomorrow, and implications for education for the 21st century.

THE WORKFORCE OF TODAY

Today's workforce is influenced by a number of factors including low productivity, *uni*-skilled workers, and changing demographics.

Low Productivity. From the time of the industrial revolution the United States has been a worldwide leader in industrial growth and development. This growth was matched by an unparalleled standard of living. Clearly this would not have been possible without an educated workforce. This growth was combined with a workforce made up primarily of immigrants who were used to hard work and who wanted better lives for their children. It was the "American dream."

It appears today, though, that the dream, if not shattered, has begun to crack. While productivity levels in this country have not declined, they have not increased since the 1970s. In fact, "From . . . 1950 through 1989, U.S. productivity growth averaged only 1.9 percent per year, which was lower than 13 other competitor countries" (Kolberg & Smith, 1992, p. 4). Kolberg & Smith further state that much of this decline in productivity may be attributed to "unsatisfactory levels of educational and skill development" (p. 26). The following example better explains this dilemma: " . . . in Japan, 19.1 manhours of labor are required to assemble an automobile. At Japanese auto plants in the United States, 19.5 manhours are expended building the average car; the average number of assembly hours for a car manufactured in U.S. auto plants is 26.5" (Kolberg & Smith, pp. 25-26).

Uni-skilled Workers. While competitor countries embraced a Theory Z or quality circles approach to teamwork, the United States remained steadfastly committed to Frederick Taylor's scientific management approach. "Taylor's system called for very specific divisions of work, with laborers doing nothing more than repetitive, physical assembly. It was the right system for the standardized, mass production needs of its time, but it is the wrong system for today" (Kolberg & Smith, p. 37).

This approach to mass production also mass produced uni-skilled workers ill-prepared to solve problems, to embrace teamwork, or to think critically. Until recently, this uni-skill development was present in high school class-rooms across the country and continues to be reflected in the limitations of the adult workforce. "The National Assessment of Education Progress (NAEP) found that practically all young adults who finish high school are able to use printed information to accomplish routine and uncomplicated tasks. For many, however, these skills are so rudimentary that comprehension and ability to utilize the information is minimal" (Bosworth, 1992, p. 39). So while today's workers can read and follow directions, they are not able to meet the more rigorous challenges of critical thinking and problem solving required of the workforce for the 21st century.

Bosworth states further that many companies request on-the-job training for specialized skill development. However, he warns, "This kind of training does not constitute a system of skill formation that will provide continuous support . . . . These firms will need multiskilled, flexible workers who com-bine a solid educational foundation with technical proficiency and learning-to-learn skills" (p. 53). In fact, Bosworth states that what is required to be successful in the workplace may not be learned in school. He further states that "Problem solving, motivation, negotiation, and leadership are skills so intimately connected to the context of the learning environment that they probably can be developed only in the workplace" (p. 55).

Changing Demographics. The workforce of the 21st century will include more older people, immigrants, minorities, women, and the functionally illiterate.

Apolloni, Feichtner, and West (1991) report that "By 2000, the average age of the work force will increase from 36 to 39. One out of every 6 Americans will be 65 or older by the year 2032 (currently 1 out of every 9 Americans is 65 or older)" (p. 6). Frequently employers have released older workers and hired younger workers at lower salaries as a cost-cutting measure. That practice may not continue as the pool of younger talent is shrinking and, in fact, is pro-jected to "decline by 8 percent in the coming decade" (Apolloni et al., p. 6).

Frequently those who immigrate to the United States do not speak English, or they speak English as a second language. Two-thirds of the 600,000 immi-grants entering the United States annually through the remainder of this century will enter the workforce and will include "23 percent of all new workers" (Apolloni et al., p. 6). These persons will have extraordinarily diffi-cult times finding a job, maturing in that job, and becoming successful long-term employees.

Because of the projected numbers of immigrants, society, industry, and education have a vested interest in their acquiring the requisite skills—both language and vocational—to enter and remain in the workforce. The more quickly these individuals can enter and remain in the workforce, the better their chances for socioeconomic success and independence. This will also benefit employers seeking qualified employees.

The following facts paint a startling picture of those who will be entering the workforce: "Thirty percent of students in grades K-12 are educationally disadvantaged due to poverty, cultural obstacles, or linguistic barriers; and

30 percent of students entering high school will leave prior to graduation" (Apolloni et al., p. 7). The worst part is that those individuals without a high school diploma have virtually isolated themselves from even marginal levels of successful employment and subsequent socioeconomic success. The impact of this loss to the individual, the workforce, and society is incalculable. In fact, one may observe that society has indeed already begun to feel the impact of this via increasing levels of violence by the disenfranchised.

Finally, the impact of increasing numbers of minorities and females will be felt throughout the workforce. The increasing influx of these groups may require employers to provide services either not needed or not valued in the past. Apolloni et al. reported "Blacks, women, Asians, Hispanics, and other races will account for more than 90 percent of all labor-force growth by 2000. Nearly 61 percent of women of working age will be employed" (p. 6). These groups may need support services such as child care, counseling, and language assistance. The availability of these services is critical to their becoming successfully employed, thus also becoming contributors to America's economic base.

Employers now complain of the cost to business and industry of providing remedial instruction that should occur at the primary and secondary school levels. Educators are caught in the twin pinches of declining revenues and rapidly rising costs of caring for the burgeoning numbers of students in special populations. It is important to note that many who are categorized as special-populations students do succeed in the workforce on their own without external support systems; however, to deny support services that might be needed by these special populations is also to deny them the opportunity to become contributing members to society, both on a personal and economic basis. Neither these individuals nor America can afford either.

An economy stifled by stagnant productivity levels, supported by a uni-skilled workforce, and faced with dramatic changes in its demographic profile is not an economy that can meet the challenges of the global marketplace. Nor is it the kind of economy that can continue to provide the economic base and standard of living for which it has become famous.

Only through a multiskilled, responsible workforce with opportunities for all for full participation can the U. S. workforce for the 21st century again become a major participant in the global economy. This means that educators must closely examine the changing demands of the workforce of tomorrow with an eye toward program review and revision to best meet the needs of all our students.

THE CHANGING DEMANDS OF THE WORKFORCE OF TOMORROW

While a "Tayloristic" model might have sufficed in the workplace of yesterday, it clearly is not appropriate for the workforce of the 21st century. No longer are employees at any level able to be uni-skilled, independent workers. A real need exists for all who enter the workforce to be problem solvers and critical thinkers, cooperative and responsible workers, and highly-skilled, multitalented workers.

Problem Solvers and Critical Thinkers. With the increase of corporate restructuring and the movement of decision making to administrative support personnel, employees need to be able to not only recognize a problem but also to have some degree of intellectual wherewithal to attempt a solution. In the best of workplace climates, employees are encouraged to think critically about a problem and/or problem situation and subsequently be creative in reaching a solution. What exactly does that mean? In most instances, it means moving beyond the normal, sequential thought processes and on to innovation. It encourages problem solving unfettered by traditional constraints.

The payoff for such encouragement may often be great for the employer. A workplace climate that fosters, encourages, and rewards creativity also fosters and encourages employee ownership and cooperation—a win-win situation for everyone.

Cooperative Workers. Cooperative workers understand the value of teamwork. Carnevale, Gainer, and Meltzer (1990) tell us that "Teamwork skills are critical for improving individual task accomplishment at work because practical innovations and solutions are reached sooner through cooperative behavior" (p. 32). Employers may need to provide specific help such as interpersonal skills training to help employees learn best how to work with others.

Carnevale, as cited in Carnevale et al. (1990), writes "that there are two ways to increase productivity. 'The first is by increasing the intensity with which we utilize [human] resources (working harder), and the second is by increasing the efficiency with which we mix and use available resources (working smarter)' " (p. 32). In fact "the ability of working teams to learn together—is the most significant among human factors in producing income and productivity growth" (Carnevale et al., pp. 32-33).

Responsible Workers. A responsible employee is one who is accountable for his or her work. Responsible individuals recognize that when they do a good job, their employer benefits, which in turn reaps benefits for the employee. It also means that a responsible worker is self-directed, able to move on to the next job when one is finished without having to wait to be told what is next.

In fact, these requirements for a responsible worker are supported by the Secretary's Commission on Achieving Necessary Skills (SCANS), which has identified these five competencies as critical for success in the workforce:

1. The ability to allocate resources, such as time, money, and materials

2. Good interpersonal skills that allow workers to work on teams, to teach others, to serve customers

3. The ability to acquire and evaluate information and data, including the ability to use computers

4. The ability to monitor and to evaluate systems and performance so that they can be improved

5. The ability to utilize technology and tools (Kolberg & Smith, p. 135).

The Commission also strongly suggests that the following three characteristics complement the aforementioned five competencies:

1. basic skills, such as reading, writing, arithmetic, speaking, and listening

2. thinking skills, such as creativity, decision making, problem solving

3. personal qualities such as individual responsibility, self-esteem, and integrity (Kolberg & Smith, p. 136).

In addition, recognizing the immediacy of need, Goals 2000 and the National Skills Standard Project sponsored by the U.S. Departments of Education and Labor have begun to address these workforce needs.

Highly Skilled, Multitalented Workers. When asked what qualities they look for in employees, employers quickly respond with "basic skills: the ability to read, write, and do math." However, further investigation by Carnevale, Gainer, & Meltzer (1988) reveal that, in fact, employers want much more and that, unfortunately, "Deficiency in basic skills stands as the final barrier to employment of the poor and disadvantaged" (p. 6). If many of those young people entering the workforce are unable to demonstrate even basic skills, there is little hope for them to become highly skilled, multitalented workers.

Based on the forecasted changes in the workplace and increased global competitiveness, Carnevale et al. (1988) have developed this list of the seven skills employers want.

Learning To Learn. While the vast majority of employees have been a part of a learning system, the odds are very good that they were never confronted with the notion of figuring out how they best learn something. Because lifelong learning is critical to long-term success in the workplace, learning to learn becomes a keystone in the route to success for all workers in the 21st century.

Reading, Writing, Arithmetic. Candidly, these skills have not always been used to the greatest extent possible in the workplace. Through no fault of their own, many employees succeeded in the past because of brawn rather than brains. The probability of that continuing in tomorrow's workplace is shrinking daily.

Listening and Oral Communication. "The average person spends 8.4 percent of communications time writing, 13.3 percent reading, 23 percent speaking, and 55 percent listening" (p. 11). While much is made of writing the English language in school, little effort is placed on developing effective listening and oral communication skills, the two avenues we use most in our professional and personal lives.

Creative Thinking/Problem Solving. As discussed earlier, a firm's success or failure may be based on its ability to quickly isolate a problem and find an appropriate solution. The extent to which employees' creative thinking and problem-solving energies are encouraged and utilized can directly impact the efficiency and effectiveness of any organization.

Self-Esteem, Goal Setting/Motivation, Personal/Career Development. Increasingly, career development literature has begun to address the important role that self-esteem and self-efficacy play in an individual's career choice and development. As the workforce includes more immigrants, minorities, and women who are seeking legitimate careers rather than jobs, more effort must be devoted to helping employees learn about the options available and how to make the best choice.

Interpersonal Skills, Negotiation, & Teamwork. Because of the increased attention to teamwork in the workplace and the increased numbers of immigrant, minority, and women employees, workers for the 21st century will need strong interpersonal skills. Success in interpersonal skills, negotiation, and teamwork does not just happen. It stems from specific training opportunities beginning in elementary school and continuing throughout life.

Organizational Effectiveness & Leadership. Simply because one is employed by an organization does not automatically translate into success. Tomorrow's workers need to be able to understand how organizations work and how they fit within that structure to become effective employees.

At the dawn of the 21st century, business as usual will no longer enable us to successfully compete with a foreign labor pool that is better trained, more efficient in the workplace, and flexible in meeting rapidly changing consumer needs. The successful employee will be able to critically analyze a situation and find a solution while working cooperatively with fellow employees. These workers will be able to make the transition smoothly from one work role to another, recognizing that both their success and the success of the organization depend on their communication and interpersonal skills as well as organizational effectiveness.

IMPLICATIONS FOR EDUCATION

In order for workers for the 21st century to develop needed job acquisition and retention skills, the educational community is faced with several challenges. These include integration of vocational and academic education, relevant learning, and career development. While these may ring of a "taste it again for the first time" mentality, like the corn flakes advertisement, they are, indeed, not only appropriate, but much needed for tomorrow's workers.

Integration of Vocational and Academic Education. It is increasingly obvious that the current, "theory based" secondary school model of instruction serves well only a small portion, perhaps 20 percent, of the student population. For those entering the workforce of tomorrow, neither an academic nor a vocational education alone is sufficient preparation. In fact, Kolberg and Smith (1992) report that "Nearly all high school students take at least one vocational course, but only 30 percent of high school students focus on vocational training in preparation for specific occupations" (p. 49).

To bring vocational and academic education together, incorporating both theory and application through contextual learning is the first step in preparing individuals for success in the workplace of tomorrow. From many perspectives, business education has been a leader in an applied approach to education and work.

Historically, business educators have successfully used simulations in accounting and office procedures classes. This is an excellent foundation from which to forge relationships with other vocational educators as well as academic educators. For example, business educators may work with marketing educators to prepare layout and designs for a marketing plan or develop spreadsheets for agriculture production classes. But business educators also need to move down the halls to the English teachers and develop situations where the students use a word processing class to further develop and refine their writing assignments.

This integrated instruction becomes increasingly important for entry-level employees for whom little or no formal on-the-job training is provided.

The recent Tech Prep and School-to-Work initiatives provide an excellent window of opportunity through which an individual can begin to develop the skills needed in the workplace by actually learning them "on the job." Tech Prep, cooperative learning, apprenticeship programs, and other School-to-Work initiatives are important in helping high school students achieve necessary skills to ensure survival in the workplace of the 21st century.

Adults who face the necessity of enrolling in advanced skills training must embrace the concept of lifelong learning. This concept is critical in order to remain competitive with the ever-changing demand for new knowledge and new levels of technical ability.

Making Learning Real Through Real Partnerships. The Tech Prep and School-to-Work initiatives provide excellent opportunities for students to work side by side with experts in a workplace setting, similar to the apprenticeship programs which are so successful in Germany. These situations are far removed from the days when students found a job—often menial—through their own initiative and for which they received some kind of credit. The apprenticeship programs really provide a situation where the student works with a master of a particular skill or trade and exits the learning experience with a real, marketable skill.

A carefully chosen, active advisory committee can also be extraordinarily useful at the secondary and postsecondary levels. Here future employers can provide valuable input with regard to both program development and emerging technology requirements. These community employers can also provide much-needed teacher training by bringing teachers into the workplace; this can quickly translate into improved student learning. This training may take on a variety of configurations: one-day, off-campus workshops; in-service workshops; or part- or full-time summer employment.

These new initiatives provide a winning situation for everyone: Students get state-of-the-art learning opportunities; teachers are able to stay current with office practices, computer hardware, and new software applications; and future employers should have a well-qualified workforce to choose from.

Early and Continuing Career Development. For some young people, the following often depicts the current student approach to career development:

Alice:	"Would you please tell me which way I ought to go from here?"
Cheshire Cat:	"Well, that depends a good deal on where you want to go."
Alice:	"I don't much care where."
Cheshire Cat:	"Then it doesn't matter which way you go."

Lewis Carroll

Alice's Adventures in Wonderland, 1865

And too often this lack of goals is compounded by the fact that students' career development begins upon their graduation from high school, leaving few, if any, windows of opportunity for career planning open.

An optimum situation for the student, the economy, and our society is for career awareness, choice, and development to be a lifelong process, beginning at the elementary school level. Here children can be exposed to a wide variety of careers, both traditional and nontraditional for their gender. The idea is to stimulate early on their thinking about the world of work.

The awareness process continues through middle school, where some career exploration begins to take place. Here the students have opportunities to "taste" a variety of courses that can lead to an even wider variety of careers. The optimum situation, then, is that somewhere along the way the student makes a conscientious decision to pursue a particular career path.

Unfortunately, it is often at the secondary level where this career train may become derailed. Indeed, Gray (1993) supports the premise that the Taylorist approach embraced by industry has also been embraced by educators. He reported on a study conducted by Oakes that "suggests that teachers (consciously or unconsciously) treat bright students as future peers and the less bright as future subordinates" (p. 372). Oakes asked teachers what they perceived to be the five most important lessons learned by high school students. Curiously, or perhaps not so curiously, "Teachers hoped the brightest would learn to think logically and critically (important skills for future leaders), while they hoped that the less bright would learn good work habits, respect for authority, and practical or work-related skills (all important attributes for future subordinates)" (p. 372).

This is a scenario which we must work to avoid. Clearly those important lessons learned by the brightest are requisite skills for all who enter the workforce of the 21st century. And having a predisposed idea or attitude about a student's abilities based on factors other than intellectual aptitude effectively prohibits that student from being a full participant in the workforce, in society, and in the economy of our country.

SUMMARY

As we move into the 21st century, it is clear that the workforce of today is quite different from that which will become the workforce of tomorrow. The impact of low productivity, uni-skilled workers, and changing demographics is already being felt throughout our nation's economy.

Our educational community is in a prime position to positively impact the workforce of tomorrow. We know that business and industry need problem solvers and critical thinkers, cooperative and responsible workers, and highly skilled, multitalented workers. It is our responsibility to provide the educational opportunities to help prepare students for this demanding employment arena.

What must education do? We need to provide ample opportunities for the integration of academic and vocational education in a meaningful way. We need to develop strong relationships with the business communities where we live and work. These relationships are required for successful school-to-work opportunities. And we must provide genuine, early, and continuing career development for all students. After all, each and every student will ultimately become a member of the workforce.

REFERENCES

Apolloni, T., Feichtner, S. H., & West, L. L. (1991, Fall). Learners and workers in the year 2001. *The Journal for Vocational Special Needs Education. 14,* 5-10.

Bosworth, B. (1992). State strategies for manufacturing modernization. In E. Ganzglass (Ed.), *Excellence at work; Policies option papers for the National Governors' Association* (pp. 15-70). Kalamazoo, MI: W. E. Upjohn Institute for Employment Research.

Carnevale, A. P., Gainer, L. J., & Meltzer, A. S. (1990). *Workplace basics, the essential skills employers want.* San Francisco: Jossey-Bass.

Carnevale, A. P., Gainer, L. J., & Meltzer, A. S. (1988). *Workplace basics: The skills employers want.* Alexandria, VA: The American Society for Training & Development.

Gray, K. (1993, January). Why we will lose: Taylorism in America's high schools. *Phi Delta Kappan. 74,* 370-374.

Kolberg, W. H., & Smith, F. C. (1992). *Rebuilding America's workforce: Business strategies to close the competitive gap.* Homewood, IL: Business One Irwin.

The American heritage illustrated encyclopedic dictionary. (1987). Boston, MA: Houghton Mifflin.

CHAPTER 2
Successful Business Alliances

RUTH K. SHAFER

Hazelwood School District, Florissant, Missouri

Education and the business community can no longer exist as separate and unrelated entities. They must join together to communicate and lead our students into a productive life for the 21st century. School/business alliances are emerging today across the country to educate each other and provide a mechanism for dialogue and planning. Each entity has a defined path that will lead into the 21st century. This chapter will outline a generic model of developing an alliance and highlight several types of successful school/business alliances that could be adapted for your local school setting.

WHAT IS A SCHOOL/BUSINESS ALLIANCE?

It is important for prospective business/education partners to understand that partnerships do not live by good will alone. They take hard work and good management. Businesses and schools are structured differently and some-times have problems communicating. Experience shows that it is essential to have someone in the school district in regular contact with someone in the business, to plan, iron out difficulties, and keep the channels open.

Well constructed partnerships between schools and businesses are a good response to concerns Americans have about education. In a complex and inter-related world, it is becoming clear that energy and resources from the wider community are needed if schools are to succeed in educating all youngsters.

A partnership is a mutually supportive arrangement between a business and a school or school district, often in the form of a written contract, in which the partners commit themselves to specific goals and activities intended to benefit students.

Partnerships may involve business employees as tutors, mentors, coaches, or guest lecturers in the partner schools; a business may or may not make material or monetary contributions as well, but people resources are the most important. In good partnerships, schools provide something to their partners in return; this may be intangible, such as good will, or a tangible benefit, such as use of school facilities or academic resources.

Partnerships are often "brokered" by a third party—chamber of commerce or school district coordinator, for example. Some partners find each other, especially if they are neighbors. Many businesses choose to partner with schools within walking distance of their offices or plants, and a school may look for a nearby business that has special resources or expertise the school needs.

These relationships have led employers toward a river of resources and helped to create a linkage bridge to improve the whole. They also are largely advisory with the primary function of promoting information exchange. For employers this may mean advising a school about labor market trends, industry skill needs, or the specifics of education or training programs that will prepare individuals to find jobs in the community. It may even mean an employer encouraging a school to train students in specific occupations by lending equipment for the training or by consulting on curriculum design or delivery. For the school, this kind of relationship hinges on providing feedback to the employer about the school's capabilities in preparing the community's future workforce or suggesting ways that employers can assist in constructing strategies to meet industry needs. Such connections should result in the employer hiring individuals trained by the school, which contributes to the whole community.

Successful partnerships have agreed-upon and well defined goals and objectives. The business may wish, for example, to support the mathematics or science program of a school or district. Together they work out activities that will implement their objectives. Once they are joined, partners should expect to stay together for a long time. Though the partnership may change and evolve, commitment and continuity are essential for success, especially when dealing with youngsters in the elementary and secondary schools.

The school needs to make clear its instructional objectives, define its needs, plan for and structure the business interventions, and monitor and report the outcomes. In good partnerships, all activities undertaken by the school and business together are intended to enhance the educational experiences of students.

The business, in turn, may offer jobs for students, incentives for academic achievement, training for teachers, use of its labs or equipment, management expertise, instructional enrichment, one-to-one support for students at-risk of failing or dropping out of school, tutoring sessions in basic skills, career awareness, or special opportunities for gifted youngsters.

STRENGTHS OF SCHOOL/BUSINESS ALLIANCES IN ENHANCING TEACHER KNOWLEDGE AND TEACHING SKILLS

Business people work directly with students, one on one, or in groups, to improve skills, motivate performance, or enrich the curriculum. Depending on the nature of the business and the identified needs of the schools, the partnership may bring business personnel into the schools as volunteer tutors, lecturers, sponsors, coaches, mentors, or classroom aides. Good partnerships try to match the special expertise of businesses in science, mathematics, technology, writing, or the arts with the instructional program of the schools, so students can see real-world applications of the skills they are studying. In some partnerships, the business partner opens its laboratories or offices to students for training on specialized equipment, or for career awareness. Other partnerships may operate after-school or Saturday coaching or tutoring programs, or staff homework hot lines.

In instructional support activities, the business partner works in collaboration with school staff to further the schools' instructional objectives. These may include scholarships and summer employment, special trips, luncheons, banquets, books, or minor items such as tee shirts, caps, or buttons. Incentives work best when people from the partnerships are in regular contact with students.

Staff Development. Businesses may help schools with staff development by offering summer internships to teachers or funding attendance at professional meetings and seminars. They may make corporate expertise in management and strategic planning available to school boards and administrators. In science, mathematics, technology, publishing, and other fields in which changes have occurred since teachers were trained, business can provide state-of-the-art updating on equipment and content. In turn, schools, particularly high schools, can offer career development courses and basic skills training for business employees. Working in conjunction with school boards and administrators in the development of guidelines and selection methods, business may create and/or sponsor recognition programs for outstanding teachers and administrators as part of the overall staff development effort.

Curriculum Development. In some partnerships, business partners with technical expertise have developed supplemental instructional materials to augment the regular school curriculum and textbooks. This is an advanced step in most partnerships and should be taken in cooperation with the school district's curriculum development staff.

Material and Financial Support. Business partners and school administrators often think of this as the first step in partnership development, but it should probably be the last. Experience has proven that involving people is more important for good partnership development and is more likely to improve education than simply having the corporation supply material and financial support. Donating a computer lab to a school, for example, may be an ineffective strategy unless the business partner and the school have worked out the problems of staff support, identification and integration of instructional objectives, training, and maintenance involved in the gift. Schools often need and welcome material support, but it should be accompanied by people support. For partnerships to succeed, it is essential that business partners "buy into" partnerships with an involved, participative level of commitment that may include, but should extend beyond material and financial support.

BENEFITS TO SCHOOL AND CORPORATE COMMUNITY

All participants of a business/education partnership benefit and realize positive outcomes. Each participant has unique experiences that provide growth and a better understanding of the other partner's role in society. The following descriptors offer a partial list of benefits:

Students

- Better understanding of real world application of abstract concepts
- Better command of the English language and its use in the workplace
- Increased confidence, self-esteem, and competence; enhanced maturity; increased pride in specific activities

- Improvements in study habits; improved grades, tests scores, and passing rates for standardized tests on practical applications of knowledge
- Better attendance; more interest in school
- Increased awareness of career opportunities; help in getting into better colleges; summer/vacation/part-time employment; scholarships

Teachers

- Help in covering the assigned curriculum; new approaches and ideas that can be incorporated into examples for teaching concepts
- Concrete examples of theory and academic concepts
- Knowledge of technical skills and abilities students need to prepare for technical careers
- Stimulation of teacher interest to teach subjects (especially important in elementary schools); increased morale
- Interaction with other professionals; respect and recognition for their efforts; higher self-esteem; building motivation and enthusiasm; rejuvenation
- Better understanding of the business community

School system

- Expansion of educational opportunities for students
- Access to experts for special courses; supplies and/or equipment that school systems couldn't justify; increased community support for school systems
- Maintenance of current and relevant curriculum; variation in the typical teaching method and setting, adding another dimension to classroom instruction
- Local and national recognition for outstanding achievements
- Link for students and teachers to an upper level of curriculum development
- Activities that can lead to a variety of assistance (gifts, donations of equipment, purchases of video tapes and other special teaching material;) persons to serve on curriculum advisory committees

Business volunteers

- Enjoyment from working with students and seeing them learn
- Sense of social responsiveness and contribution to the community
- Elevating the excellence of the school system in which volunteers and children attend
- Understanding of what is going on in school today
- Creative outlet for some employees; access to school facilities and special programs
- Way to contribute to the community; positive public image with students, school officials, and parents
- Improvement of the school system, which is helpful in recruiting new employees
- Access to a talented local labor pool of students and teachers, enlargement and enhancement of future job applicant pool
- Development of management, communication, and presentation skills and leadership abilities of employees; mechanism for team-building

STRENGTHS OF SCHOOL/BUSINESS ALLIANCES IN PREPARING STUDENTS FOR THE WORKPLACE

Vocational and job-skill training programs can be enhanced by schools utilizing business facilities, training materials and procedures, state-of-the-art equipment, and employees as supervisors and credentialed teachers. By working in partnerships in this manner, schools are able to utilize the most current trends, processes, expertise, and equipment that school budgets cannot afford or provide.

Compacts and Agreements for Employment and Employability Training. Some business/education partnerships focus specifically on the responsibility of the school to provide education for employment and the responsibility of the business to employ graduates of the school system. Compacts between schools and employers in a number of cities represent this kind of partnership, in which the businesses pledge priority hiring in return for the student's achievement of certain academic, attendance, and other standards. Cooperative work experience opportunities are available for students through a business/education partnership, and the School-to-Work initiative will provide guidelines and opportunities for cooperative curriculum-related work experience; for internships and work experiences during secondary and apprenticeship postsecondary training; and mentoring and one-on-one job shadow experiences for all students.

Counseling and Guidance. Business/education partnerships may include a component of counseling and guidance for students, for career pathway selection, career technical program selection, or a college four-year degree. This may take the form of career shadowing, in which students are assigned to business mentors for in-school and out-of-school experiences. It may involve business people as "friends" to students, listening to problems and discussing plans for the future. Career fairs and parent informational sessions during middle-school career-pathway selection will provide excellent opportunities for business partners to team with the counseling staff as they guide students.

Policy Development and Advocacy. Business partners, along with other community groups, may work with schools to develop new policies in such areas as early childhood education, graduation requirements, technology education, school management, or teacher training. Supporting change in existing school policies is a legitimate function of partnerships, whose participants may have a better understanding of school needs than citizens who are not involved in education. Business partners may choose to serve on key advisory committees.

Many schools welcome partnerships with business as a way to improve their community relations, as well as a way to improve education. Surveys show that businesses cite the desire to enhance their image in the community as the single most important reason for forming a school partnership. In many communities, this mutual desire for good public relations translates into advocacy, with businesses and schools working together to support tax levies and bond issues for education, or to promote other school-improvement strategies. As the partnership is planned, it is important to determine which option of a comprehensive partnership is developed first.

MULTIDISTRICT ALLIANCE

The North County, Inc. School/Business Partnership of St. Louis County, Missouri, was formed in 1985 as a result of an alliance between seven North County public school districts and the McDonnell Douglas Corporation. This alliance was expanded through the efforts of North County's board of directors. It now includes four parochial high schools, the Special School District of St. Louis County, and St. Louis Community College at Florissant Valley. Over 200 businesses participate each year. The purpose of this alliance is to share ideas, expertise, and enthusiasm to improve instruction in North St. Louis County schools. To date, more than 1,000 educators and 500 businesses have participated in this exciting, innovative alliance through the following activities:

- Job shadowing for teachers and students
- Curriculum development
- Career days and job fairs for students
- Business ethics seminar
- Professional development seminars
- Educator-for-a day activities
- Guest speakers and field trips
- Workplace orientation programs
- Services to the business community
- Local, state, and national conferences

INDIVIDUAL SCHOOL/BUSINESS ALLIANCE

The General Motors Automotive Service Educational Program (ASEP) is a two-year program designed to upgrade the technical competence and professional level of the incoming dealership technician. The curriculum, designed by Northern Virginia Community College (NVCC) and General Motors (GM), leads to an Associate in Applied Science Degree in Automotive Service Technology. The program involves attending classroom lectures and labs on GM products at the college and requires the student to work at a General Motors dealership. The total program lasts 21 months, including the summer between the first and second years, with over one half of that time spent in a GM-sponsoring dealership.

The ASEP program requires that each student be employed by a sponsoring GM dealer. If necessary, the student will receive some assistance in locating a sponsoring dealer. The main responsibility of the dealership is to provide employment with "real world" occupational technical experience for the student during his/her cooperative education. The student may work part-time at the dealership while attending classes if it does not interfere with studies. Dealers who have participated in ASEP find that students begin earning their way at the dealership in the second semester. Students who have graduated can often rival the performance of technicians with three to five years of experience.

The sophistication, professionalism, and competence required in today's automotive service field demand such a program. The program requires significant effort for student success; however, the benefits are worth this. The skill, knowledge, and potential of those who complete the program are far superior to those who complete most other automotive programs. The balance of qualities obtained forms a basis from which the graduate can develop and progress within the dealer's organization (Kershan, 1994).

INDIVIDUAL SCHOOL/BUSINESS ALLIANCE

The 880 youngsters at Meadow Woods Elementary School are reading, writing, and talking to one another over their own computer network. Meadow Woods has become the only elementary school in Orange County, Florida, to have its own private public foundation to underwrite specific educational programs. The Meadow Woods Foundation brought together parents, educators, and business people to finance and support fully computerized classrooms. The prototype organization, which focuses primarily on science and technology, is a creature of Landstar Homes, developer of housing developments in Central and South Florida. Landstar, which contributed $25,000 in seed money matched by businesses, parents, and other sources, expects the foundation to serve as a model for communities elsewhere. "We want to encourage others in the private sector to think about funding school programs rather than expecting the government to do it all," said Rudy Stern, president of Landstar Homes. The foundation, with a board of directors that includes public and private officials and parents, hopes to raise about $50,000 annually (Flores, 1993).

CITY, SCHOOL-WIDE DISTRICT/BUSINESS ALLIANCE

Thirty volunteers in Oregon have a 95 percent success rate in getting people to stay in or return to school. The Oregon Outreach Program received a Points of Light commendation for mentoring more than 3,000 youngsters in inner-city Portland since 1988, linking them to meaningful employment opportunities and encouraging them to continue their education.

Trained tutors teach learning skills to young people who have dropped out of or been expelled from school; minority community action volunteers provide job skills training and look for employment opportunities for youngsters who are involved with gangs; and other volunteers work directly with young substance abusers (NAPE Newsletter, 1993).

SCHOOL SYSTEMS WORKING WITH THE BUSINESS COMMUNITY

IBM Corporation has developed a partnership with schools based on its employee benefit policy. IBM has a Meal Break Flexibility policy in which employees can take up to two hours for lunch to pursue personal choice activities. IBM highlights "attending school function" as an example of an appropriate use of the policy. Many other corporations are developing flexible work policies to help employees meet personal or family needs, but have not highlighted parent-teacher conferences specifically (Soussou, 1990).

DEVELOPING A SCHOOL/BUSINESS ALLIANCE
THE EIGHT-STEP PARTNERSHIP-DEVELOPMENT PROCESS

Depicted below are the eight steps in a partnership development. Depending on the circumstances of the partnership, its goals, and the time and resources available, some steps may be emphasized more than others. However, it is important to think about all of the steps at the outset and then refer to them repeatedly during the development of the plan and as the partnership moves forward.

Each step is important but could be combined with others as the alliance is developed.

1. Awareness and Needs Assessment
2. Potential Resources
3. Goals and Objectives
4. Program Design
5. Program Implementation
6. Recruitment and Assignment
7. Orientation and Training
8. Monitoring and Evaluation

STEP ONE: AWARENESS AND NEEDS ASSESSMENT

No matter which element of a comprehensive partnership you decide to develop, the success of the partnership will be dependent upon your ability to create the right environment conducive to partnership development and growth by conducting well planned awareness activities.

Awareness is informing key populations within schools and corporate systems that a partnership is being considered as a means of improving the schools and the community. In the right environment, key education decision makers, teachers, and potential community or business partners become knowledgeable about and informed of the need for a partnership. Most importantly, these individuals become aware that a consensus strategy concerning the partnership is being sought, and that they will be part of developing the strategy.

Awareness involves aspects of networking, marketing, selling, brainstorming, public relations, and even luck. Planning and conducting awareness activities in an effective fashion is a true test of the political savvy and leadership ability of the partnership's managers and planners. Your knowledge of the power structures of the school and business, and your ability to convince key decision makers in and out of the school and corporation that a partnership is beneficial will be a major factor in the success of your partnership. An effective awareness strategy will create the climate in which your partnership can begin, grow, and continue to flourish.

DEVELOPING AWARENESS: QUESTIONS TO CONSIDER

The awareness strategy and plan that you develop is dependent on your understanding of how the school and business partners are structured. The following questions will help you analyze the structure and concerns of the institutions that will be involved in the partnership.

Schools

- What is the structure of the governance system?
- What do educators perceive their major educational problems to be?
- What effect do the problems have on the school?
- What do educators and others think is needed to solve these problems?
- How does this partnership help meet those priority problems?
- What does each key group need to know to be aware of and support the partnership?

Businesses

- What is the commitment of the company to the community?
- What financial and human resources exist within the business that could benefit education?
- How can the partnership tap these resources?
- How does the partnership relate to existing company programs and policies?
- How does the partnership benefit the company?

AWARENESS ACTIVITIES

Awareness activities will vary by target population and the message to be conveyed. Different partnership elements require different awareness activities. The initial awareness campaign will help various populations decide and propose ideas. The following is a list of common awareness activities:

- Breakfast meetings with business groups and chambers of commerce to outline partnership elements such as advocacy, staff development, curriculum development, instructional support, etc.
- After-school meetings with principals and teachers
- Presentations to the local chamber of commerce board of directors
- Meetings between representatives of a successful partnership and a potential partner
- Video presentations, computer bulletin boards
- Guest appearances on television and radio talk shows
- Editorials and feature articles in journals, periodicals, and newspapers.

NEEDS ASSESSMENT

Determining specific educational needs and designing partnership elements around the needs of schools and business is closely tied to the awareness process and feeds directly into the steps of the partnership process in which the goals and objectives are set.

Needs assessment is not an event; it is a process. Needs assessment is ongoing because business and community needs change over time. As a plan is developed for determining existing needs of the schools and businesses that will be involved in the partnership, think back on the awareness plan and the various populations devised. It is likely that many of the same populations will be involved in determining needs.

Schools. It is safe to say that all schools have unmet needs. Teachers may need additional material resources, or training in use of computers and software. Some may need additional planning time or help with making better use of existing time. The needs of math teachers may differ from those of English teachers. Principals have their own unique set of needs, which can range from professional development to help with completing required reports. Students may need tutoring in basic skills, hands-on experience in math and science, or enrichment in art, music, or history.

The task in planning a needs assessment strategy is to determine how best to determine the existing priority needs of each of these groups. Once the methods are reviewed, a method will be developed to use with each population.

Business. Addressing the needs of the schools is the primary objective of business/industry partnerships. In good partnerships, the needs of the business must also be recognized, respected, and addressed throughout the partnership relationship. For example, many companies are currently facing a shortage of qualified workers. Some businesses spend a great deal of money to upgrade the basic skills of new employees. A partnership has a better chance of succeeding if both school and business needs are met as a result of working together. If the partnership is successful, the company gets a lot of positive publicity; teachers and parents are pleased because students are getting additional help; and students show gains in their skills. Successful partnerships define common areas of need and common priorities.

STEP TWO: POTENTIAL RESOURCES

Potential resources are all the people, materials, equipment, and monies available within the school, school district, and business to help meet the needs you have identified. Resources often come to light well after the partnership begins as the result of evaluation, monitoring, and informal feedback. Where are potential resources of people, materials equipment, and money found? What is already present in the schools or in the businesses to help establish and improve a partnership?

Use the needs-assessment statement to focus the search. The needs-assessment results may indicate that the use of business facilities and personnel are needed for vocational education purposes. A review of potential company or business resources will result in light of this particular need. Other options of a partnership may also have shown up in the assessment results, such as instructional support or curriculum development in a particular subject area.

STEP THREE: GOALS AND OBJECTIVES

A **goal** is a broad statement of purpose for the partnership. It is similar to a mission statement in that it provides broad parameters for the partnership and is generally a statement of what the partnership will do and what the partnership will not do.

An **objective** is a statement of intent for an aspect of the partnership, and is measurable, specific, and determines the focus of evaluation. It is important to understand that objectives are the intended outcomes for the partnership. The objectives of the partnership will help partners to measure their successes and determine their weakness.

There is a relationship between goals and objectives. Both goals and objectives are directly related to needs and indirectly related to resources.

In the preceding two stages of the partnership-planning process, specific populations were identified in the school and business, the needs of each group were assessed, a list of priority needs for each, were created, and areas where the needs of the school and business overlap were determined. The needs that emerge in the area of overlap will shape the goals and objectives of the partnership. It should be noted that each population has its own set of values and a philosophy that creates its individual needs. Since needs shape goals, and needs differ among populations and partners, schools and businesses are likely to have different goals for the partnership. Each partner must understand and respect the other's goals. Many problems during implementation of partnerships can be traced to unclear goals.

STEP FOUR: PROGRAM DESIGN

The design of the partnership is dependent upon the education priorities of the school and the specific goals and objectives of the partnership. Program design is defined as the process of determining which options of a partnership are most likely to work effectively in the environment.

A partnership might include advocacy and policy development, staff development, curriculum development, instructional support and enrichment, material and financial resources, utilization of business facilities and resources, and counseling and guidance. Program design is really a matter of determining which options of a partnership best fit the needs, goals, and objectives. It is strongly recommended that alliances start small and build on success. Here are some other thoughts to consider:

- Instructional support and enrichment is the most popular area of partnership involvement and the most common.

- Curriculum development is often the most difficult and most challenging option. Curriculum is usually considered to be the exclusive responsibility of school board committees and central office staff.

- Staff development is somewhat easier than curriculum development; a business partner might decide to provide summer jobs for teachers, fund attendance at professional meetings, or pay for substitute teachers while teachers attend in-service training.

STEP FIVE: PROGRAM IMPLEMENTATION

Partnership planners often want to start by planning implementation. If partnership development is taken in logical steps, there will be fewer problems when you come to actual implementation. Key players in the school, district, and business will be aware and supportive of the efforts to seek their active involvement.

Implementation transforms relationships and understandings into hands-on realities. During implementation, business resources actually become a part of the school community of teachers, administrators, students, aides, other staff, and parents. In addition, the school may join the business partner in a variety of ways.

As the stages of implementation of the plan develop, keep in mind that plans will differ depending upon the options of a partnership selected. Partnerships work best when they begin with people involvement. In any case, it is suggested to start small and build on success.

STEP SIX: RECRUITMENT AND ASSIGNMENT

Recruitment is the process of engaging people and resources to become involved in the partnership, to service the needs identified by the school, community, and business. Recruitment is synonymous with promotion of the partnership.

The recruitment strategies developed for the partnership depend on which activities of the partnership are to be implemented. Whether the partnership will focus on policy, instruction, curriculum, staff development, student services, or employability skills has been determined in your planning process; the decision about which options to emphasize has been made based on specific identified needs of the school.

Recruitment is therefore driven in large part by identified needs of principals, teachers, students, and other school personnel. It is influenced, also, by the school's instructional priorities. Making clear that a real need exists for services or resources is the key element of a successful recruitment campaign.

In the recruitment stage of the partnership development, people and resources have been secured for participation in the partnership. Assignment is the process of matching the people who indicated interest in the partnership with the jobs the partnership wants done. Assignment is also the process of matching financial and material resources to identified needs of the partnership.

In many ways, recruitment and assignment are intertwined. Persons who have the necessary qualifications will have to be personally recruited. In general, however, recruiting will have brought in a number of people who offered their services generally, or in a broad category, such as instructional support. That is where the assignment process comes in, as you try to work out the best ways to use their talents.

STEP SEVEN: ORIENTATION AND TRAINING

Orientation can be described as a process that prepares people for involvement in a new situation. In a partnership, a good program orientation will acquaint all the participants with the nature of the undertaking and help them understand their roles in it. Whether orientation takes the form of a meeting, luncheon, videotape, or handbook, it can help people gain the background and overview of the program they need in order to be effective supporters and partners. It should be noted here that orientation is different from training.

Everyone involved in the partnership needs orientation. Not everyone will need training.

Training is defined as preparing individuals to perform specific tasks in predetermined situations. It is far more detailed than is a general orientation or overview. It is usually short-term, specific, practical, and is conducted in a sequence of steps. In your partnership, the major task with respect to training is to determine who needs to be trained and what skills will be achieved as a result of the training.

If the training is appropriate and adequate, teachers, business partners, and students will have a positive experience and will look forward to further participation. The purpose of the training, and its expected outcomes, must be clear to participants. The types of training you provide for the various participants in the partnership will depend on which options you have selected for emphasis. Business leaders know how to organize and lobby for policy or legislative change. They may need to be educated regarding the education issues, but they would not need training in terms of how to advocate for policy changes. If instructional support or curriculum development is selected as the partnership emphasis, then business employees may well need training.

STEP EIGHT: MONITORING AND EVALUATION

Through monitoring and evaluation, data is collected, interpreted, and used for purposes of programmatic decision making. Measurable objectives set early in the partnership planning process will determine the type of quantitative and qualitative information to be collected. Ongoing (formative) program monitoring and aggregate (summative) evaluation are designed to complement each other, one being an extension of the other. Information elicited from these evaluations provides a complete quantitative and qualitative picture of the program.

The growth in the number of partnership programs brings increased demands for assistance and support for shrinking available resources. Public and private providers of resources must make critical decisions regarding the distribution, use, and management of these resources. Currently, partnerships are just beginning to collect information about—

- How financial materials and equipment and in-kind and human resources have been, are being, or will be used by the school and community in support of partnerships in education efforts.

- What effect these resources have had on improvement in attitudes, achievement, and behaviors of the student, parent, educator, and partner and on school/school district management and governance (NAPE).

- Program evaluation should not happen in isolation. Monitoring and evaluation are integral to the overall program; it should be as much a part of the program as recruitment of partners and orientation of volunteers.

There are special techniques for collecting information. The method used should—

- Gather the best data the evaluation budget can afford

- Be welcome by all involved (both those who must provide the information as well as major audience groups receiving the evaluation)
- Allow sufficient time for gathering and analyzing the data
- Be technically sound to ensure that data collected will be reliable and valid.

Information from evaluations can be used to make informed decisions about whether or not to—

- Improve, refine, and renew an existing program or activity
- Plan and develop new programs and activities
- Eliminate a program or activity
- Celebrate and recognize the success of both partners and programs
- Document the long-term effects of the program on participants
- Review and redesign the management and delivery of instruction
- Elicit advocacy support for the school or school district (Herbourg, 1990).

REFERENCES

Creating and managing a business/education partnership (pp. 1-77). Alexandria: National Association of Partners in Education.

Herbourg, O. (1990). *How to monitor and evaluate partnerships in education; Measuring their success.* Info Media Communications.

Flores, Ike. (1993, March 15). Public school has its own foundation. *Tampa Times.* p. 8B.

Kershan, John F. (1994). Automotive service educational program. *Manager, General Motors Training Center.*

North County, Inc. school/business partnership. Hazelwood School District, 15955 New Halls Ferry Road, St. Louis, MO 63031.

Partners in education newsletter. (1993, January). National Association of Partners in Education. p. 5.

Soussou, H. (1990). *Employee time-off for public schools.* Cambridge Partnership for Public Education Inc., Plan For Social Excellence, Inc., p. 6.

CHAPTER 3

Apprenticeships for Business Students

MICHAEL G. CURRAN, JR.

Rider University, Lawrenceville, New Jersey

Apprenticing is, perhaps, the original form of on-the-job training. Examples of apprenticing may be found throughout the earliest writings from around the world. Although apprenticeship takes different forms internationally, most applications in the United States are fairly consistent in terms of development, implementation, and operation. There are differences between the states in administration of apprenticeship programs, but the concept is the same—stages of skill development through on-the-job training and classroom instruction, generally beginning at the postsecondary level. Each stage is monitored and hours of participation verified through cooperation between the employer and the apprenticeship coordinator. Monitoring includes both the classroom learning and the on-the-job training. (Bureau of Labor Statistics, 1992). The purpose of this chapter is to present options for youths in apprenticeship.

TRADITIONAL APPRENTICESHIPS

Traditional apprenticeship seemed to always include the "trades," those occupations within the construction industry. It is common to hear an electrician boasting of her journeyman apprentice, one of the stages in apprenticeship development. Apprentices in masonry, plumbing, automotive technology, diesel trades, and many more industrial trades are just as common. The U.S. Department of Labor's Office of Apprenticeship and Training publishes a list of Officially Recognized Apprenticeable Occupations (Bureau of Labor Statistics, 1992). Within those 835 occupational titles, 16 are generally used by business and marketing education students who want to enter an apprenticeship program following high school.

> They include Computer Operator; Computer Peripheral Operator; Legal Secretary; Manager, Food Service; Manager, Retail-Store; Medical Secretary; Paralegal; Post Office Clerk; Programmer; Programmer, Assistant; Salesperson (Parts); Scanner Operator; Stereotyper; Telecommunicator; Telegraphic-Typewriter Operator; and Transportation Clerk. (Bureau of Labor Statistics, 1992)

According to Dennis Fitzgerald, director of Apprenticeship and Training for the State of New Jersey, to date, very few apprenticeship programs take place in the business and marketing education area. However, the primary occupations for entry into apprenticeship are medical and legal secretary, clerical positions with the U.S. Postal System, and management positions in retail and food service. A major advantage for students entering an apprentice program is one of consistency across the nation. Apprentices completing a training program in any region of the United States have met the same criteria as apprentices completing the program anywhere else in the nation.

Detractors state that the lack of participation is due to the limited number and variety of apprenticed occupations. But, offices of apprenticeship and training across the nation are willing to apprentice new and emerging occupations (Youth Transitions to Work Partnership Program, 1995). Successful apprentice programs within states normally depend upon the relationship of the State Office of Apprenticeship and Training, and the state departments of Labor and Education. Where there is an established working relationship between these elements of the three departments (Apprenticeship and Training, Labor, and Education), ground is fertile for successful apprenticeship programs. State and federal governmental agencies are very willing to work with educators to establish sound apprenticeship programs. Participation in apprenticeship by business and marketing educators has not been significant. Perhaps the major reason can be found in the development of school-to-work programs within our discipline. Traditionally, cooperative education has been very successful at the secondary level for students wishing a school-directed program that provides in-class instruction with on-the-job supervision. Cooperative education in both business and marketing education has been successful throughout the nation. In addition, the federal and state Tech Prep and school-to-work linkage programs are popular and gaining strength daily. (See Chapter 4.)

> Today, many of the 20 million 16-to-24 year olds who skip college bounce from one dead-end job to another until they hit their mid- to late 20s. This is a big drain on both U.S. workers and the economy. It boosts unemployment, lowers wages, and leaves employers with applicants who are increasingly ill equipped for even entry level jobs. (Del Valle, 1993).

Many advocates of apprenticeship, including President Clinton, believe that a modified apprenticeship program offered at the secondary level could offset those statistics significantly (Clinton, 1991).

YOUTH APPRENTICESHIPS

Entering the school-to-work competition is a new program entitled Youth Apprenticeship, boasting a program structure much like business and marketing education's cooperative education programs. In Youth Apprenticeship a "youth apprentice" is a high school student learning a craft or occupation by working at a job under the direct guidance of a mentor or master craftsman, while attending school part time.

There are examples that demonstrate success in youth apprenticeship. Jeff Hines owns Donsco, Inc., a foundry in Wrightsville, Pennsylvania. He boasts about the benefits of apprenticeship for one of his workers, 11th-grader Chad Yoder (Del Valle, 1993). At the New England Medical Center, Tonita Dunn and Tracey Springer participate in a youth apprenticeship program set up by the Boston Private Industry Council, seven area hospitals, and three local high schools (Filipczak, 1993). In fact, there is evidence that youth apprenticeship proposals are proliferating as business and political leaders focus on the fact that half the nation's high school grads aren't headed to college, but lack the skills needed to land good jobs (Stanfield, 1992).

WHY NOT BUSINESS EDUCATION?

When polled, Americans rank work as very important (SCANS, 1992). Then, why have business educators not taken advantage of what seems to be a tried and true form of training? The primary reason is budgeting. Operating cooperative education programs is very costly. Other reasons include a lack of understanding of the apprentice system; not knowing where to start; not having the time to devote to the program; and lack of cooperation from other agencies.

In those states that have successful youth apprenticeship programs, there are major emphases on guiding students according to interest, occupational aptitude, and successive training. Many more apprenticeable occupations in business education are found in these programs. The Michigan Department of Education Vocational-Technical Education Service's Employability Skills Learning Activities Guide applies information and skills to the workplace (SCANS, 1992).

Professional Secretaries International, in its current curriculum guide, offers a course entitled Supervised Business Partnership, which is delivered through a collaborative activity between secondary schools/colleges and business establishments. Work experience in various types of office occupations is received through employment under the direction of competent supervisors. Cooperative education is a method of instruction rather than a work program (PSI Curriculum Guide, 1994).

Most organizations involved with the preparation of individuals for the world of work agree that apprenticing offers a strong program designed to force progress in classroom learning and on-the-job competency development. The Southern Regional Education Board, in their publication "Making High Schools Work Through Integration of Academic and Vocational Education," states:

> . . . another essential linkage is between high schools and postsecondary learning opportunities offered in job apprenticeships . . . high school educators and administrators must be up-to-date on the educational background that graduates will need for success in life and continued learning . . . partnerships with business and industry are vital (1993).

A TRAINING METHOD THAT WORKS!

Apprenticeship training has been found to be one of the most effective methods for training workers. States can supplement the United States Department of Labor's Bureau of Apprenticeship and Training funding. State funds could also support efforts to work with industry and unions to develop standards for certification of skills among trainees in industries that do not now have strong traditions of apprenticeship. State departments of Education and specifically their divisions of Vocational and Technical Education could charge a registration fee for each individual participating in a youth apprenticeship program or the traditional apprenticeship program. These fees could fund apprenticeship evaluation, certification, and government support staff that could be used to reduce the paperwork burden falling on training providers. States should establish a state apprenticeship council to coordinate and advocate for apprenticeship training programs (Governor's Conference, 1992).

Individual states are recognizing that participants do not enter registered apprenticeship programs until six or more years after their graduation from high school. To accelerate participation some states are issuing Requests for Proposals (RFP) for the youth apprenticeship program, officially titled the Youth Transitions to Work Partnership Program. In New Jersey, the Youth Transitions to Work Partnership Program will:

> establish new registered apprenticeship programs for high wage, high skill, labor demand occupations and link these new programs and existing registered apprenticeship programs with secondary schools and institutions of higher education. These programs shall provide effective transitions for high school graduates into registered apprenticeship programs, while sustaining or enhancing education standards (Youth Transitions to Work Partnership Program, 1995).

The initiation of these programs will create opportunities for lifelong, occupationally relevant learning and ongoing career advancement for front line workers, thereby motivating youth to great success in secondary and post-secondary education. A major component of the youth program is that participating educational institutions shall develop, to the extent feasible, articulation to postsecondary programs that provide participating apprentices with options to progress from apprenticeable trades to professional occupations. The purpose of the program is to enhance the prestige of education for skilled technical work by providing front-line workers with opportunities for lifelong, vocationally-relevant learning and professional advancement (Youth-To-Work Transitions Partnership Program, 1995). This endeavor and others like it throughout the nation hold great promise for business educators and their students in providing a sound apprenticeship opportunity.

BUSINESS EDUCATION AND APPRENTICESHIP

Business and marketing educators interested in developing a youth apprenticeship program or a traditional apprenticeship program in new and emerging occupations should contact their state's office of apprenticeship and training to get specific information including guidelines for the establishment of programs. Each state normally has an apprenticeship and training council that works with the Office of Apprenticeship and Training. The council may provide publications for establishing a program as well. State departments of Education and state departments of Labor should be used for their expertise. In fact, the thrust of the newly established Youth Apprenticeship Programs is a joint effort between the labor unions, the Bureau of Apprenticeship and Training, and the state departments of Labor and Education. Within the last few years many states have formed state employment and training councils or commissions. These commissions are generally made up of key individuals seeking to enhance the school-to-work transition. Educators may find a valuable source of information from the state commissions.

MONITORING APPRENTICESHIP PROGRAMS

For youth apprenticeship programs, monitoring will consist of guidelines developed and implemented by the student, school supervisor, and mentor or craftsperson on-the-job. The program will be established with board of education approval, state department approval or certification, and employer approval, according to the parameters set by the collaboration of the labor unions, Bureau of Apprenticeship and Training, and the state departments of Labor and Education.

Traditional apprenticeship programs are operated according to the rules and regulations of the federal Bureau of Apprenticeship and Training within the Department of Labor. At the state level the State Office of Apprenticeship and Training oversees the apprenticeship program in coordination with the departments of Labor and Education.

PROGRAM EVALUATION

Business educators choosing apprenticeship, youth apprenticeship, cooperative education, or school-to-work transition programs will find a myriad of different avenues to pursue for training excellence. Many benefits can be derived for the learner, the school, and the community no matter what form of apprenticeship training is pursued.

Program evaluation should be based upon the success rate of leavers as compared against the number of participants beginning the program. One-, two-, and five-year follow-up studies should be conducted to improve the program as it matures. If federal or state funding is requested, obtained, and utilized in the establishment of apprenticeship, youth apprenticeship, cooperative education, or other school-to-work transition programs, then the evaluation criteria detailed in the RFP must be followed.

SUMMARY

Apprenticeship or youth apprenticeship may present opportunities for you and your students. Once your interest level has been determined, seek advice from your local school administrators to see if there is support for an apprenticeship program. State Apprenticeship and Training personnel, Department of Education staff and Department of Labor staff will be happy to assist you in developing, monitoring, and evaluating your apprenticeship program.

In some states, apprenticeship programs are established with enterprise zones like the International Economic Zones. There may be tax benefits for the students, schools, and hiring business if operating out of the trade zone. In addition, apprenticeships taking place within an enterprise zone will enhance the possibility for the student to become involved internationally in the occupation of his or her choice. (See Chapter 19.)

If a school district and the local employing community want to improve the quality of life for all students, an apprenticeship or youth apprenticeship program should be considered.

REFERENCES

Bureau of Labor Statistics, (1991-1992). *Occupational Outlook Quarterly,* Winter, pp. 27 - 40.

Clinton, W. J. (1991, October 1). Apprenticeship American style, *Vocational Education Journal,* 22 - 23.

Del Valle, C. (1993, April 26). From high schools to high skills, *Business week,* pp. 110-112

Filipczak, B. (1993, December 1). Bridging the gap between school and work, *Training,* pp. 44-47.

Governor's Economic Conference: *Workforce quality task force reports.* (1991). Trenton, NJ. New Jersey State Government Printing Office.

Haynsworth, T., and Perselay, G. (1994, May 1). A United States youth apprenticeship program, *Journal of Education for Business,* 252 - 256.

Professional Secretaries International (1993). *Model curriculum for office careers.* Kansas City, Missouri.

Southern Regional Education Board (1992). *Making high schools work through integration of academic and vocational education* (p. 68). Atlanta.

Stanfield, R. L. (1992, May 2). The forgotten half, *National Journal,* 1049 - 1052.

U.S. Department of Labor: The Secretary's Commission on Achieving Necessary Skills - SCANS In The Schools (1992, June). Washington, DC. Pelavin Associates, Inc.

Youth Transitions To Work Partnership: An Initiative of the New Jersey Apprenticeship Policy Committee (1995). Request for Proposal, 1995 - 1996. New Jersey State Department of Education, Trenton, NJ.

CHAPTER 4

Business Teachers' Role in the School-to-Work Transition

JOAN W. LOOCK

Wisconsin Department of Public Instruction, Madison, Wisconsin

America's Choice: High Skills or Low Wages, issued by the Commission on Skills of the American Workforce in 1990, and the Secretary's Commission on Achieving Necessary Skills (SCANS), call for a curriculum that focuses on workplace skills and a restructuring of our schools that would deliver these skills.

School-to-Work is about people coming together to help our high school students make more informed career decisions and learn the skills they need for their future. It is about educators, business people, communities, and parents working together to accomplish important goals—goals that stem from a common vision and shared beliefs that benefit all of our young people as they embark on their career journey.

School-to-Work transition is a system of high standards combining school and workplace learning that helps transform youth from students to economically self-sufficient adults. The School-to-Work system reforms education by increasing the skills and expectations for all students so that they may succeed in both the workplace and in postsecondary education.

The purpose of this chapter is to detail the roles business teachers play in the success of School-to-Work transition programs—in planning, implementation, and administration. As schools undertake the restructuring process, business education teachers will need to take on the following roles:

- mentoring students;
- directing curriculum development;
- helping to design ongoing staff development based on local needs assessment;
- practicing integrated teaching methodologies;
- exercising control over curriculum and school policy; and working closely with parents, employers, and human service professionals to meet student needs.

THE SCHOOL-TO-WORK CONCEPT

Business education teachers need to look at instruction through practical applications of knowledge and through the integration of vocational and academic curriculum, delivered by means of innovative, creative, and exciting new strategies. The process of integrating academic and business education classes must go beyond the traditional approach of academic instruction. A study by Schmidt, et. al. (1992) demonstrates that it is simply not enough to present academic skills in vocational classes as separate activities, because students feel that they are receiving the same academics that have already turned them off.

The coordination of School-to-Work programs requires a commitment by administrators, teachers, counselors, and the community to ensure success. Such coordination should be undertaken through the integration of academic and vocational learning, work-based and school-based learning experiences, and secondary and postsecondary opportunities.

The role of the teacher in the School-to-Work transition is vital to its success, as the teacher is often the only link between education and the world of work for many youth. This is especially true at the elementary and middle school levels. In the state of Wisconsin, which serves as the basis for the examples used in this paper, the "education for employment" concept grew out of a comprehensive study of business and industry needs and the growing concern over the number of youth who failed to make a successful transition from school to the work world. One of the findings of a study of Wisconsin youth was that 60 percent of them enter the workforce at or before graduation. Consequently, the major portion of the state's entry level "skill training" and career exploration takes place while students are in school.

Starting in the budget session of 1985-87, the state legislature responded to the research and recommendations of the study by enacting a law that established an "education for employment" standard for all school districts and by creating the Governor's Council on Business and Education Partnerships. In considering what students need to be prepared for in the future working world, the education for employment initiative identified seven critical elements:

- business and education partnerships
- practical application of basic skills
- career exploration, planning, and decision making
- employability skills and attitudes
- school-supervised work experiences
- knowledge of business operations and economics
- contemporary vocational education programs.

School-to-Work refocuses the mission of public elementary and secondary education by saying all youth should be prepared for work and for lifelong learning. The School-to-Work concept embodies John Dewey's notion of "learning by doing" and, therefore, links education to real-world learning. Teachers at all levels need to assist students in connecting what they learn in school to how it is used in the workplace; understand and plan for career awareness; and teach human relations skills needed for success in the workplace. Students learn the need for basic skills in the working world through practical applications. Employers and educators gather on a regular basis to discuss what should be considered basic education for the future. The answers they find help to refocus the content taught in the classroom.

Business teachers have a history for involvement with these skills but now is the time that all teachers will have to take an active view of learning that includes not only these cognitive requisites but also a broader look at their role in career guidance for all youth. They must have a vision; they must look to the future and become involved in the learning process themselves. As technology changes our global economy, so must our teachers change and seek new ways to direct and guide children.

Teachers must have a personal commitment to implement this vision and must be willing to learn and experiment with new ideas and technologies. They must gain firsthand knowledge of the skills and expectations of the changing workplace. They must also reflect on their actions and use of that knowledge to influence change. Teachers are community role models, and, as such, they must reflect a positive image of a progressive learning environment. They serve as the window to the community; they can be open and create interaction between the school and the community, or they can be closed and separate the learning process from the community.

The implication of this process is that business teachers must develop a coherent sense of personal meaning regarding change in their programs. They need more than an opportunity to learn new curriculum. They need time to design, implement, and reflect on change based on personal convictions. There are four basic characteristics that influence the change process in educators:

- setting high expectations for all students
- supporting and influencing integration of curriculum
- connecting curriculum to the world of work
- assessing and teaching methodologies consistent with student learning styles.

There is an increased focus on what students should know and be able to do. Curriculum needs to be systematically developed to connect school with work activities. It will be the role of the teacher to provide leadership in the change process. Teachers have the closest connection to curriculum and the school support systems to affect all the necessary elements within the school. Partnerships between educators and business can provide many opportunities for students. One such partnership established in Racine, Wisconsin, with the Racine Area Manufacturers and Commerce has established over 138 such partnerships with area schools. Activities include Volunteers in Action, Shadow Days, Teen Parent Day Care Program, Mentorships, Coops, and Youth Apprenticeships. The Racine businesses promise to help improve the quality of education and to foster increased cooperation between teachers and the business community.

Teaching must reflect on current curriculum design, teaching methods, and assessment criteria. Quality of these processes must be determined and improvements made based on student needs. Business teachers will have to look beyond the typical resources for curriculum and build even stronger partnerships with business, industry, and labor to assist in identifying realistic outcomes. A curriculum that involves all aspects of higher education as well as the employability skills of the industry is the key to ensuring the content is delivering the necessary skills and knowledge for the future.

New roles for teachers, administrators, and business/industry partners are essential in order to provide the learning tasks and experiences and assure high performance outcomes for all students. Teachers will play a variety of roles in this process—coaches, mentors, resource providers, and learning facilitators. In some cases, business, industry, and labor representatives, social service providers, and community members will work closely with teachers to provide specialized support services and assistance.

The new role has been more closely associated with business and vocational teachers due to their training and experiences in the area of work-based learning. Most business teachers have established and maintained advisory committees from the business and industry community, formulated work-based training agreements, and supervised students in work experience programs.

THE ROLES AND RELATIONSHIPS OF ACADEMIC AND BUSINESS TEACHERS

Historically, academic and business teachers have been worlds apart in the schools—both physically and philosophically. In the comprehensive high school, most classes are segregated according to disciplines. Vocational classrooms are often located in opposite ends of the building from academic classrooms, and many are located in separate buildings. In addition, even the vocational areas are segregated according to disciplines—business classrooms, technology education classrooms, family and consumer education classrooms, etc., are all clustered separately, making communication and cooperation among teachers extremely difficult. Another factor that has nurtured separatism is the need felt by teachers to protect their enrollments. Vocational teachers feel that they must compete with one another as well as with the academic teachers for student enrollments that will maintain their full-time employment. Over the years, state and local policies have mandated more academic requirements for high school graduation as well as entrance into colleges and universities. This trend has narrowed the time available for students to enroll in elective courses.

Business departments attempt to meet the academic departments on their own ground by securing course requirements in business such as an English credit for Business Communications and math credit for Business Math or by seeking dual credit for some courses. Such strategies require that business teachers work with their academic colleagues and school administrators to identify what business topics are of sufficient importance to be required of all students, or that certain courses are sufficiently academic in content to warrant academic credit.

A number of programming options can be considered, depending on availability of staff and resources. One option is for business and academic teachers to collaborate to enhance the academic competencies in business classes or vice versa. Another option is to modify and align the curriculum in both business and academic courses so that similar content is taught at the same time in both program areas. Other schools use the project method where students are engaged in a long-term project that requires the integration of skills through research and development of a major project. One of the most successful methods is the team-taught approach composed of business and academic teachers working together to facilitate learning. If this method is not possible, the curriculum should be team-planned. In La Crosse, Wisconsin, a business teacher and a world language teacher are team teaching two courses in International Business. The semester course, International Business I, was developed by two world languages and two business teachers. After just one semester, students who were enrolled in the course were so excited they petitioned the school board to approve an International Business II course the following school year.

In order for the School-to-Work transition to succeed, there must be a common vision of all teachers working together for the benefit of their students. The integration of business and academic education will improve students' basic academic skills and strengthen both business and academic coursework so that it is more meaningful for students. Integration involves making business courses stronger academically and making academic courses more applied and relevant. When students see the connection between what they are doing in class and what they plan to do in the future, they become motivated and interested in learning. Teachers who have become involved in this collaboration and cooperation in designing and implementing applied and integrated courses are excited and feel rewarded at the results they see in their students. These teachers find that they have new roles focusing on business teachers reinforcing academic skills and academic teachers using applied instructional methodologies. Central to the collaborative instruction is teacher teamwork and cooperation.

As integration takes place within the instructional framework, both academic and business teachers progress through the following stages:

- Establishing relationships with one another. Teachers need time to build trust in one another and feel comfortable to share their personal ideas about curriculum and education.

- Learning from one another. They need time to learn and understand each other's content so connections can be made.

- Instruction through teaming. As teachers work together, they develop a teaching style that plays off the strengths of each other.

The practice of team teaching can take a variety of forms depending on the strengths of the individual teachers. Some teams split the responsibilities between lecture and lab; some play off each other to stimulate the creative thinking of students; while others divide the content to take advantage of their own strengths. Whatever method is used, it will require time for sharing, time for planning, time for implementing, and strong administrative support. Schools that have progressed in the School-to-Work areas of integrated and applied curriculum and work-based learning systems have done so with strong leadership by their principals and district administrators. The teachers must have ownership in the curriculum, but they must also have the support of the entire school district and community for the implementation process. The relationships and the planning and the sharing of instruction all take time for the in-depth commitment needed for success. Teachers and administrators need to work together to ensure there is adequate time to change instruction and to help identify what will be needed to implement changes.

To create improvement around the School-to-Work philosophy, the entire educational system must be addressed. This improvement effort includes the following elements: the classroom teachers, the organization and the curriculum, guidance and counseling services, student assessment, and administrators. Sound changes will not occur throughout a department, school, or district if only the teachers are the focus. All of the support systems associated with the school must also reflect and assess their quality functions and responsibilities.

RELATIONSHIP AND RESPONSIBILITY OF COUNSELORS IN THE SCHOOL-TO-WORK TRANSITION

The role of counselors is a very important link to the success of any School-to-Work program, but at the present time, it is a very weak link. A major concern is that an insufficient number of counselors are available in schools to support the activities necessary to implement a School-to-Work philosophy. There is no regular source of labor market information available to students whether it is termed "career guidance" or "college counseling." Student connections with the world of work and the world after high school are neither systematic nor organized to provide effective learning experiences. Another concern is that many schools rely on community social service agencies, and yet most believe these agencies are unable to accommodate the counseling needs of students. However, it is also clear that counselors need effective linkages with social service agencies and community health providers to offer support to those students whose social, emotional, or medical problems interfere with their ability to learn.

Business and industry must join the effort with counselors to make clear to students the relationship between instruction, curriculum, high performance standards, and the world of work. It is not sufficient simply to refocus the role of counselors in the K-12 system unless government agencies streamline delivery systems to address the bewildering array of services, programs, and providers of education, job training, and access to employment.

Parents and young people need to understand their career options, the education required, and the importance of maintaining adequate flexibility for change of direction. The counseling role is beyond that of the school counselor and must include all teachers, administrators, municipal and state agencies, and business and industry. Counseling has to be delivered via the curriculum, giving students the opportunity to explore a variety of options and then to base their decisions on those explorations.

To meet these ends, the role for the school counselor focuses on providing all youth with comprehensive career development. The essential elements of a current guidance and counseling model that supports a School-to-Work initiative are:

- Systematic, regularized career awareness activities that begin during the early middle school years and are delivered through regular instruction. This might include career days, field trips, or release time from school to enable children to go to work with a parent or neighbor.
- Structured job shadowing during the late middle school years, continuing into the ninth and tenth grades, that gives students direct, in-depth, hands-on (to the extent practicable) experiences with employers. (This may be the responsibility of the work experience coordinator or the classroom teacher as it relates to curriculum content.)

- Preparation of a specific career plan that builds on practical knowledge gained in job shadowing. Under the direction of the career guidance counselor, parents, and teacher mentors, the student uses all resources available to help express a proposed focus in a career plan that lays out some clear, realistic options for completing high school and continuing on to postsecondary experiences.

- Continuous career counseling that helps a student constantly reevaluate the continued validity of a career plan by reviewing the impact of school-based and work-based experiences.

- Community-based career center that contains reliable, easy-to-use information about employers, occupations, wages, job openings, skill qualifications, and education or training options.

- Career guidance and counseling services that are fully integrated with the school curriculum.

At the heart of these components is a transformed role for school counselors that focuses on providing all youth with comprehensive career development. It must also be assured that each of these components operates as part of a fully integrated system utilizing the expertise of counselors, all educators, and the community.

The Wisconsin Developmental Guidance Model identified career competencies for elementary, middle/junior high school, and high school students in three areas: learning; personal/social, and career/vocational. At the elementary level, student career competencies are focused on learning about each of the three areas just identified. For example, one competency is that students will learn how to cooperate and coexist with others in work and play. In the middle school/junior high school, student career competencies are focused on understanding. An example is that students become informed about alternative educational choices and preparation for them. The high school career competencies are focused on application. An example is that students form tentative career goals and strategies to reach them. This system of guidance and counseling has proven to be an asset to student career planning.

With the demands on counselors that go far beyond the career guidance component, it is vital that career counseling be integrated throughout the curriculum and across the experience of teachers and community resources to assist in the guidance process. Teachers must recognize the value of career guidance and work with counselors to ensure that all students receive instruction or information on occupations, employability skills, and current job market information.

IMPACT OF SCHOOL-TO-WORK ON PROFESSIONAL DEVELOPMENT, CERTIFICATION, AND LICENSURE

Attention must be directed to the professional development, certification, and licensure of all educators at all levels of education starting with the teacher preparation programs in colleges and universities.

The new vision of secondary education requires a new vision of preparation of business teachers. Requirements for teacher preparation should not only be thought of in terms of numbers and types of courses required but also in terms of what is learned in these courses. Business teachers need to learn the content knowledge when they participate in preparatory courses, but they also must learn new teaching strategies and methodologies. They must be exposed to teaching methodologies that encompass all learning styles, applied and integrated practices, and utilizing the community as a resource. They should be able to formulate and utilize community partnerships, advisory committees, and student organizations.

Business teachers of the future must be able to teach content in the way that is practiced, pursuing real questions about the world and incorporating learning-style methods with knowledge of the important concepts of the discipline. A solid preparatory program will include the following:

- the ability to relate their particular field to related fields—for example, science and technology or business and economics

- the ability to look beyond traditional fields of study and look for ways to connect the curriculum; and the ability to connect their curriculum to real-world applications

- alliances between business teachers and the community to make important decisions affecting student learning, thus increasing greatly the attention paid to the needs of all students and equalizing education opportunities for all.

Business teachers need to be able to plan, organize, actuate, control, and evaluate the learning environment as it relates to: curriculum design, laboratory methodologies, delivery of instruction, student assessment, and student management. They also need to feel comfortable with accessing and integrating technology across the curriculum to facilitate student learning.

The current curriculum in teacher preparation programs does not meet the needs of future teachers. It is essential that teacher preparation programs include the School-to-Work initiative. Business teachers of the future ought to be able to develop programs and curriculum that will assist students in career awareness, exploration, and preparation. They must provide a variety of experiences related to career clusters and make students aware of the preparation required for the different levels of entry into the world of work. Teacher preparation institutions must explore and model a variety of instructional methods such as team teaching and cooperative learning so that new teachers are coming to the profession with stronger abilities in integrated settings.

The changes required to establish a School-to-Work model may require an examination of state teaching license requirements, especially in licensed curriculum instruction areas. Care must be taken as cross certification of disciplines and grade levels are explored. Teachers may feel threatened and compelled to protect their "turf" rather than enthusiastically joining the restructuring of schools around the School-to-Work transition. Any of these programs that have an impact on licensure and certification should be approved by a variety of instructor constituencies, bargaining units, and appropriate state agencies. This would help to alleviate the apprehensions relating to cross certifications.

In an effort to build a skill-enhanced curriculum model for secondary students who are enrolled in courses at the high school level and who would benefit by the availability of postsecondary courses, the Wisconsin Technical

College System, The Wisconsin Department of Public Instruction, The Wisconsin Education Association Council, and the Wisconsin Federation of Teachers have entered into an agreement that allows secondary school teachers to provide technical college introductory level occupational or occupational-related course work to high school students for technical college credit. This partnership and commitment is built upon trust and collaboration to improve the opportunities for a smooth transition for students into the postsecondary system.

The University of Wisconsin System has also made it possible for over 120 course transfers from the technical college system to the four-year system. This type of cooperation must continue in order to build an educational system that is built on the concept of lifelong learning.

Professional development programs for instructors are a necessary component of the implementation and institutionalization of any innovative curriculum change. Well-planned, well-funded professional development programs for instructors are necessary to the establishment of quality School-to-Work programs. Since instruction in School-to-Work programs requires the knowledge of a variety of instructional techniques, the differences in teacher preparation between business and academic teachers should be a focus of any professional development programs. This is especially true when instruction goes beyond the sequencing of coursework to the establishment of an integrated approach to the curriculum.

An aspect of this professional development should be the opportunity for release time during the school year for teachers to shadow a variety of occupations and to make arrangements for partnership activities. Business teachers should also be encouraged to become involved in work experience programs where they can gain a better understanding of "applied academics" and update their curriculum, making it more relevant to the working world of today—by making the business experience their own personal classroom for a period of time.

SUMMARY

The School-to-Work transition initiative will improve the quality of secondary and postsecondary education and will advance student entry into the workforce. However, it is the teacher who makes the rhetoric of School-to-Work initiatives a reality! This will only happen if the front-line workers, the teachers, are empowered to lead the many reform efforts associated with School-to-Work.

Several trends reinforce the importance of such an initiative. School-to-Work programs across the nation help address serious issues created by—

- rapid advancements in technology
- global economic competition
- dramatic changes in the workplace
- new workplace literacy skills
- increased dropout rates from secondary schools.

Schools and communities can address these problems through partnerships with key stakeholder groups—educators, employers, labor unions, and community leaders. To ensure the success of School-to-Work programs, an honest partnership must occur between:

- academic and vocational teachers—to facilitate interdisciplinary cooperation and stimulate academic and vocational education curriculum integration

- secondary and postsecondary business teachers—to provide opportunities for students to transition smoothly from one level of education to another and to share resources that increase the students' overall education experience

- employers and teachers—to clearly communicate and establish high expectations for academic and business areas and to provide opportunities to gain exposure to educational and workplace needs.

Business teachers have a vital role in the development and implementation of School-to-Work programs. They must be involved at the beginning so that they can help create a better understanding of the initiative and develop a shared ownership of the activities. They can facilitate communication and decrease "turf" battles if they are a part of the development of the program. The program will also obtain better results and in a shorter time frame if educators value the program.

Teachers will play a variety of roles and assume new responsibilities in the School-to-Work initiative. Therefore, it is critical that business teachers have the opportunity to help shape those responsibilities.

REFERENCES

Commission on Skills of the American Workforce. (1990). *America's choice: High skills or low wages!* Rochester, NY: National Center on Education and the Economy.

Kane, M., Berryman, S., Goshn, D., & Meltzer, A. (1990). *The Secretary's commission on achieving necessary skills: Identifying and describing the skills required by work,* Washington, DC: Pelavin Associates, Inc.

Schmidt, B. J., Finch, C. R. & Faulkner, S. L. (1992). *Helping teachers to understand their roles in integrating vocational and academic education: A practitioner's guide,* Berkeley, CA: University of California, National Center for Research in Vocational Education.

United States Department of Labor, The Secretary's Commission on Achieving Necessary Skills. (1991). *Skills and tasks for jobs: A SCANS report for America 2000,* Washington, DC: U.S. Government Printing Office.

United States Department of Labor, The Secretary's Commission on Achieving Necessary Skills. (1991, June). *What work requires of schools: A SCANS report for America 2000,* Washington, DC: U.S. Government Printing Office.

Wisconsin Department of Industry, Labor and Human Relations. (1992). *Wisconsin youth apprenticeship guidelines,* Madison, WI: Wisconsin Department of Industry, Labor and Human Relations.

Wisconsin Department of Public Instruction. (1991). *Business and education partnerships,* Madison, WI: Wisconsin Department of Public Instruction.

Wisconsin Department of Public Instruction. (1993). *Wisconsin focuses on career guidance report,* Madison, WI: Wisconsin Department of Public Instruction.

Disclaimer: This chapter is a revision based on a paper written for the Academy for Educational Development's National Institute for Work and Learning Study of School-to-Work Transition Reform, which is part of the Studies of Education Reform program, supported by the U.S. Department of Education, Office of Research, contract No. RR 91-172012. The program supports studies and disseminates practical information about implementing and sustaining successful innovations in American education. The opinions in this document do not necessarily reflect the position or policy of the U.S. Department of Education or the Academy for Educational Development, and no official endorsement should be inferred.

CHAPTER 5

Programs Meeting the Needs of Business and Students

PETER F. MEGGISON

Massasoit Community College, Brockton, Massachusetts

Many excellent business education programs are found throughout the county at all levels—elementary, secondary, postsecondary, and college. Illustrated in this chapter are nine very different programs at various levels that have been extremely successful. This panorama of educational programs provides a blueprint of offerings that serve the diverse needs of today's students and thereby business and society in an especially effective manner. The programs described have been selected to be illustrative only; far more important are the general principles of effective program development and planning that each program represents.

CURRICULUM INTEGRATION

Since one of the requirements of the 1990 Carl D. Perkins Vocational and Applied Technology Act includes the integration of academic and vocational education in the context of job skills preparation, business teachers need concern themselves with how this can best be accomplished. The process of integration involves developing meaningful relationships between school subjects and student experiences in an interconnected, holistic fashion.

To meet the needs of students at Cedar Bluffs (Nebraska) High School, the Business Department has designed a curriculum that provides opportunities to practice employability skills in an integrated curriculum environment. Additionally, students gain experiences with a wide variety of computer software programs and technology tools. Students enrolled in Information Processing, for example, learn word processing, database, spreadsheet, and essential telecommunication skills.

Students in computer application courses have the opportunity to showcase their human relations, time management, creativity, problem-solving, critical thinking, oral communication, and written communication skills in an integrated Business/English employment unit entitled, *How to Land a Job and Keep It*. Moreover, students learn invaluable technology skills including how to digitize images and sound (using *Computer Eyes* software, *Zap Shot* camera, and *Digispeech* adapter); create computer graphics; use authoring software (*LinkWay*); use research CDs (SIRS—Social Issues Resources and Grolier's *Multimedia Encyclopedia*); and use the Internet. The culminating project for this unit is the development of a group multimedia presentation that is delivered to a panel of judges that includes peers, teachers, administrators, and community members. In addition, students in the computer applications class complete an international business unit which requires a considerable amount of research via the Internet and integration with family science, world history, and economics classes. Again, students utilize numerous computer skills while developing a multimedia presentation that depicts what a business employee should know in order to conduct business with a foreign country.

Another project for this course requires students to monitor an integrated curriculum project developed by the staff at Cedar Bluffs High School. This integrated curriculum project includes all subjects and all students in grades 7 through 12. It utilizes a thematic-based approach, with the themes changing yearly in a six-year rotation. The 1994 theme was the *Platte Attack*—a focus on the nearby Platte River. Students in the computer applications class monitored what teachers did in their respective subject areas and then created a multimedia presentation that illustrated each teacher's *Platte Attack* curriculum from beginning to end. Then, they presented their work at community functions and to other nearby school districts. The 1995 theme was *The Railroad*. The final project for this group of students was to take an issue that MTV's Community of the Future addresses and develop a computer presentation using information and materials supplied by MTV to be given to elementary students to educate them in one of the following areas: violence in America (*Enough is Enough*); drug use among young people and its consequences (*Straight Dope*); teen violence and how guns have become the weapon of choice for many young people today (*A Generation under the Gun*); and sexual activity among teens (*Smart Sex*).

The Advanced Computer Applications class requires students to complete a variety of telecommunication kits that incorporate numerous subject areas. In order to successfully complete the kits, the Internet must be used. Additionally, the activities can be competitive against other schools across the nation, which increases interest and raises achievement due to the competitive spirit within students. More importantly, the kits are designed to solve problems that require students to demonstrate critical thinking, creativity, and problem-solving skills. To illustrate, the *Ring of Fire* kit requires students to collect data via the Internet on the locations of earthquakes around the world for a period of one school year. Then, based on their findings, students predict the location of a future quake. Other kits address social problems, environmental issues, and controversial issues by bringing together knowledges and skills acquired in science, social studies, English, math, and business courses.

Higher student achievement, a greater interest in the business curriculum, and growing enrollments in all business courses are the positive outcomes brought about by this integrated approach to teaching and the implementation of projects and activities that afford students the opportunity to practice employability skills. Students at Cedar Bluffs High School understand how math, science, the social sciences, and English relate to business because they have had an opportunity to practice their employability skills in a contextual environment through an integrated curriculum, telecommunication, and student-centered technology projects.

BANKING PROGRAM FOR URBAN YOUTH

Cambridge, Massachusetts, is populated by nearly 100,000 people representing a diverse spectrum of customs, talents, and backgrounds. Rich in culture, ethnic activities, and industry, Cambridge maintains its strength though the cooperative efforts of a multicultural population that represents over 64 nations. Educationally, the city's public education system consists of 15 elementary schools and one comprehensive high school, Cambridge Rindge and Latin (Grades 9 to 12), which has a 2,200-student enrollment. An estimated $9000 is spent per year on each pupil in the system.

Since Cambridge is considered to be one of the most cosmopolitan intersections of individuals and ideas in the world, innovation is expected and, therefore, encouraged in its school system. Operating within such a framework led to the establishment of an operational bank at Cambridge Rindge and Latin High School as a joint venture between the Cambridge Public Schools and the East Cambridge Savings Bank in 1989.

In order to participate in the school bank program, students must adhere to high standards of conduct including: (1) proper attire, (2) punctuality and attendance, (3) confidentiality, and (4) security consciousness. Although these requirements are stringent for high school students, the rewards and skills developed remain with the students and enable them to obtain challenging positions in the banking profession.

The keystone to this collaborative effort is the Introduction to Banking course. Students interested in participating in the operation of the branch bank must complete this course in their junior year. The course teaches students about banking as a service industry and how a bank helps its community. Students also learn the basic principles of banking including organizational structure and the history of banking. Students who successfully complete the Introduction to Banking course are eligible to be part of the school bank operational team in their senior year. Students receive paid training in the summer of their junior year from the East Cambridge Savings Bank in order to be ready to fully participate in the operation of the school's bank once classes start in September. The school bank is designed to expose students to banking and business practices, accounting and economic principles, and banking and consumer laws and regulations in a branch office environment.

Under the supervision of East Cambridge Savings Bank employees, students perform all transactions including opening accounts, accepting deposits, and making withdrawals. Some of the services offered at the school bank include saving and investment accounts, consumer loans, student loans, and check cashing. The bank is open on school days from 11:05 to 12:25. The school branch is not open to the general public; only students, faculty, and school department personnel are eligible to utilize its facilities.

The program is operated by a full-time business education teacher, who implemented the program, and is chartered under regulations set forth by the Commonwealth of Massachusetts, State Banking Commission.

THE FIRM

THE FIRM is a computer applications and management training program offered to seniors by the Business Education Department of the Virginia Beach (Virginia) City Public Schools. The goal of the program is to provide the highest quality technical education through training on state-of-the-art equipment in a simulated office environment. Graduates of the program are assured of a smooth transition from high school to college or for entry into mid-management positions.

The class is block scheduled for two hours each day and is set up as an actual company. The philosophy behind the program is that high school seniors are ready for realistic work experience, and this program is intended to provide that experience. The teachers are the employers and the students are the employees. Employees earn two high school elective credits while they report to work each day and complete the goals and projects that have been scheduled.

All employees must complete a core of study each quarter that consists of two modules in word processing applications, data processing applications, English communication skills, and management principles. In order to complete a module and receive validation of those competencies, the employee must score a minimum of 88 on the final test. If employees fall below this score, they are required to refine their skills and retake the test. Since this demonstrates true competency-based learning, no employee is allowed to go to the next module until the required competencies have been demonstrated on the previous module. Employees receive over 200 hours of hands-on computer training on a networked system that includes application software that is used by local businesses and industries. In addition to the required core, employees choose an area of specialty they wish to pursue; and they complete modules in those areas.

Each employee has a cubicle, which becomes the professional space where weekly goals are set. The facilities are designed and furnished like a modern office, where the latest principles of ergonomics have been considered in its design. The textbooks of THE FIRM consist of motivational cassettes, professional periodicals, instructional films, and actual application projects needed by the Green Run High School staff. Because the employees are needed at various locations in the building, picture ID badges are worn as a pass to allow the employees access through the parts of the building during their scheduled FIRM time.

Total Quality Management concepts are also taught and applied as students hold management positions in THE FIRM. Each employee submits a goal contract each week listing modules/goals that he/she intends to complete. The principle of accountability is taught through this goal-contract program.

The on-the-job learning environment students experience in working for THE FIRM is practical rather than abstract. The training is personalized and begins at the level of competency that each student possesses upon entering the program. Employees can exempt any module where they can demonstrate proficiency.

The principles of time management, organization, prioritizing, and goal setting are also taught in THE FIRM. Employees learn to effectively use their company time each day so that they can complete their weekly goal contracts. Individual day planners and company calendars are kept so that each employee knows when company meetings will be held and how much individual work time can be planned each day.

Management principles are typically taught as conceptual units; however, unless a student can actually apply the knowledge presented, retention is minimal. In THE FIRM, one employee each week becomes the office manager and is responsible for keeping the organization functioning effectively. Employees also have an opportunity to be a testing manager. For one week the testing manager is responsible for scheduling test times and administering, timing, correcting, and verifying tests. Other managerial positions include vice president of resources, various production managers, and administrative assistants. Employees work in teams on projects where assignments must be delegated and completed by a deadline. Employees receive competency certificates upon completion of the program. The educational philosophy behind THE FIRM is based on the "law of expectation," a concept whereby teachers expect students to do great things, to succeed, and to achieve. This program represents a paradigm shift where the teacher no longer has to be all knowing but rather becomes a director of learning—a facilitator. It is a shift in focus from the teacher being responsible to the student being responsible for learning.

PROFESSIONAL PORTFOLIOS

At Westbrook (Maine) High School, senior business students who are enrolled in the office simulation course are required to prepare professional portfolios. Originally designed as a document for students to begin their job search, the portfolio has evolved into an evaluation tool for students, teachers, and employers.

The professional portfolio is an assemblage of the student's background, accomplishments, interests, and aspirations as prepared by the student. It becomes the focus of discussion during an interview, showing the interviewer how the student is trained, organized, and structured. It can be an effective device for selling the student's skills and abilities.

The parts of the portfolio will vary depending on the talents of the student. At Westbrook High School, the portfolio consists of seven parts:

1. *The title page* with a photograph helps the applicant become a person rather than just a name.

2. *The foreword* consists of one or two paragraphs explaining what the reader may expect.

3. *The table of contents* lists each page of the portfolio, is prepared last, and does not list the appendices.

4. *The resume* is updated at the time the portfolio is prepared.

5. *The work samples* include documents that reflect the student's talents. Some suggestions include timed writings, computer-generated activities, newsletters, FBLA activities, professional workshop reports, research reports, and office simulation documents such as payroll, plotting activities, and statistical reports.

6. *The certificates, awards, and commendations* section also reflects the student's talents. Some suggestions include certificates of proficiency in skill subjects, FBLA and other extracurricular awards, extracurricular citations, letters of recommendation, and evaluations from teachers, advisors, or employers.

7. *The appendices* are the last section of the portfolio and should be removed before using the portfolio in an interview. This section contains letters that a student may need when applying for a job. The letters are composed by the student based on a current newspaper advertisement chosen by the student. They include applying for a position, thanking an interviewer for the interview, accepting a position, refusing a position, requesting use of a name as a reference, thanking a person for a recommendation, and resigning from a position.

The portfolio is designed by the student and should reflect his or her personality. All work included should be accurate samples of the student's best efforts and should be placed in a new binder with index tabs for easy reference. The type and quality of the supplies will again depend on the student's individual taste and motivation.

Once the portfolio passes the mailability grade, the students are asked to present their portfolios before their teachers and peers. Using his or her graded portfolio, the student makes a three-to-five minute oral presentation. Following the presentation, the student must be prepared to answer a minimum of three questions from the following list:

- What one thing from your portfolio preparation do you believe will help you the most? Explain.
- If you could change one thing about your portfolio, what would it be?
- Why did you choose the advertisement (that you chose) for developing your appendices?
- What did you mean by the statement (or sentence), "_____" from your document or presentation?
- What do you consider to be your strengths? How are they reflected in your portfolio?
- What did preparing your portfolio prove to you? Explain.
- Is there a section of your portfolio in which you wish you had more material to present? Explain.
- Did preparing your portfolio help you identify any of your weaknesses? Explain.
- What are your goals for the next two or three years? How will this portfolio tie to these goals?
- Pick one section of your portfolio and explain it in more detail.

The oral presentation is graded as follows: 50 percent—Content and Delivery (10 percent, Poise; 10 percent, Appearance; 10 percent, Oral Expression; 20 percent, Organization); 25 percent—Ability to Defend Portfolio Against Questions; 25 percent—Listening Skills.

The development of a professional portfolio is an effective instrument for answering these questions for the student, the teacher, and the potential employer: Who are you? What is your background? What can you do? What are your skills, abilities, and experiences?

BUSINESS EDUCATION FOR TEEN PARENTS
AT HONEYWELL

New Vistas School is a Minneapolis Public High School program for pregnant and parenting teens and their children located in Honeywell's Minneapolis, Minnesota, corporate headquarters. The school represents an innovative collaboration among community resources.

Founded in 1990 for students in grades 10 through 12 who are mothers or are expecting a child, New Vistas offers individual, outcome-based instruction for the teen mothers and child care and early childhood education for their children. Parenting classes, as well as a wide range of other health and social services, are also available. New Vistas accommodates 60 students as well as up to 70 infants, toddlers, and preschoolers in child care. The school is a component of "Success by 6," a United Way of Minneapolis community-wide initiative designed to overcome barriers to health development of preschool children and to have them school-ready.

New Vistas has four primary goals:

- completion of a high school diploma
- successful transition to postsecondary education and employment
- development of good parenting skills
- enhancement of early childhood development for students' children.

Some of the provisions for New Vistas include:

- instruction and funding by the Minneapolis Public Schools
- parenting and early childhood education by Minneapolis Public Schools Early Childhood Family Education
- 15 personal computers donated by IBM
- mentoring by Honeywell employee volunteers
- apprenticeships, internships, and summer jobs in various Honeywell departments.

Honeywell's Youth Apprenticeships offer part-time employment and guided work experiences in accounting and business administration, professional secretarial training, and consumer banking and finance. Apprenticeships begin in grade 11 and continue through completion of a community or technical college program. Work responsibilities and training are aligned with a prescribed academic curriculum. Students participating in the secretarial program, for example, follow the Professional Secretaries International Model Curriculum. At the conclusion of the program, they are tested through Professional Secretaries International Office Proficiency and Assessment Certification Program and also sit for the Certified Professional Secretary Examination.

Honeywell's Business Administration/Accounting apprenticeship prepares students for successful employment in accounting and finance-related fields. This apprenticeship program emphasizes accounting principles, computer applications, teamwork skills, information analysis, and communication skills. The banking and finance apprenticeship develops some of these same skills with an emphasis on consumer financial products and customer service. All Honeywell interns are provided guided, paid work experiences; a trained mentor to counsel and guide each student; and a certificate of competency upon completion of the program.

New Vistas School utilizes individualized, self-paced, outcome-based instruction, which enables each student to reach her potential. Computer-assisted instruction is used for about one-third of the classwork; other instruction is one-on-one and small-group cooperative learning. The school is staffed full time by four teachers, a support services coordinator, a school social worker, and child care staff, as well as part-time staff. New Vistas School is a unique partnership that attempts to solve critical social problems by assisting in the development of disadvantaged teenagers. Graduates of the program, most often from poor families, are able to escape the cycle of unemployment and poverty by becoming educated, productive adults.

BUSINESS TRAINING FOR THE BLIND AND DEAF

The E. B. Gentry Technical Facility of the Alabama Institute for Deaf and Blind, located in Talladega, is a comprehensive evaluation, personal adjustment, and vocational facility serving blind, deaf, and other severely handicapped adults 16 years of age and above. The Business Education Department offers clerical technology training, along with specialization areas such as medical transcription, legal transcription, and accounting. The general curriculum includes modules in typing, recordkeeping, filing and records management, business mathematics, oral and written communication, office procedures, computer applications, and occupational essentials.

The facility's computers are equipped with large-print screen access for persons with low vision as well as speech output for persons who are totally blind. Adaptive technology products are used to assist this group of individuals such as closed-circuit televisions, refreshable braille displays connected to the computer so that one may read—in braille—what is on the computer screen, braille notetakers with 640K memory, scanners, and braille and traditional printers. Specialized equipment such as voice-activated computer work stations for hands-free computer operation as would be required by a quadriplegic is also available. The facility attempts to research, test, and ultimately provide specialized equipment to meet the requirements of any particular disability group or individual as the need arises.

Persons completing Gentry's program do not necessarily work as receptionists, transcriptionists, or computer operators. Many are totally blind or visually impaired social workers, teachers, clergy, lawyers, and others who have taken advantage of the facility's training opportunities to learn to meet their communication needs through the use of computers uniquely adapted for use by blind or visually impaired persons.

Field services are also available for the purpose of doing job analyses, determining special equipment needs, installing equipment and software, and making job modifications to help graduates succeed on the job.

While students are enrolled in a specific trade area such as business education at the E. H. Gentry Technical Facility, there are a wide variety of other services offered to the students. These include GED preparatory classes, braille or sign language classes, therapeutic recreation, home management, independent living classes, and mobility training.

COURT REPORTING PROGRAM PREPARES
MORE THAN JUST COURT REPORTERS

Many people think of a court reporter as someone who is highly skilled in reporting verbatim testimony and possesses an intense interest in the legal justice system. Nearly everyone saw the court reporter in Judge Ito's courtroom quietly taking down the proceedings for the O. J. Simpson case. Not everyone may have realized, however, that the court reporters were providing instant translation for Judge Ito, the prosecuting attorneys, and defense attorneys.

For many years, court reporting graduates chose between working for the state or the federal government in a courtroom setting and becoming an "official reporter" or working for a freelance agency or business, taking pretrial depositions and hearings, as a "freelance reporter." As a result of recent advancements in technology, the skills of a court reporter can provide for a range of opportunities other than these traditional settings.

Medical transcription is a relatively new area for persons with high-level machine shorthand skills. A trained court reporter can use computerized machine shorthand transcription technology to produce documents more rapidly and accurately than with a QWERTY keyboard. Transcribing medical dictation is done by using machine shorthand software interfaced with word processing software. A medical transcriptionist can work for hospitals, doctors' offices, agencies, or be self-employed and own a home-based transcription service.

A requirement of the Americans with Disabilities Act is for public employers to provide disabled employees "reasonable accommodations" to be able to perform their jobs. To the hearing-impaired person, those accommodations may include a computerized note taker or real-time assistance. Since many hard-of-hearing people are not familiar with sign language, real-time steno interpreting is a valuable aid to them in any group setting.

Real-time steno interpreting, the process whereby a verbatim transcript of the speaker is instantaneously translated on a computer screen, monitor, or an overhead screen as it is being written by the machine shorthand writer, is currently being used in many nonlitigation settings such as training seminars, Americans with Disabilities Act seminars, board of directors meetings, council meetings, public forums, and other relevant settings. Educational institutions are employing steno interpreters to provide classroom captioning for hearing-impaired students.

Trained court reporters also work for television stations or captioning corporations to provide the captions that are now available on almost all home televisions. A captioning company in Colorado is currently employing a trained court reporter in Plymouth, Massachusetts, to provide captions via a modem.

Massachusetts Bay Community College, at its suburban campus in Framingham, has been preparing reporters for traditional and nontraditional jobs since the inception of its court reporting program in 1973. The Associate of Applied Science Degree in Court and Conference Reporting is approved by the National Court Reporters Association and is strongly supported by the Massachusetts Shorthand Reporters Association. Graduates of the program must demonstrate machine shorthand dictation competency at the following speeds for five minutes with 97 percent accuracy: 180 words per minute, Literary; 200 words per minute, Jury Charge; and 225 words per minute, Question and Answer. As part of the court reporter's preparation, a 40-hour internship with local reporters, both freelance and official, is included in the program. Students are required to write Question and Answer material at 200 words per minute before being placed at an internship site.

Students in the program are trained with the latest court reporting technology including 35 computers with Premier Power software and 15 computer writing machines. In addition to high-level machine shorthand dictation skills, the program provides intensive training in real-time transcription; all facets of court procedures; medical anatomy, physiology, and terminology; legal terminology; and business and criminal law. Since CART (Computer-Aided Real Time) has been added to the program, the department works with the learning disabilities staff of the college in providing hard-of-hearing students a court reporting student in their classes. The lecture is written in real time, and an ASCII disk is provided to the student for study purposes.

The future will see more and more trained court reporters in places other than courts as they combine existing needs with current technology in a variety of settings.

COMMUNITY COLLEGE BUSINESS AND INDUSTRY PROGRAM

Middlesex Community College (MCC) is one of 14 community colleges in the Commonwealth of Massachusetts. During the 1980s, the college developed a Business and Industry Program as an outgrowth of it strong academic program and community outreach activities. Currently, it is considered to be one of the largest and best of its types in New England.

The Business and Industry Program has developed a number of relationships with area companies, which have taken on various designs, including:

- Education and training for large-, medium-, and small-size companies
- Corporate contracts to provide employee education and training
- On-site workplace courses (credit and noncredit) which address specific education and training needs.

Although MCC is located in the heart of the state's high technology industry, Business and Industry programs consciously market this education and training assistance to a broad spectrum of potential employers including hospitals and health centers, banks, insurance companies, manufacturers, research and development firms, and telecommunications companies.

MCC's Business and Industry programs also provide a broad array of education and training services for the local community such as:

- a comprehensive Business Administration Associate Degree program on-site at a local firm

- an Electronic Technology Certificate Program for employees of an area high-technology firm
- Criminal Justice/Security Administration courses for employees of an area high technology firm
- noncredit professional development workshops for managers and supervisors
- international trade seminars in cooperation with the Massachusetts Office of International Trade and Investment
- workplace literacy programs, including English as a Second Language and Adult Basic Education instruction.

A second major focus of the Business and Industry Program is to work with the various academic divisions of the college to develop specialized career programs to address the needs of company consortia or to meet area-wide occupational needs. These programs prepare the unemployed or under-employed for jobs in demand, upgrade the skills and knowledge of the currently employed, retrain workers who are changing careers or are being reassigned within a firm, or fill an educational gap in the technical training market. The Business and Industry Program also manages a Small Business Institute which provides workshops for current and prospective small business owners and works with Salem State College to offer free one-on-one business counseling through the Small Business Development Center Program.

One of the reasons for the success of the program is that from its inception, an attempt has been made to integrate its activities with the overall fabric of the college. The Business and Industry Program's staff works closely with academic division deans, department chairs, program coordinators, and faculty members to ensure that its offerings are high quality, academically sound, and are in conformity with overall college standards and policies. Specifically, the Business and Industry Program staff is responsible for:

- developing initial business contacts; i.e., sales and marketing
- arranging a first planning meeting with the employer and working with the academic staff to develop an on-going approach
- preparing the contract mailing proposal
- pricing
- program administration
- quality control and evaluation
- using satisfied customers at a company to develop other prospects at which to implement programs and courses and for "repeat business"
- starting up every course; i.e., attending the first class to introduce the instructor; finalizing registration details; answering company and employee/student questions; and otherwise ensuring that the program/course starts in a smooth manner
- closing out each course; i.e., visiting the final class to administer an evaluation, answering questions, discussing the next steps with students/employees, etc.

During the 1993-94 academic year, approximately 2000 students participated in the Business and Industry Program, generating $450,000 in revenues. It is a self-supporting program, with excess revenues being made available to the college to support other programs.

TRAINING AND DEVELOPMENT INITIATIVES

In response to local area needs for employee training and retraining, the University of Houston (UH) established a Training and Development undergraduate degree program in the early 1980s. By 1985, a master's program was in place. Today, the need is greater than ever for individuals who can assess and evaluate an organization's training needs and who can design, implement, and evaluate training programs.

Both of the UH Training and Development degree programs are administered through the Industrial Technology (ITEC) Department within the College of Technology. The curriculum prepares its majors to analyze performance problems, identify training needs, write instructional materials, furnish and equip corporate classrooms, and implement training using a variety of delivery systems. Training and development students also complete coursework in several support areas such as supervision, computer applications, communications, and technology.

In 1995, the undergraduate Training and Development program was revamped into a specialization called Training/Human Resources and was placed within the ITEC Department's Industrial Supervision major. This move was taken to assure that students get a solid base of knowledge, skills, and applications related to technology as well as comprehensive coursework in training and human resources.

Students in the Industrial Technology Department, especially those with training and development career objectives, frequently complete a paid internship in a local business or industry. Some students, including those who may be currently employed, may pursue an internship to gain experience with their newly acquired skills and/or to expand their employment opportunities. Internship opportunities vary widely and have become an ideal way for an employer to select future employees. Frequently, employers seek interns from both the UH undergraduate and graduate Training and Development programs since an internship is an excellent way to evaluate potential employees. If a position exists or opens up where the student is interning, usually the intern is given first preference to fill it.

Another offering of the ITEC Department's Training and Development Program is the "Certified Training and Development Manager" program. Participants in this 200 contact-hour train-the-trainer certification program are usually industry employees who want to learn the latest in instructional methodologies, multicultural training, and train-the-trainer techniques and management skills. The training certification program is divided into nine modules and is offered over a period of nine months within the following three phases: Accelerated Learning and Cross-Cultural Communication, Instructional System Design, and Managing the Training and Development Function. Successful completers of each phase of the program receive specific subject-area certificates: Phase I—Instructor/Facilitator; Phase II—Instructional Designer; and Phase III—Training Manager. In order to receive a Certified Training and Development Manager Certificate, however, all three phases of the certificate must be completed. This certification may be applied toward an ITEC Department Bachelor's or Master's degree.

Since 1992, a yearly "Supervision Workplace Seminar Series" has been offered. This series is a service to employees within the local community who need to learn or update their supervisory/managerial and facilitation/training skills. Seminars are one day in length and are offered once a month over a 10-month period.

All of the described programs have recently been expanded into instructional television (ITV) delivery. Students are able to complete all upper-division courses via ITV in the Training/Human Resources specialization of the Industrial Supervision program. Local community colleges are offering ITV lower division courses; thus, ITV provides an excellent means for articulation between nine of the Houston-area community colleges and UH. The entire Master's program with an emphasis in Training and Development is planned for ITV.

While the demand for graduates from the Training and Development programs remains strong, reengineering and restructuring of organizations in the Houston area appear to be contributing to the demand for its graduates. No doubt the popularity of UH training programs will grow as marketing efforts help to publicize the track record of the program!

SUMMARY

President John F. Kennedy said, "Actions deferred are all too often opportunities lost." The programs described in this chapter illustrate concrete ways in which business educators have taken action to meet the needs of business and students. In today's changing social and business climate, opportunities will continue to abound for the business educator who is willing to venture into new, unchartered areas to create innovative programs that meet the needs of businesses and students. Now is the time to act!

CHAPTER 6
Alternative Scheduling and Delivery

JACQUELINE M. SCHLIEFER
Western Kentucky University, Bowling Green, Kentucky

MARY M. CRISP
Western Kentucky University, Bowling Green, Kentucky

GINNY HELD
Corvallis, Oregon

". . . change—constant, accelerating, ubiquitous—is the most striking characteristic of the world we live in . . . our educational system has not yet recognized this fact," said Postman and Weingartner in their 1969 book, *Teaching as a Subversive Activity.* Now, 27 years later, the educational system is beginning to recognize this fact.

From Kentucky to Oregon (and many places in between) educational reform is creating an exciting climate of change. In Kentucky, change was precipitated by the passage of KERA, the 1990 Kentucky Education Reform Act; and in Oregon, the legislature passed the School Reform issue in 1991. Kentucky and Oregon high school business education teachers have been involved in examining not only their business curriculums but also in re-evaluating the traditional school day and delivery system. One important piece of the change puzzle is alternative scheduling.

In this chapter we will discuss how educational reform and block scheduling, a form of alternative scheduling, will affect business education programs across the nation. High schools in Kentucky and Oregon will be used as examples of two basic types of blocks that are changing the "fragmented schedules" that Jacobs (1989) and others have described so vividly.

DIFFERENCES BETWEEN BLOCK AND TRADITIONAL SCHEDULES

Marilyn Ferguson, an American futurist, said, "It's not so much that we're afraid of change or so in love with the old ways, but it's that place in between that we fear. It's like being between trapezes. It's Linus when his blanket is in the dryer. There's nothing to hold on to" (*Changing Times,* 1994). One of the significant changes brought about by educational reform is the restructured school day. Over 100 Kentucky high schools had implemented block scheduling by the 1994-95 school year. A Bell County High School teacher put it this way: "Thus began the search for a different way to handle one of the notorious high school sacred cows: the daily schedule" (*Changing Times,* 1994). Block scheduling seems to be an idea whose time has come—

again. Unlike the office procedures block of former years, however, today's block scheduling represents a radical departure from the traditional school day.

Sample block schedules run from 73 to 120 minutes. In this discussion, 90 minutes will be used as the average block length, and the traditional class period will be assumed to be 55 minutes unless otherwise indicated. The following comparison chart shows some of the general differences between block and traditional schedules.

Block Schedules (90-minute classes)	Traditional Schedules (55-minute classes)
Students can earn 8 credits per year	Students earn 6 credits per year
Students can earn 32 credits by graduation **or** begin post-secondary work early	Students earn 24 credits by graduation
Planning time for teachers is 90 minutes per day	Planning time for teachers is 55 minutes per day
Number of students per day per teacher, approximately 75 (3 classes w/25 students each)	Number of students per day per teacher, approximately 125 (5 classes w/25 students each)
Teaching minutes per day, 270 (three 90-minute classes)	Teaching minutes per day, 275 (five 55-minute classes)
Role-taking time, 45 minutes per week (3 min. x 3 classes x 5 days)	Role-taking time, 75 minutes per week (3 min. x 5 classes x 5 days)
Students absent a whole day miss four classes	Students absent a whole day miss six or seven classes

In talking with teachers, examining sample schedules, and reviewing the literature, two basic types of block schedules (the straight block and the alternate-day block) are evident. Variations on the straight block and the alternate-day block also abound.

STRAIGHT BLOCK SCHEDULE

So, what exactly is a straight block schedule (also known as the concentrated model, intensive model, 4 x 4 model, or four-block model)? Schoenstein (1995) describes the straight block as four 90-minute classes each day, five days a week. Full-year courses now meet for half a year, and classes that were completed in one semester under the traditional schedule may be completed in nine weeks, giving students opportunities to take more electives.

An informal survey of business education teachers in Kentucky schools showed many variations of the straight block schedule; however, here is one of the most commonly used models. A sample one-year teaching schedule of a business teacher at Warren East High School in Bowling Green, Kentucky, is shown here:

Block	First Semester	Second Semester
1st Block 7:58 - 9:30	Business Principles and Applications	*Business Law *Business Management
2nd Block 9:40 - 11:10	Computer Applications	Business Principles and Applications
3rd Block 11:20 - 1:20 (includes lunch)	Planning	Planning
4th Block 1:30 - 3:00	Business Principles and Applications	Business Principles and Applications

*These classes were traditionally one semester; they are now each completed in nine weeks.

ADVANTAGES AND DISADVANTAGES OF STRAIGHT BLOCK SCHEDULES

Edwards (1993) describes the advantages of straight block scheduling as ". . . better, more efficient use of teacher time, student time, and existing educational resources." Kentucky business teachers seemed to agree with Edwards. These teachers reported that the biggest advantage of straight block scheduling is their ability to spend more time with students. A Kentucky teacher said: "In computer class, I can now present a new topic, demonstrate it, and students can do activities for practice all in one day." Teachers were also asked to indicate what they think the advantages of the straight block schedule are to the students. Here are their responses:

Advantages to the Teacher	Advantages to the Students
Fewer classes for which to prepare	Fewer classes for which to study
Fewer students per day; time to get to know students better	Learn fewer teachers' styles and expectations
Fewer papers to grade each night	Less homework and fewer tests
Less time lost in opening and closing classes	Less time wasted
More planning time	Opportunities to take more classes (electives)
Fresh start each semester and sometimes at mid-semester	Courses can be repeated next semester, if necessary
Increased opportunities for field-based experiences	Experience the business world
Shift to hands-on learning, critical thinking activities, and student-centered learning	Higher quality instruction: realistic, active learning, increased motivation
Increased opportunities for team teaching and collaboration	Increased opportunities for work with fellow students

The literature repeatedly mentions longer planning periods and fewer students per day as primary advantages. More effective use of time has also been an often-mentioned factor; Canady and Rettig (1993) said, "If three class changes are eliminated each day, an hour of instructional time is gained each week."

Another interesting advantage of fewer classes per day also appeared. Teachers at Bell County High School found that fewer classes improved attitudes and reduced stress levels of both teachers and students (*Changing Times*, 1994). Schoenstein (1993) believes that longer classes with longer passing times (his school has 15-minute passing periods) makes for a less frantic pace; and this arrangement, he feels, has contributed to a calmer, safer high school. Canady and Rettig (1993) also found that discipline problems were reduced with fewer class changes.

The Kentucky business teachers were asked what they consider to be the disadvantages of the straight block schedules. Teacher disadvantages were determining critical content and keeping students focused for 90 minutes. Student disadvantages were the difficulty of catching up after absences and transferring from one school to another.

One of the disadvantages often cited in the literature of straight block scheduling is that not as much content is covered as with the traditional schedule. Schoenstein's (1993) response is, "I cover less content, but the kids can still leave class with more, not less, of the subject to take with them." He went on to say that the Coalition of Essential Schools' belief that "less is more" and "student as worker" makes more sense to him now. The key seems to be in determining the critical content—what exactly do students need to know when they leave a particular class? With the knowledge explosion, teachers find that it is increasingly difficult to cover "everything." Teaching fewer big ideas more thoroughly and helping students learn how to learn on their own have become more important than completing chapters in a business textbook.

ALTERNATE-DAY BLOCK SCHEDULE

The alternate-day block schedule (also known as the rotating block) is used at Philomath High School in Oregon. The beginning of this change at Philomath was a change in the school's schedule. During Philomath High School's first semester of alternate-day block scheduling, each day consisted of three 90-minute block classes and two shorter 47-minute "traditional" classes. The periods were numbered 1 through 8 with 5 and 6 being short classes/lunch hours. One of the advantages of this schedule was that block- and single-period classes were both available. Disadvantages included:

- teachers spread too thin with multipreparations

- different daily schedules confusing

- interrupting events (assembly, snow day) could cause a class to meet only once a week

- classes held during lunch periods, which eliminated lunch meetings for students or staff and caused problems for intramural programs

- MAC Lab scheduled every period so that no extra time was available for out-of-class work.

During their second semester of the first year, Philomath changed to a four-block schedule on Monday/Wednesday and four different blocks on Tuesday/Thursday. On Friday, all classes met for 30 minutes; three half-hour flex periods were added for study time, tech labs, assemblies, club meetings, or individual help.

An advantage of this schedule was that it followed the same pattern from week to week with Friday being a good time to give short tests, reviews, assignment sheets, etc. Disadvantages were that for many teachers the short Friday periods were a nightmare. Classes were still held during lunch periods, and teachers had to "account" for students assigned to them during flex period as well as help other students or advise students at a meeting.

By the second year of block scheduling, their seven-period day went to eight periods over two days. Here is how their two-week period of time looks:

90 min. Blocks	M	T	W	TH	F	M	T	W	TH	F
1st Block	1	5	1	5	1	5	1	5	1	5
2nd Block	2	6	2	6	2	6	2	6	2	6
3rd Block	3	7	3	7	3	7	3	7	3	7
4th Block	4	8	4	8	4	8	4	8	4	8

Periods 4 and 8 are "flex" periods—most freshmen and sophomores have period 4 flex and are scheduled into small or large groups for a study or lab situation with teachers of freshmen and sophomores. Most juniors and seniors have period 8 flex, and they have the freedom to move within the building with passes.

ADVANTAGES AND DISADVANTAGES OF ALTERNATE-DAY BLOCK SCHEDULES

Many of the advantages and disadvantages of an alternate-day block schedule are similar to those of the straight block schedule, for example, fewer students per day and longer class periods to plan more student-centered activities. The primary advantage of the alternate-day schedule, however, is the year-long continuity of instruction. For example, Accounting I is scheduled every other day for a full year (instead of being completed in one semester in straight block) in preparation for Accounting II the following year.

Philomath High School teachers found a few unique advantages to the alternate-day schedule. Additional opportunities for team teaching, integration, and group meetings were available. They also found that unassigned time for students encouraged personal responsibility. Gerking (1995), a Wyoming science teacher whose high school chose the alternate-day block schedule, said that although she was not able to cover as much material, the learning was far more intense. ". . . we waste less time and value every minute. . . . We tend to emphasize the concepts that are really important." She also stressed that the schedule change had facilitated curriculum change.

A major disadvantage of the alternate-day schedule is that the number of students and class preparations does not change from that of the traditional schedule. Classes meet for longer periods of time, every other day, for the whole year. Other disadvantages are not seeing students every day and the confusing rotating schedule.

BLOCK SCHEDULE VARIATIONS

Variations of the straight block or the alternate-block schedules go from a one-day block every two weeks to a different block schedule four days of the week. Frequently, a shortened flex period is included to provide for club meetings, special school functions, extra library work, and computer lab activities.

Scott High School (Kentucky) has adopted a variation of the straight-block schedule: a combination of 54-minute periods on Mondays and Fridays when all six classes meet and 73-minute periods on Tuesdays, Wednesdays, and Thursdays when four of the six classes meet. With this schedule, each class meets four days a week, two times for 54 minutes and two times for 73 minutes. As shown on the following table, on Tuesdays, Wednesdays, and Thursdays there is also a 45-minute flex period.

Monday 54-min. class periods	Tuesday 73-min. class periods	Wednesday 73-min. class periods	Thursday 73-min. class periods	Friday 54-min. class periods
Homeroom 15 min.	Homeroom 15 min.	Homeroom 15 min.	Homeroom 15 min.	Homeroom 15 min.
1st period	1st period	3rd period	2nd period	1st period
2nd period	45-min. flex	45-min. flex	45-min. flex	2nd period
3rd period	2nd period	1st period	3rd period	3rd period
4th period w/lunch	4th period w/lunch	5th period w/lunch	4th period w/lunch	4th period w/lunch
5th period	5th period	6th period	6th period	5th period
6th period	*			6th period

*School ends every day at 2:30; however, on Tuesday, Wednesday, and Thursday, students have four 73-minute class periods and a flex period instead of six 54-minute periods.

McLean County High School in Kentucky uses another variation on the straight block schedule; their blocks are 77 minutes with one 24-minute flex block per day and three staggered 25-minute lunch periods. Another Kentucky school, Rockcastle County High School, has four 85-minute blocks, three staggered 25-minute lunch periods, and a 30- minute homeroom at the end of the day.

Combinations of traditional and block schedules are also being experimented with in Oregon. One school district combines block periods (90 minutes) with a few short periods (45 minutes). The block classes meet daily allowing students to take a full year's course in one semester. The 45-minute periods meet for the full year to provide for continuity when prerequisites are required.

Canady and Rettig (1993) describe an alternate-day block schedule variation that features three double-block periods of 104 minutes on an alternate-day basis and one single-block period of 52 minutes every day. Another variation features four 104-minute blocks (two of which meet each day) and three 52-minute blocks that meet every day.

BENEFITS TO THE BUSINESS COMMUNITY OF BLOCK SCHEDULING

Block scheduling could conceivably help to prepare better trained employees. Two of the five competencies from the SCANS (Secretary's Commission on Achieving Necessary Skills) report (1991) that are particularly relevant to business classes in the restructured high school day include (1) interpersonal: works with others and (2) technology: works with a variety of technologies. The SCANS report also recommends a foundation of basic skills, thinking skills, and personal qualities.

Business education teachers have always been in the unique position of providing opportunities for the development of these skills and professional/technical competencies in realistic classroom experiences. Block scheduling provides even more opportunities to incorporate activities that will encourage students to develop the skills discussed in the SCANS report—the skills that will be required by 21st century employers.

In working with the local business community, one of the greatest benefits of block scheduling is its flexibility. Students will have more time for work-based learning, which includes visitation, mentoring, shadowing, and cooperative education. Because more electives are possible, students may take additional business courses to increase their professional/technical training.

CHANGES IN TEACHING METHODS/STRATEGIES

Business teachers across the nation are expanding their teaching repertoires to take advantage of the longer class periods that block scheduling provides. In fact, Kentucky and Oregon business teachers' perceptions of the disadvantages of block scheduling would seem to indicate that changes in teaching methods and strategies are essential. One teacher said, "I now have the ability to use many methods/strategies within one period."

Group activities, cooperative learning, and simulations are just some of the classroom activities that can be used more effectively with block scheduling. Students will learn to take more responsibility for their own learning, will learn to work productively with other class members, and will, therefore, be better prepared for employment in the 21st century.

Slavin (1995) tells us that three concepts are essential to group activities and cooperative learning: team rewards, individual accountability, and equal opportunities for success. Block schedules provide additional time for all students to develop the interpersonal skills necessary to successful group work. One successful strategy is a discussion of group roles and what students like/dislike about working with their peers. Teachers serve as facilitators and guides but let students plan how they can work together more productively.

Gerking (1995) talked about different ways in which the 90-minute blocks can be subdivided. Popular plans are three 30-minute sections or two 45-minute sections. She went on to say, ". . . we divide the block into times for more group work and activities. Lectures are limited to 10- to 20-minute segments" (p. 23). These "mini" lessons will hold the students' interest, especially when they know they will be required to put the information into practice immediately on the same day.

Teachers find that to use their time more effectively, they must reexamine their courses to determine critical content. The current trend with Tech Prep and the School-to-Work movement is to teach fewer big ideas in a more integrated and realistic way so that students learn essential skills and concepts well.

Academic/vocational integration and team teaching are facilitated in career academies which use block scheduling ("Career Academies" 1995). An example is Philomath High School's (Oregon) school-within-a-school concept, where two business teachers team teach and integrate work with an English teacher and a social studies teacher. In their alternate block schedule, all junior and senior business students spend one full day—every other day—with the four teachers for business/academic integration. The ideas for all-day activities—in the classroom or out in the community—are endless.

Learning concepts and principles through exploration, problem solving, and discovery learning are what students will be doing on the job. Why not give them that experience in the classroom? As business teachers encourage students to become life-long learners, teachers, too, will be learning and growing. Schoenstein (1993) put it this way: "Try new ways of operating in your classroom, and drop them if they don't work. Give yourself permission to experiment—and to foul up as well."

SUGGESTIONS/RECOMMENDATIONS

Teachers are being asked to rearrange the student day in creative ways to provide for more effective instruction and learning. With these increased expectations, we believe that teachers need additional individual and collaborative planning time to determine critical content. Schools are experimenting with late-start and early-release days, four-day student weeks, joint planning periods, and extended employment days.

To allow for greater flexibility of the school day, consideration should be given to a minimum number of hours of instruction per course per year rather than a minimum number of school days. The Kentucky High School Restructuring Task Force (1993) recommended that the 6-hour, 175-day minimum be replaced with a minimum number of organized school hours per year. Schoenstein (1995) reports that Colorado mandates a minimum of 1,080 hours of instruction per year. Oregon requires 990 hours.

We recommend that class size be reduced to 20 or fewer students. Research shows a relationship between class size and pupil learning. Gene V. Glass reviewed nearly 80 studies on student achievement and class size and found that ". . . for every pupil by which class size is reduced below 20, the class's average achievement improves substantially" (Ryan and Cooper, 1984). The Kentucky Task Force also recommended establishing an ideal daily student-teacher ratio of 80:1 as the long-term goal for Kentucky schools.

Consideration should also be given to streamlining the traditional four-year sequence of high school classes. Edwards (1993) suggests that students be allowed and encouraged to complete all "foundation" courses in the first two years of high school. For example, students would take Algebra I, Geometry, and Algebra II in the first three semesters rather than in the first three years of high school. Edwards goes on to recommend that "students could then complete an intensive college preparatory program, a full two-year technical or vocational program, or even an associate degree program." Another of his suggestions is to allow students who complete the required high school work in less than four years to continue their education at public expense. Students could receive from a one-semester to a two-year scholarship for advanced study to round out the traditional four years they would normally attend high school.

We advise teachers involved in the change process to give themselves time to change. Schoenstein (1993) says to not expect everything to be different in the first week or month of the new schedule. He also reminds teachers that no one else's restructuring plan will fit their situation exactly and urges that teachers modify others' ideas, plans, and schedules to fit their identified needs.

Educational reform is providing the impetus for teachers, school districts, and states to reexamine the traditional school day. One teacher said, "The schedule is God. You can implement any innovation you want in your classroom as long as you don't mess with the schedule" (Watts and Castle, 1993). Now seems to be the time to "mess" with the schedule. Henri Bergson, a French philosopher, once said, "To exist is to change, to change is to mature, to mature is to go on creating oneself endlessly."

REFERENCES

Canady, R. L., and Rettig, M. D. (1993, December). Unlocking the lockstep high school schedule. *Phi Delta Kappan. 75*, 310-314.

Career academies and other education choices. (January, 1995). *Keying In. 5, 6.*

Changing times. (1994). Pineville, Kentucky: Bell County High School.

Edwards, C. M. (1993, May). The four period day: Restructuring to improve student performance. *NASSP Bulletin. 77,* 77-88.

Jacobs, H. H., Ed. (1989). *Interdisciplinary curriculum: Design and implementation.* Alexandria, Virginia: Association for Supervision and Curriculum Development.

The Kentucky Education Reform Act of 1990: A Citizen's Handbook. Frankfort, Kentucky: Legislative Research Commission.

Newmann, R. A. (1994, March). A report from the 23rd International Conference on Alternative Education. *Phi Delta Kappan. 75,* 547-549.

Postman, N., and Weingartner, C. (1969). *Teaching as a subversive activity.* New York: Dell Publishing Co., Inc.

Ryan, K., and Cooper, J. M. (1984). *Those who can, teach,* Fourth Edition. Boston: Houghton Mifflin Company.

Schoenstein, R. (1995, February). Making block scheduling work. *The Education Digest.* 60, 15-19.

Schoenstein, R. (1993, September). Some comments on a block schedule. Colorado Springs, Colorado: Wasson High School.

Slavin, R. E. (1995). *Cooperative learning,* second edition. Boston: Allyn and Bacon.

Task Force on High School Restructuring. (1993, June). Final Report. Frankfort, Kentucky: Kentucky Department of Education.

U. S. Department of Labor. (1991). What work requires of schools: A SCANS report for America 2000. Washington, D.C.: U. S. Government Printing Office.

Watts, G. D., and Castle, S. (1993, December). The time dilemma in school restructuring. *Phi Delta Kappan. 75,* 306-310.

PART II

TEACHING IN TODAY'S CLASSROOM ENVIRONMENT

CHAPTER 7

Principles of Learning

COLLEEN VAWDREY

Utah Valley State College, Orem, Utah

Webster defines the word "teach" as "to impart the knowledge of" or "to cause to know a subject." The traditional notion of teaching has embraced the teacher as the dispenser of knowledge; his or her job is to talk while the students' job is to listen and accept. Information is transmitted from the teacher to the student in a one-way process, and the student is expected to absorb the truths in a sponge-like fashion. The teacher decides what to transmit, how much information is necessary, and how quickly it should be absorbed. Although this pedagogical approach has much merit, it should not be the sole source of learning, as it puts the teacher in the role of the all-wise source of knowledge and leaves little room for student input into the process.

Recently, more emphasis has been placed on the role of the learner. Giving the learner responsibility for his or her learning changes the education process, as the student becomes an active rather than a passive participant. This philosophy, known as andragogy, is usually associated with adult education and is based on the assumption that adult students bring more experience and motivation to the classroom. Although this assumption is usually true, most students approach the learning process with some degree of motivation; and all students bring some past experiences with them. The more actively students participate in the learning process, the more they retain; hence, the learning becomes more effective. This difference in philosophy is similar to the Theory X vs. Theory Y principles of management. When an employee is presumed to lack ambition and to need external motivation, the manager must direct and control the situation. On the other hand, when the employee is assumed to be goal-oriented and have an interest in the outcome, the role of the manager shifts to one of shared ownership and achievement. Translating these assumptions to an educational setting, the process shifts from the teacher being the information disseminator to the student being the center of information collecting with the teacher as a mentor or facilitator in the learning process. Initially, this shift in the approach to learning may be uncomfortable for teachers and even difficult for some learners. But the learners will soon thrive in this student-directed atmosphere, and the teacher will find a much less frantic pace to his or her input. The initial threat to some educators may be due to the fact that teachers tend to teach as they were taught (Heinen, Sherman, & Stafford, 1990). The commitment to change may be a drastic alteration from tradition.

This shift does not mean, however, that the teacher's role has become less important; actually, the teacher as a facilitator may have additional influence on the students' achievement. Wittrock (1986) found three teaching factors that seemed to have a great influence on student success. The first was the teacher's expectations about student achievement. The greater the teacher's verbal expectations to students, the higher the student achievement; in other words, the self-fulfilling prophecy seemed to apply. Second, teacher-directed praise or reward increased student learning; and third, the amount of time teachers allocated to the learning seemed to correlate directly with student achievement.

A popular adage about teaching—"if students haven't learned, the teacher has not taught"—no longer seems to apply. As a result of the change in emphasis from teaching to learning, this chapter focuses on principles of learning rather than the principles of teaching that have been part of the traditional teacher-education curriculum.

REVIEWING THE BASICS

Most educators have had exposure to Bloom's taxonomy of educational objectives, wherein he designates levels of teaching. The theory is that the lower levels teach simple conceptual knowledge but that teachers need to teach at higher levels so students have application experiences and can synthesize the ideas presented. However, Gagne's categories of learning (Bell-Gredler, 1986) better represent the point of view of the student. Each category uses different learning steps and leads to different acquired skills.

Verbal information includes the acquired knowledge of students about facts and certainties. When learned, these truths can be recalled as needed. For example, a computer user should be able to recall the keyboard home row, "a-s-d-f-j-k-l-;" in its proper order. As can be readily seen by this example, however, long concentration on verbal information alone will not lead to educational mastery of the subject. Yet many times students and teachers alike concentrate on the "learn and parrot back" type of education.

Intellectual skills include the learning that makes the student able to function in society. These skills are the "knowing how" as opposed to the verbal skills of "knowing that." To be effective with technology, students must know more than recall regarding the keyboard. The understanding of the application of word processing software is an example of an important intellectual skill for business students.

The category of motor skills involves the ability to perform actions. This category is, of course, essential in business education since performing skills —particularly computer skills—are basic and pervasive to the curriculum. Knowing about a skill, of course, is much different from the ability to perform the skill. All the textbooks about driving do not develop a student's ability to operate the vehicle correctly and develop the awareness of the road necessary to become a successful driver. Similarly, reading about or watching someone else operate a computer does not give the student the computer expertise. Motor skills learning is enhanced with both theory and demonstration, but the majority of learning time should be devoted to practice. Because new learning is uncomfortable and novice learners quickly become tense, leading to a decrease in performance, short sessions of practice are more likely to provide a learning situation with continuous improvement than long sessions. Although stress can lead to tenseness, a certain amount is necessary for the learner to remain effective. A learner faced with a low stress task becomes very ineffective. The data also suggest that improvement in motor skills takes place best with many practice sessions over long periods of time.

In addition, an important part of the practice is feedback about what the student is doing correctly and incorrectly with the practice. One danger in motor skill development is the tendency to concentrate on what the learner is doing incorrectly, assuming the student translates a lack of correction to be praise for correct performance. Positive reinforcement should outweigh negative feedback to ensure successful skill development; positive and prompt feedback to students—whether verbal, nonverbal, or written—is desirable for optimal learning. The feedback from the teacher also influences the affective component of the student's learning.

Attitudes influence the learner's choices about endeavors through preferences for or against certain activities. Although attitudes may not determine what acts a learner may do, they certainly determine the desires of the learner toward or away from future learning. This desire, in turn, may have a great effect on the student's motivation toward learning. And as noted above, the feedback from the teacher can greatly affect the student's attitude as well as the student's learning.

The last of Gagne's categories, cognitive strategies, encompass the learner's ability to manage learning. In other words, these strategies involve the capability to use remembering skills, critical thinking, and analysis to solve problems and adapt learning to other situations. These skills are developed over long periods of time and help the student become a self-learner. Therefore, the learner who develops cognitive skills has the capability to be successful in applying the other categories of skills. Educators, then, must give attention not only to assisting the learners develop "knowing that, knowing how, ability to, and positive attitude about" but also to helping students acquire the ability to continue with their own learning. This capability has increased in significance with the emphasis on lifelong learning and the constant changes in the workplace the learners will face in their careers.

Traditionally, education has included learning only some of Gagne's categories. Most noticeably missing has been the development of the cognitive strategies. Students must learn how to learn, how to think, and how to motivate themselves. Norman (1980) indicates

> It is strange that we expect students to learn yet seldom teach them about learning. We expect students to solve problems yet seldom teach them about problem solving. And, similarly, we sometimes require students to remember a considerable body of material yet seldom teach them the art of memory. It is time we made up for this lack, time that we developed the applied disciplines of learning and problem solving and memory. (p. 97)

LEARNING ABOUT LEARNING

Learning is a complex task, and experts agree that students use a variety of methods. The senses collect information from both internal and external sources, and students process information from the senses differently. Some students are visual learners, others are auditory learners, and still others are haptic or tactile learners. This fact requires students to receive material in multiple forms for best success. Visual, hearing, and touch systems are all capable of handling large amounts of information; and all should be considered in the learning process. However, the visual system seems to be the best method of gathering information for most people. Also, the fact that verbal information can be processed at a much higher rate than it is usually spoken should be considered. Many learners actually recode the auditory information into visual images for storage. Although information may be spoken, the learner may form a mental picture of the material to more effectively process the ideas. This neurolinguistic theory is being used by trainers and managers.

> These learning preferences influence communication style . . . . For example, people who are visual tend to reveal themselves by using expressions like, "I see," or "I get the picture." Auditory learners may say "I hear you," or "That doesn't ring a bell." Kinesthetic [tactile] learners talk about "getting a grasp" on things, or "feeling" one way or another. (Learning-Style Theories p. 91)

Those who learn best visually should be given picture images of concepts. Flowcharts, visual maps, and graphic representations are effective learning tools for visual learners. Auditory learners do best by listening to instructions. Because the majority of a traditional classroom is listening, these learners seem to thrive without many additional learning tools. Tactile, or hands-on learners, however, need to experience the concepts to best retain the information being presented. This type of learner can be especially challenging for teachers since many knowledge concepts are difficult to turn into hands-on forms. As a beginning step, helping students understand their best learning styles will support them in choosing those aspects of the concepts being presented that will best aid retention. Since teachers cannot always know each student's learning style, care must be taken to use multiple forms as much as possible when presenting ideas.

PROCESSING INFORMATION

The process of entering information into the brain involves the learner's perception. The brain does not simply file information, but it analyzes the information and relates it to other information already received. The information storage and retrieval system is the memory. Memory is linked to perception since what is learned at one time is related to what is already known. Both perception and memory are part of the complex system of information processing.

Perception. Before information can be stored for future reference, it must be processed into long-term storage. Each person uses past knowledge and experiences to help process new information being received. This processing is different not only because each person has different past experiences but also because the material may be perceived in a different form from one person to the next.

People see what they expect to see, and something expected may be seen even though it is not present. Therefore, visual perception may not always be accurate. This fact is evidenced by listening to two people's descriptions of the same experience. Although the explanations may differ, one person is not necessarily lying; he or she has simply perceived the information according to his or her own situation.

Verbal perception may also be distorted based on the person's past knowledge. Upon first hearing an unfamiliar language or even unfamiliar terms in a native language, the listener may believe the sounds are jumbled and make no sense. With some understanding of the language or specific terms, however, the jumbled sounds become recognizable and can be repeated by the listener.

Learners are selective about the information they choose to process and store. They may search through a large amount of information to select the desired material. This task, known as scanning, is valuable in allowing the learner to search an abundance of information for the specific items needed, saving the time of having to read everything in detail. Most students have developed this skill to a certain degree, but other learners can increase their learning ability with some instruction in scanning.

The activities related to the processing of information are known as attending to the material. The amount of attention given is determined by the type of activity and the information involved. When the learner is searching for specific information, either by scanning or by another method, he or she may use a filtering technique. This task allows the learner to quickly discard those items not important to the particular activity and search only for those items that fit the criteria being sought. Another closely related inputting task is known as pigeonholing. This method is a slower process since the learner must categorize the information according to where it should be placed rather than simply discarding it as unimportant in the current situation. Although these activities may be performed subconsciously for some learners, the outcomes are important in helping them process the information in an organized manner.

Another important aspect to perception involves time. Learners must be given an adequate period to process the information. Although some learners process faster than others, visual information can be processed more quickly than auditory information. The visual information is seen in a more holistic way, whereas the auditory information must be entered word by word. Single words often cannot be processed until the entire communication has been delivered, as word meanings are affected by the surrounding words. Also, the capacity of the learner will influence the amount learned. Although advocates of mastery learning have long insisted that all students can learn the same material given enough time, Palady (1994) indicates the notion does not extend to higher-level thought processes of synthesizing and evaluating, which may be beyond some students' capacities.

During the process of gathering information, students often acquire knowledge that was not part of the originally intended learning. This incidental learning may rival the intentional learning in importance. For example, a student may learn more in the college environment by virtue of living with roommates and managing his or her own circumstances than in the actual classroom situation. Although no one will dispute the importance of the classroom knowledge, that incidental learning will likely contribute more to the student's lifetime success than the academic degree. Some learners absorb more incidental learning than others, and the amount does not seem to be related to the individual's intelligence. However, incidental learning seems to decline with learners who are highly motivated or driven to success. Many psychologists agree that incidental learning is perhaps the greatest source of learning.

One factor that determines how well information is processed is the learner's motivation. Information that is important to the learner will be processed more efficiently than information that is considered unimportant. Consequently, giving learners information about the relevance of the concepts being learned is important in motivating them to process the information well. The student who is "learning" only to pass a test will not retain the knowledge to the same degree as the learner who is motivated to "internalize" the information. Often this understanding of the material's relevance is a component of maturity on the part of the learner. Immature learners are more concerned about external rewards such as grades, whereas mature learners are concerned with retaining the knowledge for future use. Although the external motivation may be needed initially, students should be "weaned" from external rewards even though the process is not a simple one. By relating the information to the student's personal needs, the teacher may be able to influence this aspect of motivation.

When information is entered into the system, it does not enter a vacuum but instead is stored in an organized fashion to be retrieved at a later date. The memory part of the system ties the past with the present and the new information. These links, called schemata, are the structure around which learning is arranged and retained in organized chunks. Teachers can help students with this linking process by giving encoding clues. Because the information is new to the learners, they cannot always easily determine the most relevant information from the material presented. Discussing specific points to watch for in upcoming reading assignments, for example, will give learners an advantage in organizing the information for storage and retrieval. This linking becomes an important aid to learning. Some educators hesitate to give these clues, playing "keep away" instead, as if these prompts would make learning "too easy" for students. Much research has shown the effectiveness of this linking process.

Ausubel (1963) proposed a structure called an advance organizer to help students organize large amounts of material. He indicated the purposes of the organizer are to provide a framework for the learning that is to follow, to serve as a link between the student's present knowledge and the new material being studied, and to facilitate the encoding of material to be assimilated. These organizers may take many forms. The use of incomplete notes, where students are given partial information with the rest to be filled in as the material is presented, is a simple form of an advance organizer. Other examples may take the form of lists comparing old and new material in an outline framework. Another advance organizer is the use of mnemonic devices. Learners can use these devices to help memorize certain concepts; for example, comparing the "e" in "letter" to the one in "stationery" to distinguish it from "stationary." However, care must be taken not to mislead students while trying to simplify learning. A commonly used example in teaching students the difference between "principal" and "principle" is telling them, "The principal is your pal." This example provides a misconception since students then believe that all other examples must be "principle." Advance organizers are especially effective for visual learners since they can process information in a picture form.

Memory. Memory concerns transforming data to the brain for later recall. Just as everyone does not perceive situations the same way, all learners do not store knowledge in their memory with the same degree of efficiency. However, some fundamental principles can help students store and retrieve information more effectively.

Typically, the progress of learning begins at a slow pace, is followed by a more rapid spurt, and finally slows again toward the end of the curve. One reason may be the student's overcoming initial difficulties with the learning that then leads to a more rapid pace of learning. When the learning is satisfied or incentives for learning are no longer present, the speed of learning slows down. Therefore, both the teacher and the learner must have patience when the learning does not appear to be as rapid as desired. An example is evident with novice keyboarding students. At the beginning of the learning, the keyboarders are clumsy and slow in both learning and performance. As they become more adept with the keyboard, their ability increases not only in actual words per minute but also in the time required for skill development.

Learning is successful, of course, when the learner can later recall the stored information. This learning is usually measured by some type of testing, whether formal or informal. Different levels of recall are tested by different types of questions.

Free recall is used when a student is expected to explain what he or she knows, often in an essay-type question. The teacher must take care, however, to give the student clues about the information recall expected; students cannot be expected to read the teacher's mind. Yet many times teachers fail to give the students adequate clues about what is expected. Learners should not be expected to recall all they know about a topic or to reconstruct the text. Conversely, the recognition method of recall requires the student simply to select correct items from choices, such as a multiple-choice test. Recall requires more detailed information to be stored and is more dependent on complete retention of information than recognition. Requiring students to give short answers when clues are given about expectations compels learners to recollect information that has been stored internally.

When learners have "forgotten" information, they have actually lost the ability to retrieve information. This loss of response capability is a decay process where information fades from the system. Most often, all learning of the information has not been lost, but perhaps only bits and pieces remain. Initially this forgetting occurs rapidly and becomes slower as time passes. Although initial forgetting may be rapid, less time is required to relearn the same material. The amount of relearning that is necessary depends on how well the material was learned originally and how efficiently the information was stored. Also, the greater the time between practice sessions, the more time required to relearn. Because pictures are more easily recalled than words, visual images again become a source of increased learning.

When people refer to memory, they actually may mean one of several systems. Most often, experts refer to three types of memory systems. The trace memory refers to the very quick analysis of information. For example, a person may repeat a phone number or address to keep it in the memory just long enough to use the information and then promptly forget it. The short-term or working memory is limited in the amount of information that it can hold. The long-term memory is the permanent storage system. Information first enters short-term memory and must be transferred to the long-term storage. To be transferred, the material must be organized in some way. Somewhat like a filing cabinet, information that is not filed in some organized way will be lost rather than retrieved quickly. The better the organization and the more rehearsing the information receives in the short-term memory, the more effectively it will be stored in the long-term memory.

Travers (1982) refers to learning material in pieces as chunking. He indicates that most people have a limit of seven "chunks" of material that can be remembered at the same time. This chunking is most effective if the material is organized in some manner.

Several techniques may be used to help learners organize the information for permanent storage. Teachers should organize the material before presenting it to the learner so he or she will have fewer difficulties with both processing and storage. An example of this organization can be seen in the changes in computer software over the last few years. Earlier versions included templates listing the various functions available with the software. These functions were different with each software package and required the learners to memorize which function keys to use in performing various functions. Later versions, particularly windows packages, use visual icons and menu bars with well-organized terms to help the software user more easily find and perform the various functions of the software.

Next, helping the students understand relevance of the material being studied will also aid in storage since the long-term memory is reserved for material that has high utility for the learner. The student's perception of the relevance of the material affects the storage. If the student believes the material will be useful in the future, he or she is more likely to store material efficiently. This perception may help explain why teachers become frustrated with students' inability to recall information learned earlier. Rather than assuming the earlier teacher did not teach the information, a better assumption may be that the student did not perceive the information as something important enough to organize and store for future use.

The use of rehearsal is an important learning strategy. This rehearsal may take the form of reciting the information, copying the material, underlining important ideas, or taking notes on selected material. Howe (1970) found that students who took notes of presentations were more likely to learn the information than those who did not. Specifically, information found in the students' notes could be recalled 34 percent of the time whereas information not in the notes could be recalled only 5 percent of the time. This fact supports the idea that rehearsal strategies help learners acquire and store information.

The point beyond which immediate and complete recall is possible is known as overlearning. This strategy is accepted as the single best way to prevent forgetting. Overlearning does not mean the material has to be attended to in the same way again and again; it is actually more effective if presented in different contexts. Distributed practice over several sessions instead of one long session greatly enhances retention of information. Research indicates spaced and comprehensive reviews are essential to students' remembering information. According to Palady (1994), "if 'it' is worth taking time to teach, 'it' must be worth taking time to review."

Homework. If students are to be as successful as possible in processing, storing, and retrieving information, they must have continual experience with the concepts. One of the most valuable strategies for success is frequent homework. In essence, homework extends the school day, and the more time students spend studying, the more information they will learn. In studying research on homework, Walberg, Paschal, and Weinstein (1985) found that homework benefits both achievement and attitudes. Homework that is assigned without any comment raised students' scores from the 50th to the 60th percentile. When the teachers graded or commented on the homework, the increase was from the 50th to the 79th percentile. Daily homework had a greater effect than sporadically assigned homework.

PUTTING IT ALL TOGETHER

Although learning theory can be fascinating, its worth is questionable unless the theory is translated into practice. The following suggestions are given in list form to help the reader follow the ideas readily. The list is an example of an advance organizer of how to implement the ideas presented throughout the article.

Learning theory:

- Use higher level teaching strategies of analysis, transfer, and synthesis along with the concept knowledge.
- Plan several spaced practice sessions instead of one long session to teach a concept.
- Teach students to scan information to find specific items.
- Present relevant concepts. Students are more likely to assimilate the information if they understand the importance.
- Bridge the gap between what the learner knows and what he or she needs to learn, using advance organizers.
- Consider using short-answer test questions to compel students to more completely retain information.
- Introduce students to mnemonic devices to help with memory.
- Devote time to teaching students to take notes. Try giving learners incomplete notes to be filled in as the learning progresses.
- Make recall of information less dependent upon the context by presenting it in more than one setting.

Teacher behavior:

- Provide positive reinforcement in the classroom. Although a certain amount of stress aids in learning, too much can shut it down completely.

- Avoid playing "keep away" with important clues. Rather, give students hints about what to expect before they begin projects. These hints will help learners more easily meet the frustration of learning.

- Summarize for one or two minutes at the end of class.

- Assign meaningful homework assignments often. Then attend to the information by grading it and making helpful comments to the students.

Student focus:

- Give students responsibility for their learning.

- Review previously learned material frequently.

- Use high but reasonable expectations of all students.

- Keep in mind that some students are visual learners, others are auditory learners, and still others are tactile learners who achieve better by "doing." Learning activities should be varied to include all three groups.

- Help students develop an appreciation for life-long learning.

- Enjoy the results of students' increased success!

REFERENCES

Ausubel, D. P. (1963). In Joyce, B. & Weil, M. (1986). *Models of teaching.* Englewood Cliffs, NJ: Prentice Hall.

Bell-Gredler, M. E. (1986). *Learning and instruction: Theory into practice.* New York: Macmillan.

Heinen, J. R. K., Stafford, K. R., & Sherman, T. M. (1990, Dec.). Role of learning theory in educational psychology. *Psychological Reports,* pp. 763-774.

Howe, M. J. A. (1970). In Weinstein, C. E., and Mayer R. E. (1986). The teaching of learning strategies. In M. C. Wittrock (Eds.), *The handbook of research on teaching,* (pp. 315-327). New York: Macmillan.

Learning-style theories. (1992, Sep.). *Personnel Journal,* p. 91.

Norman, D. A. (1980). In Weinstein, C. E., and Mayer R. E. (1986). The teaching of learning strategies. In M. C. Wittrock (Eds.), *The handbook of research on teaching,* (pp. 315-327). New York: Macmillan.

Palardy, J. M. (1994, Dec.). Principles of learning: A review. *Journal of Instructional Psychology,* pp. 308-312.

Travers, R. M. W. (1982). *Essentials of learning: The new cognitive learning for students of education.* New York: Macmillan.

Wahlberg, H. J., Paschal, R. A., & Weinstein, T. (1985, April). Homework's powerful effects on learning. *Educational Leadership,* pp. 76-79.

Weinstein, C. E., & Mayer, R. E. (1986). The teaching of learning strategies. In M. C. Wittrock (Eds.), *The handbook of research on teaching,* (pp. 315-327). New York: Macmillan.

Wittrock, M. C. (1986). Students' thought processes. In M. C. Wittrock (Eds.), *The handbook of research on teaching,* (pp. 297-314). New York: Macmillan.

CHAPTER 8

Diversity in the Classroom

BERYL C. McEWEN

North Carolina A&T State University, Greensboro, North Carolina

THADDEUS McEWEN

North Carolina A&T State University, Greensboro, North Carolina

In the last few years we have seen an upsurge in interest in diversity in businesses and in the classroom. Conferences, speeches, articles, and books on education constantly mention the need for educators to help students develop the skills necessary to function in a culturally diverse workplace. Accrediting agencies as well as legislative bodies in many states (including California and Texas) are requiring the inclusion of cultural diversity in teacher education programs (Larke, 1990). In fact, it seems that everyone, from the President of the United States to presidents of major U.S. corporations, is talking about diversity.

Business educators, therefore, must address diversity in the classroom. Now, more than ever before, it is imperative that teachers become more sensitive to the needs of all students. Teachers should not be uncomfortable with individual differences in the classroom. Instead, they should carefully consider these differences to create a learning environment that is effective for all students, regardless of ethnicity, socioeconomic status, or other differences (Larke, 1990).

This chapter focuses on teaching in a culturally diverse classroom, rather than on what to teach in a cultural diversity course. The following will be discussed in the chapter:

- Meaning of diversity
- Importance of diversity
- Differences in culturally diverse students
- Needs of culturally diverse students
- Strategies for teaching in a culturally diverse classroom
- Ways of increasing cultural diversity awareness.

MEANING OF DIVERSITY

Ask business teachers what comes to mind when they hear the word "diversity," and we are sure to get a variety of responses—"multiculturalism," "minority," "ethnicity," "race." Defining diversity strictly in terms of race and ethnicity, however, artificially limits one's perception of diversity (Mungo, 1992). Diversity should include race, ethnicity, gender, exceptionality, age, and many other factors. Ownby and Perreault (1994) also provided a similar definition—"Diversity includes differences such as physical disabilities, educational levels, gender, sexual orientation, age, and religion as well as cultural background" (p. 27).

In fact, Loden and Rosener (1991) categorized diversity factors into two groups—primary dimensions and secondary dimensions of diversity. Primary dimensions include unalterable characteristics, such as age, gender, race, ethnicity, and physical ability. Secondary dimensions include educational level, marital status, religion, socioeconomic status, and educational background, which might change over time. It is important to understand that diversity goes beyond the primary dimensions to include the secondary dimensions. Many factors make students different and can affect their interests, values, how they interact, and how they learn.

IMPORTANCE OF DIVERSITY

Two important factors are fueling current interest in cultural diversity. The first is changes in societal demographics and the other is increasing awareness of the value of diversity in businesses.

Changing Demographics. A demographic revolution has been taking place in the United States. Between 1970 and 1980, the United States has become increasingly multicultural. The Hispanic population grew by 61 percent, Native-Americans by 71 percent (Cortes, 1986), and Asian-Americans by 141 percent (Banks, 1987). Between 1980 and 1990, the minority populations continued to grow—African-Americans by 13.2 percent, American Indians by 37.9 percent, Asian and Pacific Islanders by 107.8 percent, and Hispanics by 53 percent.

The 1990 census revealed that one of every four residents of the United States is a person of color and that by the turn of the century one of every three will be a person of color. Not surprisingly, the ethnic and racial makeup of schools is also changing significantly. Students of color constitute a majority in 25 of the largest school districts. They will account for nearly half, (46 percent) of the school-age children by the year 2020, and about 27 percent of those students will be victims of poverty (Banks, Cortez, Gay, Garcia, and Ochoa, 1991). As such, education must face the challenge of the demographic revolution and help students develop the skills needed to succeed in the culturally diverse workplace.

Value of Diversity in Businesses. Like society, the workplace is also diverse and will continue to be that way as we move into the 21st century. According to the Hudson Institute's "Workforce 2000" report (Johnson, 1987), in the year 2000 new entrants to the workforce will be about 85 percent minorities, including women and immigrants. Organizations are therefore requiring new employees to come into the workplace with the skills needed for working with and managing people with culturally diverse backgrounds. In a study of 645 companies, 74 percent considered cultural diversity a corporate concern (Wilcox, 1991). And Winikow (1991) agreed with Wilcox's findings, noting that the challenge is not just to accommodate diversity but to actually use it to bring new and richer perspectives to jobs and customers.

Recognizing the needs of businesses, the Report of the Secretary's Commission on Necessary Skills (1992) listed the ability to work well with people from culturally diverse backgrounds as a foundation competency that students need to succeed in the workplace. Similarly, Michigan's Employability Skills Task Force (Stemmer, Brown, & Smith, 1992, p. 33) also listed the ability to "work in changing settings and with people of different backgrounds" as an employability skill. As companies continue to value diversity, business education must take advantage of the diversity in the classroom in providing all students with effective workplace skills. We can begin by trying to understand and work with the differences in culturally diverse students.

DIFFERENCE IN CULTURALLY DIVERSE STUDENTS

Comments such as, "diversity doesn't matter; I treat all students alike," though genuine and truthful, indicate a problem. Since students bring the values of their dominant culture to the classroom and all cultures are not identical, recognizing and responding to the differences is preferred to "trying to treat all students alike."

As teachers, one of our jobs is to make the classroom a place where all learners feel comfortable enough to participate. One way to do this is to be aware of those behaviors that make some students feel unwelcome or excluded. Longstreet (1978) listed five guidelines for recognizing and understanding cultural differences in the classroom: verbal communication, nonverbal communication, orientation modes, social value patterns, and intellectual modes.

Verbal Communication. Students need to be proficient in standard American English. Many minority students, however, do not speak standard English in their home communities. As such, they often have to translate to their dominant language in order to think and process information. This translation slows their response time, often suggesting lack of knowledge. Many also experience cultural conflict because they are forced to ignore the language they have known from birth. Standard American English also may be a problem for African-Americans and students from some rural areas. For example, students who speak "country," Black vernacular, or any other nonstandard dialect are usually perceived as uneducated or less intelligent.

Discussion modes also vary among ethnic groups. During discussions Anglo-American students tend to follow the "you take a turn, then another takes a turn" model. Black students, however, tend to find this model restrictive, while Asian-American students are also uncomfortable for different reasons. Asian-American students tend to think through a position before verbalizing it and are unlikely to express their thoughts in the midst of a spontaneous, seemingly loud discussion.

Nonverbal Communication. Between 50 and 90 percent of what humans communicate is nonverbal. Messages are sent through body movements, expressions, gestures, space, and touch. The literature contains numerous examples of cultural differences in nonverbal communication such as eye aversions (looking down or away), which is a source of intercultural misunderstanding. With the dominant culture, direct eye contact signifies that one is listening to the speaker, is honest, and is telling the truth. In some African-

American communities, as well as among Native-Americans, Asian-Americans, and many international students, however, eye aversion is a sign of respect for others.

Orientation Mode. Difference in the perception of time in Anglo-American and African-American cultures is well acknowledged. For Caucasians, things are usually accomplished one-at-a-time, in a linear fashion. Events are carefully scheduled. For Blacks, many activities take place simultaneously, and schedules are less visible. Events begin when people get there and end when people leave. School life, however, operates according to schedules and procedures, therefore requiring serious adjustments on the parts of some students.

Social Value. Social values are beliefs about acceptable and unacceptable behaviors. For example, most academic activities are competitive, affirming the belief that individual achievement is important and commendable. Teachers often motivate students with competitive games. Many Anglo-American students enjoy working on their own; however, African-American youths tend to value cooperation. They are prone to seek the assistance of classmates at least as frequently as the teacher's. Behaviors that resemble cheating, copying, or frivolous socializing may, sometimes, be attempts to seek help from a peer.

Intellectual Mode. Intellectual mode refers to the types of knowledge that are valued most and to preferred learning styles. Students who are practically-oriented are often frustrated when their course work is too theoretical. Also, the dominant culture emphasizes visual learning through reading while African-Americans have a more aural tradition. For example, they perform better if they listen to a tape of the text while reading it. On the other hand, many Caucasian students prefer to read without the background noise. These patterns do not mean all Blacks learn aurally and all Caucasians learn visually.

Motivation. Motivation in multicultural classrooms is related to learning styles and perceived relevance of course materials. Teachers need to recognize that both motivation and learning styles vary in the multicultural classroom. Motivational activities that are effective for one student or a group of students may have little effect with others.

Creating interest in a multicultural classroom will provide a challenge for the instructor because of the varied backgrounds and needs of students. Minor changes in the instructor's behavior, however, can create a learning environment that encourages participation by minority students. Teachers need to establish a comfortable classroom atmosphere in which all students are encouraged to participate. Creating such an environment requires an understanding of the cultural orientation of students. Even the most sensitive and dedicated teachers can be frustrated in their attempts to reach individual learners if they are unaware of how their own cultural orientations may cause learning difficulties for some students.

DETERMINING STUDENTS' NEEDS

Longstreet (1978) lists three factors that can influence an individual's predisposition to learn: classroom atmosphere, relevance of the information, and appropriateness of the teaching materials. The heterogeneity of the diverse classroom suggests that students will respond differently to these factors. For example, not all students require or even prefer a quiet learning environment. To develop an understanding of students' needs, business teachers must carefully observe how students interact with their learning environment. As Kendall (1983) noted, the goal is to accurately determine the work habits that each student uses in her or his most successful encounters.

Learning Style. Learning style describes the way in which different types of stimuli affect an individual's ability to absorb, retain, and use information. Learning opportunities that appeal to an individual's preferred learning style will yield more permanent learning (Kendall, 1983). In the context of business education, the classifications of learning styles presented by Romero (1992) seem most appropriate. According to Romero, "Cognitive Learners" are those who learn through group instruction (e.g., lectures, books, and assignments). These students learn in the traditional way in which schools expect learning to occur and in which most teachers teach. Probably, because of this, they are often the high achievers. "Affective Learners" learn through group interaction. They like to talk and are very people-focused. These learners have difficulty conforming to the "quiet, orderly environment" of the typical classroom. "Psychomotor Learners" learn best through activity and movement. They need to touch, feel, and manipulate things and have great difficulty sitting still and listening. Of course, as Green (1989) noted the importance of viewing learning style as a matter of preference rather than absolutes. ". . . students need opportunities to exercise their preferred style as well as develop their weaker styles" (p. 142). Teachers who expect all students to conform to their teaching style will undoubtedly frustrate some students. Using a variety of learning activities will enable students to exercise their strengths as well as develop their nonpreferred styles.

Responding to Students' Needs. Romero (1992) noted that cooperative learning is highly valued among Hispanic, African-American, and Native-American students. They tend to be "affective learners." Asian-American students tend to be more "cognitive learners," but they also tend to be more quantitative than verbal—having been socialized to exercise restraint, especially of strong feelings.

Demanding that African-American or Hispanic children sit quietly and work might be counter-productive when their dominant cultures focus heavily on cooperative activities. Such students may want to move around, ask their peers for help, offer assistance to those who need it, and may even be tempted to behave in this manner under testing conditions.

Teachers who are committed to promoting diversity in the classroom and providing all students with equitable learning opportunities must vary their teaching styles to respond to the varying learning styles of their students. The following are some suggestions for varying the teaching/learning approaches:

Collaborative Approach. The collaborative approach involves students in the curriculum process—deciding what to teach and how to teach. At the high school level students may be somewhat reluctant to tell the teacher what to do; but games, group work, brainstorming, and other such activities can be used to solicit students' suggestions. The teacher or, better yet, a group of teachers involved with each course can then decide how to incorporate the students' suggestions. If all students are involved in the process and their opinions and suggestions are carefully considered and utilized, this approach can lead to a curriculum that represents the diversity of the group, both in what is taught and in how the teaching is structured.

Cooperative Approach. Cooperation is highly valued in many ethnic minority groups and among people with disabilities. Sharing is at the core of the cooperative approach. Students are allowed to support each other in the learning process—ensuring that all benefit. This approach also allows the teacher to help all students develop such skills as diplomacy, leadership, delegation, responsibility, and respect. Although the cooperative approach involves working together in groups, other formats, such as coaching or peer tutoring, can also be used.

When structured group work is assigned, teachers in a diverse classroom should assign students to groups instead of allowing them to form their own groups. Assigning students to groups will ensure that students form multiethnic, multigender groups and so get to know each other and work together better.

Competitive Approach. Through the competitive approach, students can develop the type of independence that will allow them to compete successfully in the classroom and in the workplace. Business teachers should design classroom activities in which students are required to perform tasks alone and within specific time frames. They should, however, also be aware that many ethnic minority groups discourage competition; and, as such, competing is difficult for some of these students. Minority students will therefore need more assistance in developing competitive learning skills as some majority students will need more assistance in developing teamwork skills.

Inquiry Approach. The inquiry approach involves questioning students and engaging them in oral discourse. For many minority students, the inquiry approach presents great difficulty because they tend to be less comfortable in oral communication than are Anglo-American students. They often fear ridicule if they give the wrong answer or use incorrect grammar or diction. When using the inquiry approach, teachers need to provide enough "wait time" for students to prepare their responses before being asked to speak. Efforts must also be made to ensure that all students are asked "thinking questions" as well as questions that allow them to draw answers from their dominant culture. At the same time, instructors should not assume that minority students can represent their entire ethnic group and therefore be asked to give the opinion or position of the group. Many minority students resent this, insisting that they are individuals who can speak only for themselves. Notwithstanding, the inquiry approach provides unique opportunities for students to develop their oral skills and their critical thinking skills. It should be used frequently and well.

TEACHING STRATEGIES

The teaching strategies that the instructor chooses will determine not only the quality of instruction but also the comfort level of the diverse classroom. Teaching strategy underlies the quality of interaction that occurs between teacher and students. The diverse classroom needs responsive teachers—teachers who treat each student with respect and empathy. Selakovich (cited in Romero, 1992), however, found that ethnic and economically deprived students received significantly—

1. less teacher praise and encouragement
2. less teacher acceptance of their ideas
3. fewer teacher questions
4. less positive teacher response
5. less non-criticizing teacher talk.

On the other hand, Sandhu (1994) reminds us that: "As educators, we teach *students* first, and then the subject matter" (p. 14). Responsive teaching is therefore critical for the diverse classroom.

Responsive Teaching. Sandhu (1994) suggested a three-step model for culturally responsive teaching, which includes awareness, acceptance, and action.

Step 1: **Awareness** involves seeking knowledge about other cultures and ethnic groups, learning how to create equitable classroom conditions for all students, and examining how one's values and beliefs may affect interaction with students.

Step 2: **Acceptance** should be based on the notion that cultural diversity is a strength and that all students can learn and excel in their areas of interest. Acceptance also means respecting divergent thinking and various viewpoints.

Step 3: **Action** involves empowering students through personal attention, encouragement, and support; practicing behaviors that are free of prejudice, biases, and stereotypes and encouraging students to do so; being genuinely considerate of students, both inside and outside the classroom; and being open to new experiences and challenges.

Jackson (1994) also suggests seven ways to "Culturally Responsive Pedagogy."

1. Build trust, e.g., learn students' names and pronounce them correctly.

2. Become culturally literate, e.g., observe students in nonschool settings like churches, community organizations, or the home.

3. Build a repertoire of instructional strategies, e.g., limit assumptive teaching in the classroom—all students can perform but some are unwilling—and try instead to understand and respond to the students' learning styles.

4. Use effective questioning techniques, e.g., include higher-order questions and address them to all students.

5. Provide effective feedback, e.g., communicate how to correct errors and improve overall quality instead of commenting only on such things as neatness.

6. Analyze instructional materials, e.g., avoid material that includes racist concepts, cliches, or phrases.

7. Establish positive home-school relations, e.g., at the beginning of the school year, send home a note that expresses your enthusiasm at having each student in your class. Follow up later with a phone call to discuss the students' strengths,

weaknesses, and interests with the parents.

Of course, some of these suggestions are more appropriate for grades 6-12 than for postecondary levels. For responsive teaching at the college level, Reyes (1991) suggests the following:

1. Review important learning prerequisites.
2. Provide several examples of abstractions used in lectures.
3. Distribute questions equally among students in terms of quantity and quality.
4. Ask higher level questions of all students.
5. Give culturally diverse students enough wait time to frame responses to difficult questions.
6. Provide prompts for students who seem to be having difficulty responding to a difficult question.
7. Reinforce students only for correct responses or productive lines of thought (don't patronize low ability students).

Teaching/Learning Activities. The diverse classroom will demand creative activities that will appeal to the varied learning styles and interests of students. Traditional types of activities like projects, library research, term papers, work books, computer-aided instruction, and case studies are certainly applicable. Diverse classrooms, however, will also require more multimedia and cooperative activities.

Multimedia, which appeals to many different senses, increases the likelihood of reaching students of varied backgrounds. Activities that require students to work in teams will almost certainly appeal to Hispanic, African-American, and Native-American students whose cultures tend to emphasize the achievement of the group over individual successes.

The following strategies are well suited for diverse classrooms at both the secondary and the postsecondary levels:

- class discussions in small groups
- presentations by members of culturally diverse groups (including parents and community leaders)
- group research projects and presentations
- field experiences involving small groups of students
- simulations and games, including the use of multi-media
- interactive videos
- multimedia computer-assisted or computer-based instructions
- well-structured and managed debates
- peer tutoring.

The following are examples of specific learning activities:

1. Assign small groups of students to review various news media (radio, newspapers, magazines, and television), looking for examples of advertising to people of various ethnic groups or national origins. Have students discuss how the ads are similar or different.
2. Have students visit a local mall or shopping center (in small groups) to find examples of how businesses market their product or services to diverse populations, e.g., ethnic minorities, females, disabled people, bilingual or nonEnglish speak-

ing people. Have students discuss the effectiveness of various marketing efforts.

3. Have students design a marketing plan for increasing sales of a particular product within a particular ethnic group represented in the class. Encourage students to consult with the members of the group being targeted.

4. Divide students into small groups and have each group develop a calendar for one of the ethnic groups represented in the class, including Anglo-Americans. Require students to use desktop publishing software to create a professional product, if necessary, consulting with other students to get assistance to complete the assignment. Each calendar should contain at least one entry per month. (Adopted from Zeliff, 1994).

5. Have each student in the class speak with at least one individual from a different cultural or ethnic group to his or her own and learn from that individual one short verse, anecdote, or quotation that has some special meaning for that group. Present the material on an 8.5 x 11 poster for the wall. The poster should contain the quote and the explanation, as well as a citation. Leave the display up for as long as is possible.

6. Have students, in small groups, create a brochure of "Do's and Don'ts" for building relationships with various diverse groups. Require students to use their desktop publishing skills to produce a professional product.

7. Require small groups of students to research and present a table of weights and measures for all the various countries represented in the classroom. If all class members are from the same country, encourage them to do it for some of the countries that they have visited or hope to visit. Require accuracy both in mathematics and in translations.

Assessment Strategies. Because of the diversity that exists in the classroom, instructors need to use a variety of assessment techniques. Most textbooks are supported by test banks that primarily consist of objective-type questions. Students with language deficiencies will find objective tests to be more difficult, or they will require more time because of the need to translate to their native language to understand the questions or statements.

To cater to the needs of all students, therefore, several different types of evaluations should be planned for each course. These should include:

1. Criterion-referenced quizzes and tests

2. Essay questions that allow for some expression and discussion

3. Oral reports, followed by questioning (sometimes in small groups)

4. Products of individual or group efforts

5. Portfolios of students' work over a specific period

6. Video-taped performances that can be done in students' comfort zones

7. Observations of students in individual or group processes

8. Critical incidents

9. Assessment Centers, where students can select their peers for supporting roles while simulating a specific job scenario

10. Peer evaluation.

These strategies can be used very effectively in assessing students. The key is to use several throughout a semester so all students can find assessment situations in which they can perform well. To insure objectivity, instructors should prepare and use answer keys as well as checklists and rating scales. Students should be encouraged to discuss their performance with a view to understanding what is needed to make improvements.

Cross, Baker, & Styles (1977) noted that assessment of results must give attention to attitudes, understandings, and interactions of students. They further noted that while attitudes and understandings can be measured, interactions must be observed. Observation is probably the most powerful tool for assessing student interaction in the context of the diverse classroom. Teachers should use it, and students who show progress in building working relationships with others who are different from themselves should be rewarded for their achievement.

LEARNING MORE ABOUT DIVERSITY

To better understand culturally diverse students, teachers can visit students' homes and speak with their parents and other family members; start a class newsletter to which all students contribute stories about their communities, families, and interests; and invite parents to visit and participate in classroom activities. Many parents will be delighted to be guest speakers in their children's classrooms. Teachers should also participate in community activities, such as international and other cultural festivals, read about other cultures, watch non-majority television shows and movies, try listening to a foreign language station for a few minutes each week, develop working relationships with colleagues from minority populations, and listen to the international news. A variety of print and nonprint resources are also available.

RESOURCES

The following resources will help business teachers develop diversity awareness in their classrooms.

Articles/Microfiche/Books:

Banks, J. A., Cortes, C. E., Gay, G., Garcia, R. L., & Ochoa, A. S. (1992). Curriculum guidelines for multicultural education. *Social Education, 56*(5), 274-294.

Bennett, C. I. (1990). *Comprehensive multicultural education: Theory and practice.* (2nd. ed.). Boston, MA: Allyn and Bacon.

Codina, W. (1994). *Accessing culture and language through the Internet.* Maryville, MO: Northwest Missouri State University.

Jenkins, C. A., and Bainer, D. L. (1990). *Common instructional problems in multicultural classrooms.* (ERIC Document Reproduction Service No. ED 330 279)

Kohls, L. R. (1981). *Developing intercultural awareness.* Washington, DC: SIETAR.

Larke, P. J. (1991). Effective multicultural teachers: Meeting the challenges of diverse classrooms. *Equity and Excellence, 25*(1), 133-144.

Sandhu, D. S. (1994). *Cultural diversity in classrooms: What teachers need to know.* (ERIC Document Reproduction Service No. ED 370 911)

Tiedt, P. L., and Tiedt, I. M. (1990). *Multicultural teaching: A handbook of activities, information and resources.* (3rd. ed.). Boston, MA: Allyn & Bacon.

Wright, D. J. (1987). Minority students: Developmental beginnings. In D. J. Wright (Ed.), *Responding to the needs of minority students.* San Francisco, CA: Jossey-Bass.

Games/Simulations/Videos:

Bafa Bafa

Smile II
P. O. Box 910
Del Mar, CA 92014
Simulates two diverse cultures. Develops sensitivity to diversity.

Heelotia: A cross-cultural simulation

Spice
Stanford Program on International and Cross-Cultural Education
Littlefield Center, Room 14
Stanford University
Stanford, CA 95305-5013

Videos by Copeland-Griggs Productions

302 23rd Avenue
San Francisco, CA 94121

"Beyond Culture Shock" - 30 minutes
"Bridging the Culture Gap" - 30 minutes
"Champions of Diversity" - 30 minutes
"Welcome Home, Stranger" - 15 minutes
"You Make the Difference" - 30 minutes

Organizations:

Advisory Committee on Education of Spanish and Mexican-Americans
400 Maryland Avenue, S.W.
Washington, DC 20202

African-American Institute
833 United National Plaza
New York, NY 10017

American Indian Cultural Development Program
3315 S. Airport Road
Bismarck, ND 58501

Association for Asian Studies
Service Center for Teachers
The Ohio State University
29 W. Woodruff Avenue
Columbus, OH 43210

Indian Education Resources Center
123 Fourth Street, S.W.
P. O. Box 1788
Albuquerque, NM 87103

Japanese-American Curriculum Project
P. O. Box 367
San Mateo, CA 94401

SUMMARY

Diversity factors include primary dimensions such as age or race and secondary dimensions including educational level and marital status. Cultural differences exist in the classroom and business educators need to understand, appreciate, and value the diversity. Using a variety of teaching and assessing strategies will provide all students with opportunities to succeed. As business teachers, we undoubtedly have a significant role to play in preparing students for the diverse workplace. This will involve exploring ways for helping students in our diverse classroom to reach their potential. It will also involve helping diverse students develop good working relationships with each other.

Businesses need workers who have a genuine understanding of and respect for diversity. This need will undoubtedly continue into the 21st century. The proverbial "ball" is in the teachers' court. Business teachers must take a leadership role in developing students' awareness of and appreciation for cultural diversity.

REFERENCES

Banks, J. A. (1987). *Teaching strategies for ethnic studies* (4th ed.). Boston, MA: Allyn and Bacon.

Cortez, C. E. (1986). The education of language minority students: A contextual interaction model. In California State Department of Education. *Beyond language: Social and cultural factors in schooling language minority students.* Los Angeles, CA: Evaluation Dissemination and Assessment Center, California State University.

Cross, D. E., Baker, G. C., & Stiles, L. J. (Eds.). (1977). *Teaching in a multicultural society: Perspectives and professional strategies.* New York, NY: The Free Press.

Green, M. F. (Ed.) (1989). *Minorities on campus: A handbook for enhancing diversity.* Washington, DC: American Council on Education.

Jackson, F. R. (1994). 7 ways to a culturally responsive pedagogy. *The Education Digest, 59*(6), 47-51.

Johnston, W. B. (1987). *Workforce 2000: Work and workers for the 21st century.* (Executive Summary). Indianapolis, IN: Hudson Institute, Herman Kahn Center

Kendall, F. E. (1983). *Diversity in the classroom: A multicultural approach to the education of young children.* New York, NY: Teachers College Press.

Larke, P. J. (1990). Cultural diversity awareness inventory: Assessing the sensitivity of preservice teachers. *Action in Teacher Education, 12*(3), 23-29.

Loden, M., and Rosener, J. B. (1991). *Workforce America! Managing employee diversity as a vital resource.* Homewood, IL: Business One Irwin.

Longstreet, W. (1978). *Aspects of ethnicity: Understanding differences in pluralistic classrooms.* New York, NY: Teachers College Press.

Mungo, S. (1992). Teachers for culturally diverse classrooms. In J. Q. Adams, and J. R. Welsch (Eds.), *Multicultural education: Strategies for implementation in colleges and universities.* Macomb, IL: Western Illinois University.

Ownby, A. C., and Perreault, H. R. (1994). Teaching students to understand and value diversity. *Business Education Forum, 48*(3), 27-29.

Purkey, S. C., and Smith, M. S. (1985). Effective schools: A review. *Elementary School Journal, 83,* 52-78.

Reyes, D. (1991). Using effective teaching concepts in the multicultural classroom. In J. Q. Adams, J. F. Niss, & C. Suarez (Eds.), *Multicultural education: Strategies for implementation in colleges and universities.* Macomb, IL: Western Illinois University Foundation.

Romero, J. R. (1992). *Multicultural education: Valuing diversity.* Norman, OK: Center for the Study of Small/Rural Schools Continuing Education and Public Service, The University of Oklahoma.

Sandhu, D. S. (1994). *Cultural diversity in classrooms: What teachers need to know.* (ERIC Document Reproduction Service No. ED 370 911)

Secretary's Commission on Necessary Skills (1992). *Learning a living: A blue print for high performance. A SCANS report for America 2000.* (U.S. Department of Labor) Washington, DC: U.S. Government Printing Office.

Stemmer, P., Brown, B., & Smith, C. (1992). The employability skills portfolio. *Educational Leadership, 49*(6), 32-35.

Wilcox, J. (1991). The corporate view. *Vocational Education Journal, 66*(8), 32-33.

Winikow, L. (1991). How women and minorities are reshaping America (Transcript). *Vital Speeches, 57,* 242-244.

Zeliff, N. (1994). *Internationalizing your curriculum.* Paper presented at the American Vocational Education Association Conference, Dallas, TX.

CHAPTER 9

Authentic Assessment

NANCY D. ZELIFF

Northwest Missouri State University, Maryville, Missouri

KIMBERLY A. SCHULTZ

Central Decatur Community School, Leon, Iowa

"Not everything that counts can be counted and not everything that can be counted counts."
Author Unknown

In agreement with the assessment reform underway in education, the above quotation succinctly states that traditional methods of evaluating student learning may not adequately assess student achievement. By responding correctly to multiple choice questions, does a student reveal what he/she has learned? No guarantee exists because the probability rate of 25 percent or more may allow luck and good guesses to measure student achievement inaccurately. One may be simply "counting" a student's test-taking ability. By responding to short-answer or true/false questions, does a student reveal competency in a skill? No, the performance of a skill observed by an evaluator would better demonstrate student competency.

Traditional means of assessment do not provide an instructor with a complete picture of what a student can or cannot do. Only by using several different forms of evaluation does an instructor gain insight into the student's depth of knowledge. It is the purpose of this chapter to provide the reader with (1) a background of authentic assessment research; (2) a variety of authentic assignments; and (3) alternative ways to evaluate the student in the forms of portfolios and rubrics.

AUTHENTIC ASSESSMENT

The emphasis on authentic assessment today is a result of the concern that objective tests do not accurately assess the critical thinking, problem solving, and self-directed learning of students (Sugarman, Allen, & Keller-Cogan, 1993). Objective assessment includes true/false, multiple-choice, and short-answer questions. These measures are appropriate for evaluating lower level cognitive learning but often give a choice of answers. Choices give students the opportunity to rely on the probability of selecting the correct answer. Objective evaluation may not, therefore, be an accurate means of assessment.

Projects, presentations, and portfolios are examples of performance and authentic assessment. Meyer (1992) states that with performance assessment, the student demonstrates the behavior to be measured with little or no inference. If a student's competence in producing a block letter is desired, the student prepares a block letter. Correctly answering multiple-choice questions on formatting block letters may lead the assessor to presume the student can format a block letter when in fact he/she cannot.

With authentic assessment, the student not only demonstrates the behavior but also completes the behavior in real-life context (Meyer, 1992). When completing a block letter authentically, the student composes or selects a business letter to prepare in block style. More authenticity can be added when the letter is mailed by the student or prepared for someone else.

Assessment considerations. Important considerations with all types of assessment are validity and reliability. Validity in assessment refers to the degree to which the results (scores) represent the knowledge or ability intended to be measured. For example, the intent or objective of completing an income statement is to measure an accounting student's knowledge of the parts and placement of income and expense accounts and to figure net income/loss. Completing true/false questions about the income statement would only measure a student's lower-level cognitive knowledge. Likewise, a valid measure of a computer programmer's skills would be the creation of a computer program, rather than multiple-choice questions about programming in the C++ language.

Reliability measures refer to the consistency of the measurement over time and/or by multiple evaluators. The completion of an income statement by an accounting student each quarter would be a more reliable measure of the student's competence throughout the year than a single test given at the end of a unit of instruction. Reliability also is achieved in assessment when multiple evaluators judge student competence. The evaluators must use the same criteria when judging. Gymnastic, diving, and figure skating competitions use multiple evaluators for reliability. When a gymnast falls from the balance beam, the same point deduction is recorded by all judges; when a difficult dive is completed, points for difficulty are recorded by all evaluators; and when a required jump is not executed, all judges deduct the same points for the skater. The same concept should apply when multiple evaluators grade income statements. Identical grades should be given by each assessor.

Assessment strategies that are less valid and more reliable usually take less time of the assessor when determining student achievement. Objective test questions, spelling tests, and standardized tests have definite right and wrong answers. Computerized scoring is also possible to reduce grading time for the assessor. These measurements are more reliable because multiple evaluators would agree upon the same answer.

Assessment strategies that are more valid and less reliable take more time of the assessor when determining student achievement. Observations of skills, performances, writing assignments, and portfolios are valid because they measure a student's ability to competently perform a skill, write concisely, and synthesize information. Less reliability is present when criteria, however, are not specifically stated.

Authentic assessment strategies are valid measures and become more reliable with the addition of stated criteria. Checklists and rubrics provide this necessary reliability. Another way to increase reliability is to use multiple evaluators.

AUTHENTIC ASSIGNMENTS

Business instructors have always used forms of authentic assignment. Textbooks for keyboarding, computer applications, and accounting provide ample examples for a student who is beginning to practice concept learning. Simulations take the student a step further by placing him/her in the shoes of an employee in a contrived business. Authentic assignments are the final step.

Authentic assignments place the student in the real world with deadlines, revisions, technological mishaps, and teamwork. Authentic assignments are real because the student's product is actually used. The knowledge of the product's future use drives the student to create the best product possible.

A teacher may create many authentic lessons if he/she is willing to turn the project over to the student. Lessons are only authentic if students, not the teacher, have control over the work being completed. Authentic lessons provide the student with the opportunity to budget time, access reference manuals, "test drive" the product, and seek expert advice when needed—all skills that employers demand. Authentic assignments work well in computer-based classes, keyboarding, accounting, and other business classes.

Computer-based classes. Computer-based classes are the easiest in which to use authentic assignments. Desktop publishing software allows the student to create programs, pamphlets, brochures, and business cards. The instructor need only consider the following limiting factors:

✓ deadlines (Can an eight-page program be completed in two class periods?)

✓ graphics availability (Does a variety of clip art exist from which to choose?)

✓ software knowledge (How long has the student been working with the package?)

✓ individual or joint project (Is a project available for each individual?)

An obvious authentic project is designing a program used for athletic, drama, and music events. Securing a master list of the school year's activities will aid the instructor in planning and assigning to students the programs for all events. Students can prioritize their schedule, plan when to begin the project, secure needed information, search for graphics, and build page layout.

Students can create worksheets, tests, review sheets, and typed work for other teachers. Special consideration must be given when pairing the student and the teacher. Questions that must be addressed include these: How well do student and teacher get along? Is the student in the class in which the project will be used? Does the student have friends in the class in which the project will be used?

Other authentic projects may include:

✓ advertisements for school dances

✓ school or community newsletters

✓ department, school, or community promotional pamphlets

✓ department checklists or grade cards

✓ department or office inventories

✓ business cards for teachers, community members, or student organization officers

✓ letters or other documents

✓ sports score charts

✓ envelopes

✓ forms for classroom, school, or community use

✓ application letters and resumes.

Keyboarding. Collaboration with other teachers, particularly those in the English department, can provide a host of authentic assignments for students. After learning how to format various documents, the student is ready to tackle an authentic project. Instead of keyboarding a textbook assignment, the student may choose to key a personal research paper. Two copies can be printed, one for the English instructor and one for the business instructor.

Science experiment data and mathematics or economic survey data readily provide table unit information that can be substituted for a textbook assignment. Corresponding with foreign language pen pals requires letter typing skills and can be integrated with the foreign language curriculum if the student must first translate the letter or reply in the foreign language being studied. Keyboarding students can also practice composition skills by writing and sending request, thank you, or application letters.

Another authentic assignment in which beginning keyboarding students can have success is keying peer or faculty papers. This project allows the student to view many writing styles, learn about topics not otherwise known, and appreciate legible handwriting.

Accounting. In accounting, authentic assignments are hard to find. Businesses can be reluctant to turn over important financial material to a novice accounting student. A copy of financial material can, however, be obtained for student use. Examples of material that can be acquired include ledger balances; inventory, depreciation, or payroll figures; and personal or business income tax information. The project can be done in place of a simulation, reinforcement activity, or chapter problem. Upon completion, a comparison of the student's and accountant's work should take place. An interview with the accountant to explain why the differences occurred can be arranged when figures do not match.

Accounting students also may have the opportunity to solve business problems with which area business people are faced. City council members or area business representatives can supply "case study" scenarios. The students can research the problem, present pros and cons in a written or oral assignment, and, as a class or small group, determine a solution. The solution can be compared with what the council or business decided to do.

Job shadowing an accountant provides another opportunity for accounting students to experience authentic accounting work. Before students leave for the experience, expectations are recorded, providing a benchmark for comparison. Students will maintain a journal in which daily activities are recorded. Accountants may give students work to complete, explaining how to compute the solution and verifying the figures later. Upon returning home, students analyze their journals and determine which events were expected and unexpected. Preconceived ideas and misconceptions are also recorded with explanations. If none of these options is available, textbook reinforcement activities and simulations provide students with valuable accounting experience, even if contrived.

Other business classes. Authentic assignments can be created in other business classes as well. Business law students can view a court case. The students can then write a newspaper account of the trial or write a play based on the court case. The play can be acted out in class or for other students. Also, after reading actual cases, an original case can be written based on researched information and legal advice from attorneys.

Information processing students can plan and present a Professional Secretary's Day Seminar. Each student is responsible for a written and an oral part for the seminar. Photos can be taken and a booklet compiled for each student to keep as a record.

Business management students can contact alumni working in business to research office parties. Based on the replies, the class then can plan a party. The students set up committees, complete the necessary work, and videotape the event. School support staff can be invited or students can be the only participants. Either way, students practice acceptable business and social etiquette.

Creating a business is another authentic assignment. Local businesses can be used as consultants or guest speakers. The students each choose a business, survey the community to learn the need for the business, write a business plan, select a suitable site, create an advertising campaign, and arrange for financing. As an alternative, the entire class selects one business, completes the planning process, and produces the product or service. In both cases, evaluation can be either conducted as the project progresses or at the end.

The department's advisory committee can also be used to generate several projects. Often small businesses cannot afford printing costs or advertising consultant prices. The advisory committee can serve as a liaison, linking business community needs to services the business students can provide. Students can furnish their time and knowledge and use the school's technology to produce the requested services.

PORTFOLIOS

Reynolds (1992) defines portfolios as, "A purposeful collection of student work to evidence his/her learning, effort, progress, and achievement." Murname (1993) describes portfolios as "A multidimensional collection of a student's work assembled in an organized fashion" (p. 1). More simply, a portfolio is a "scrapbook of learning." All three definitions indicate that the portfolio is a collection of student work, but why collect and store the work when a student's cumulative file contains a grade sheet?

Purpose. To a prospective employer, research indicates the grade card represents only what the student might know. Borthwick (1995) interviewed employers to determine qualities sought in new employees. "When I'm considering a kid for a job, I want him to be able to show me some examples of his school work, so I can see what his writing and math are like. . . grades don't mean very much. The only way I can find out what the kid can actually do is to test him myself" (p. 24). The portfolio provides an opportunity for students to demonstrate what they have learned not only to employers but to teachers as well.

Types of portfolios. The type of portfolio the student will compile determines what items should be included. The school, teacher, and student suggest what is included in each type of portfolio. All three make recommendations on what to eliminate and how often to "weed" the portfolio. Three types of portfolios students can develop are district, career, and classroom.

A district portfolio will contain items that best demonstrate what the student can produce from each academic area. Included will be grade sheets, absentee and tardy reports, annotated teacher observations, and school activity participation notes.

A career portfolio concentrates on items that will enable a student to obtain a job. The first item included is a resume. The student can create several resumes, generic or job specific in format. Artifacts demonstrating the student's competence in workplace basic skills should be included (O'Neil & Schmidt, 1992). Papers, projects, and/or pictures illustrating the student's skill level in areas such as leadership or teamwork can be available for viewing. An accompanying explanation defining the skill, explaining the need for developing the skill, and demonstrating that the student possesses the skill may be included. Although the student may decide not to attach this information, creating the explanation sheet will prepare the student for possible interview questions. Final items to be included are job specific products that reveal the student's level of understanding. For example, accounting students can include a textbook reinforcement activity or parts of a simulation while keyboarding students can include sample documents.

The classroom portfolio is the most difficult to design. Instructors know what the curriculum objectives are; often students do not. Students must, however, learn to evaluate their knowledge and select items that demonstrate this knowledge. A combination of student- and teacher-directed items is the safest path. Instructors can create and distribute a "Table of Contents" page to students at the beginning of the school year (Reynolds, 1992). The contents page (see Exhibit 1) can consist of items the teacher believes are important in showing what the student can and cannot do. The items can either be best-shot (student-selected) or one-shot (teacher-selected) activities. Best-shot or low-stake activities are those in which the student had many opportunities to practice. The student selects the best of these activities to place in the portfolio. One-shot activities are those in which the student demonstrates competency in one sitting. Tests, quizzes, and timed productions are all examples of one-shot or high-stakes activities (See Exhibit 1).

Folders, notebooks, binders, and art portfolios are choices from which the student and instructor may select portfolio items. Students can select their own "container" although legal-size folders and three-ring notebooks with sheet-protected pages are common choices made by students. Completed student portfolios are valuable in the employment process. Business students use portfolios during the job interview to illustrate their skills and work attitudes. Potential employers are impressed with a portfolio presentation of student work.

Portfolios are now required in many university teacher-education programs. Graduates from these programs can authentically demonstrate to school district administrators their teaching abilities and characteristics. Portfolio contents with completed rubrics and checklists better depict competence than recorded grades on a transcript.

Exhibit 1

KEYBOARDING PORTFOLIO TABLE OF CONTENTS PAGE

Linda Jensen

REQUIRED ELEMENT	1st Quarter ✔	GRADE	2nd Quarter ✔	GRADE	3rd Quarter ✔	GRADE	4th Quarter ✔	GRADE
Student's Quarter Grade	mrs. S.	B+	mrs. S.	A-	mrs. S.	A-	mrs. S.	A
Productivity Grade (Work Ethic)	✔	B	✔	B+	✔	A-	✔	A
International Activity	✔	A	✔	A-	✔	A	✔	B+
Resume	✔	A	✔	A	✔	A	✔	A
Business Article Summary/Critique	✔	C	✔	B-	✔	B+	✔	A-
Timed Writing Chart	✔	A	✔	A	✔	A	✔	A
Competency Check Sheet	✔	A	✔	A	✔	A	✔	A
Self-Evaluation	✔	A	✔	A	✔	A	✔	A
Form	✔	B+	✔	B	✔	B+	✔	A-
Production Quizzes Grade Sheet	✔	B	✔	B	✔	C+	✔	B+
Learning to Learn	✔	B	✔	B+	✔	A-	✔	A
Listening/Oral Communications	✔	B	✔	B+	✔	B+	✔	A-
Reading/Writing/Computation	✔	C	✔	B-	✔	B	✔	B+
Adaptability/Creative Thinking/P-S	✔	B	✔	B+	✔	A-	✔	A
Personal Management/Career	✔	A	✔	A	✔	A	✔	A
Group Effectiveness	✔	B+	✔	A-	✔	A-	✔	A
Organizational Effectiveness	✔	B-	✔	B	✔	B+	✔	A-
Student's Choice	✔	A	✔	A	✔	A	✔	A
Book Report/Short Report	✔	A-	✔	A	✔	A	✔	A
Announcement	✖	✖	✔	A+	✔	A+	✔	A+
Numbered List	✖	✖	✔	A-	✔	A	✔	A+
Personal Note	✖	✖	✔	A+	✔	A+	✔	A+
Simplified Memorandum	✖	✖	✔	A-	✔	A	✔	A
Teamwork Paper	✖	✖	✔	B	✔	B	✔	B
Calculator Test #1	✖	✖	✔	A-	✔	A-	✔	A-

$\frac{162}{18}$ 9 $\frac{266}{27}$ 9.85 $\frac{374}{36}$ 10.39 $\frac{529}{50}$ 10.58
                              10   11

Calculator Test #2	✖	✖	✓	A-	✓	A-	✓	A-
Personal/Business Letter	✖	✖	✓	A	✓	A	✓	A
Small Envelope	✖	✖	✓	A+	✓	A+	✓	A+
Business Letter	✖	✖	✖	✖	✓	A-	✓	A-
Large Envelope	✖	✖	✖	✖	✓	A+	✓	A+
Timed Production--Letters	✖	✖	✖	✖	✓	B+	✓	B+
Outline	✖	✖	✖	✖	✓	A	✓	A
Unbound Report	✖	✖	✖	✖	✓	A	✓	A
Table of Contents Page	✖	✖	✖	✖	✓	A+	✓	A+
Title Page	✖	✖	✖	✖	✓	A+	✓	A+
Work-Cited Page	✖	✖	✖	✖	✓	A	✓	A
Bound Report/Term Paper	✖	✖	✖	✖	✓	A	✓	A
Simple 2-Column Table	✖	✖	✖	✖	✖	✖	✓	A
Simple 3-Column Table	✖	✖	✖	✖	✖	✖	✓	A
Complex 2-Column Table	✖	✖	✖	✖	✖	✖	✓	A-
Complex 3-Column Table	✖	✖	✖	✖	✖	✖	✓	A-
Complex Table With Extras	✖	✖	✖	✖	✖	✖	✓	B+
Timed Production--Tables	✖	✖	✖	✖	✖	✖	✓	A-
E-Mail Assignment	✖	✖	✖	✖	✖	✖	✓	A
Conflict Resolution Paper	✖	✖	✖	✖	✖	✖	✓	B
Application Letter	✖	✖	✖	✖	✖	✖	✓	A
Application Form	✖	✖	✖	✖	✖	✖	✓	A
Fun & Games International Table	✖	✖	✖	✖	✖	✖	✓	A
Fun & Games International Letter	✖	✖	✖	✖	✖	✖	✓	A+
Fun & Games International Report	✖	✖	✖	✖	✖	✖	✓	A-
Fun & Games International Memo	✖	✖	✖	✖	✖	✖	✓	B+

Experienced teachers are also building portfolios for promotion and tenure. While resumes list only courses taught or duties undertaken, portfolios showcase many desirable teacher attributes, including innovativeness, creativity, and curriculum development.

RUBRICS

Grading authentic assessment is challenging to the teacher. Rubrics help immensely. The word "rubric" is derived from *rubrica terra*, a Latin term referring to red earth. Centuries ago, the earth was used to mark or signify something important. Today, rubrics describe significant levels of performance (Marzano, Pickering, & McTighe, 1993). A rubric describes criteria that clearly define the range of acceptable and unacceptable performance (Herman, Aschbacher, & Winters, 1992). "Because rubrics describe levels of performance, they provide important information to teachers, parents, and others interested in what students know and can do. Rubrics also promote learning by offering clear performance targets to students for agreed-upon standards" (Marzano, et al., 1993, p. 29).

Purpose. Rubrics, in one form or another, have been used by teachers for a long time. When designing curriculum and then specific lessons, instructors know where the class is beginning and where the class should end. Often students are left in the dark until the teacher announces that "they have arrived." The "bright" students are already at the destination. The "average" students accept the fact that they have arrived and hope that they can figure out quickly where they have arrived. The "lower ability"students have not even started the car, much less looked at a road map! As the teacher grades "the tour," he/she may make a short list at the top of the page or notations in the margins. If the student is studying the same "site," high marks will be recorded on the assignment. If the student is looking in the "wrong direction," low marks will abound until the student finally figures out where the teacher is and how to get there. The lower level student will not even understand the checklist or abbreviated red marks found in the margins for he/she is still trying to unfold the road map!

To alleviate detours, instructors can make sure students are arriving at the same destination by using a rubric. Rubrics take the guess work out of turning left, right, or going straight ahead. A rubric places on paper where the destination is and how the student will know when he/she has arrived. The instructor used to have this information in his/her head, leaving the students without a legend to interpret the map.

Development and design. When beginning to create rubrics, an instructor may prefer starting with a checklist. First, the instructor determines precisely what he/she will be looking for when grading the student's work. Total points possible will also be decided. The items and associated points are "listed." When grading, a check mark (✓) is placed next to the listed item. The checklist may either add up to the total points possible (see Exhibit 2) or subtract from the total points possible (see Exhibit 3). The adding-up method is preferable as it is viewed as a positive reaction to the student's work; however, subtract-down checklists are easier to write. Some instructors may wish to begin with designing a subtract-down checklist and later revising it into an add-up checklist.

A rubric, like a checklist, has a set list of criteria. The criteria descriptions, however, are now detailed, and several levels of achievement for each criterion can be given. Suggestions for writing rubrics are:

1. Determine how many levels of performance you wish to define.
2. Write the standard for the performance, product, or understanding first—the level you want all students to achieve.
3. Begin to brainstorm ideas—knowledge, skills, and qualities—that would be exhibited by a person who has attained the proficiency.

Exhibit 2

Add-up Rubric

		KEYBOARDING Letter Checklist
Pts.		Letter Feature
5	5	Paper Size (Executive, Standard, Government, Monarch)
20	20	Margins (Top, Bottom, Left, Right)
5	5	Style (Block, Modified Block, Indent Paragraph, AMS, Government)
2	2	Centering (Not Required, Horizontally and Vertically Balanced)
2	2	Alignment (Not Required, Material Aligned)
5	4	Enumeration (Not Required, Aligned, SS w/in, DS Between, Indent Left, Right)
4	4	Table (Not Required, Row Spacing, Gutters Equal, Material Aligned)
2	2	Envelope (Not Required, Keyed)
3	3	Return Address (Letterhead, 1st, SS w/in, Horizontal Placement, Used)
4	4	Dateline (2nd, DS above, QS Below, Horizontal Placement)
4	4	Inside Address (3rd, SS w/in, DS below, Horizontal Placement)
3	3	Salutation (Not Required/4th, DS below, Punctuation)
3	3	Body (5th, SS within, DS between)
4	4	Comp. Close (Not Required, 6th, DS above, Punctuation, Horizonal Placement)
3	3	Typed Signature Line (7th, QS Above, Horizontal Placement)
2	2	Typed Position (Not Required, Horizontal & Vertical Placement)
3	3	Enclosure (Not Required, DS above, Horizontal & Vertical Placement)
3	3	Photo Copy (Not Required, DS above, Horizontal & Vertical Placement)
3	3	Typed Co. Name (Not Required, DS above, Horizontal & Vertical Placement)
3	3	Postscript (Not Required, DS above, Horizontal & Vertical Placement)
3	3	Subject Line (Not Required, DS below, Horizontal & Vertical Placement)
2	2	Attention Line (Not Required, Horizontal & Vertical Placement)
12/6/0	6	Keyed Material--Mailable (Perfect), Mailable (Minor Errors), Unmailable (Major)
93/100		Percent 93	Grade B+

Exhibit 3

Subtract-Down Rubric

KEYBOARDING	
Letter Checklist	
-2 Each	Notes
Paper Size/Letterhead	*Standard / used*
Margins	*ok*
Vertical Spacing	*ok*
Correct Style *-2*	*open punctuation – not mixed*
Format Features	*ok*
-5 Each	
Section Missing	*-5 handwritten signature missing*
-1 Each	
Typos *-6*	*their, satisfy, worthy, four, necessary, said*
Total Points *87* /100	Percent *87* Grade *B*

4. When possible, focus on presence of behaviors rather than absence of behaviors; avoid negatives.

5. When possible, avoid relying on adverbs and adjectives to define the distinctions between levels of performance. Try to identify clear distinctions in behavior.

6. Use your first draft over a period of time as you observe students in the classroom. Continue to revise rubrics until they provide an accurate description.

7. Use demonstrative verbs such as the following:
expresses
discusses
selects
interprets
modifies
conceives
corrects
connects
monitors
(McRel Institute, *Verb*).

When determining the number of achievement levels, a three-column rubric format is an acceptable style (see Exhibits 4 and 5). The "commendable" column aims for perfection. The "acceptable" column illustrates usefulness within a realistic time-frame constraint. The "unacceptable" column simply represents unacceptable outcomes. Numeric values can then be assigned to each column, row, and even individual cell. The instructor must determine which criteria, if any, are more important.

Exhibit 4

COMPUTER PRESENTATION RUBRIC

CRITERIA	COMMENDABLE	ACCEPTABLE	UNACCEPTABLE
Design: Template	Template used sets tone and establishes focus of presentation. (5 pts)	Template used distracts viewer from presentation. (3 pts)	No template used; blank background. (1 pt)
Design: Chart Choice	Chart choice(s) selected exercise simplicity and consistency; represent intended data or info appropriately. (5 pts)	Chart choice(s) selected represent intended data or information; cluttered or sparse appearance. (3 pts)	Chart choice(s) selected do not represent data or info appropriately; cluttered or sparse appearance. (2 pts)
Design: Color	Color(s) used enhance, illustrate, and/or emphasize data or info appropriately. (5 pts)	Color(s) used are distractive to viewer and/or not consistent throughout the presentation. (3 pts)	No color(s) used; black on white only. (1 pt)
Design: Text	Text provides concise information; uses phrases of parallel structure; adheres to "Rule of 49;" avoids abbreviations and acronyms. (5 pts)	Text provides information or parallel structure; is wordy and too lengthy per slide; uses some abbreviations and acronyms. (3 pts)	Text does not provide useful information; is not of parallel structure; is wordy and too lengthy per slide; uses abbreviations and acronyms. (1 pt)
Content	Content of slides enhance, illustrate, and/or emphasize data or info of the oral report appropriately. (18-20 pts)	Content of slides frequently supplement the oral report. (13-17 pts)	Content of slides do not supplement nor compliment the oral report. (0-12 pts)
Integration	Presenter integrates slide show well into oral report and manipulates equipment in nondistractive manner. (9-10 pts)	Presenter at times lacks fluidness in integrating slide show into oral report. (6-8 pts)	Presenter is awkward at integrating slide show into oral report. (0-5 pts)

(handwritten: +/9 in Content row; +9 in Integration row)

Comments: $+44$/50 total points

(handwritten)
Your type color changed
from neon green to
white inconsistently.
Green was better choice on
background.
Remember "Rule of 49".
Enhanced oral report well!

Exhibit 5

BUSINESS DEPARTMENT Work Ethic			
CRITERIA	COMMENDABLE	ACCEPTABLE	UNACCEPTABLE
Attendance	Understands importance of work--here everyday and makes up excused absences; no unexcused absences	Attempts to make up some of his/her excused absences; absences are never unexcused	Four or more days absent; no attempt to make up excused absences; some absences are unexcused
Punctuality	Always on time; makes every effort to attend class on time by arriving early	Periodically arrives late, but always has an acceptable excuse as to why late	Frequently arrives late; makes no attempt to explain why; some unexcused
Deadlines	Continually works hard to meet deadlines; willing to come in during free time to ensure meeting of deadlines	Meets deadlines, but has to scramble and work product may suffer	Deadlines hold little or no meaning to student; deadlines are disregarded most of the time
Productivity	Begins class early or promptly; works up to the last minute; high concentration skills	Tends to follow lead of class; at times appears unmotivated; concentration level varies each day	Easily distracted and is distracting; closes up shop early and must be asked to begin working
Work Product	Listens, reads, and understands directions; assignment is perfect	Sometimes must ask for more guidance in completing work or misinterprets directions; sometimes hands in assignments with correctable errors	Frequently asks questions that were just addressed; no comprehension of what final product should look like resulting in several redos

A+ = 15 points	B+ = 13 points	C+ = 10 points	D+ = 7 points
A- = 14 points	B = 12 points	C = 9 points	D- = 6 points
	B- = 11 points	C- = 8 points	

Commendable--You are in line for a raise, promotion, or both. Keep up the good work!

Acceptable--You are doing a fine job; we will keep you on. However, if you wish to be considered for a raise or promotion, we expect you to expend more time and energy in the tasks you undertake.

Unacceptable--The Accounting Department has your last check. Please clean out your desk and make room for a more productive employee.

Writing rubrics forces a teacher to clearly define expected student outcomes (see Exhibits 6-9). The teacher determines the following: How important is writing in complete sentences? How much emphasis is placed on creativity or format? How have students connected prior learning with new knowledge? Rubrics will require refinement and change as lessons and content are updated.

Exhibit 6

BUSINESS DEPARTMENT Opinion Paper Rubric			
CRITERIA	COMMENDABLE	ACCEPTABLE	UNACCEPTABLE
Deadline	Handed in Early	Handed in on Time	Handed in Late
Format	Typed	Neatly Handwritten	Scrawled
Topic Sentence	Clearly states author's opinion	Has one, but could be worded clearer	No topic sentence
Three Reasons	Three explicit reasons are given in support of topic sentence	Three reasons are given, but are undistinguishable or contradictory	Less than three reasons are given
Examples/Details	Each reason is supported by distinct details and specific examples	Each reason is supported by details and examples stated in general terms	No supporting details or examples are given
Conclusion	Succinctly summarized thoughts	Merely repeats opening paragraph	No concluding paragraph or it in no way relates to paper
Thinking Level	Perceptive and analytical; sees big picture; ties in prior learning	Some evidence of insight is shown; may tie in prior learning or make prediction	Bare basics
English	Perfect; No grammar or spelling errors	No spelling errors; Minor errors occur but message can still be interpreted	Major errors occur that distract reader; message cannot be understood

A+ = 24 points	B+ = 21 points	C+ = 18 points	D+ = 12-13 points
A = 23 points	B = 20 points	C = 15-17 points	D = 10-11 points
A- = 22 points	B- = 19 points	C- = 14 points	D- = 9 points

Exhibit 7

ESSAY QUESTION RUBRIC

Organization
    Exemplary   (4) -   Answer is well organized *Headings were helpful.*
    Good   3 -   Answer is organized.
    Average   2 -   Answer needs organization and clarity.
    Poor   1 -   Answer is weak and shows little organization.

Understanding Course Content   *Check*
    Exemplary   (8)-9 -   Evidence of thorough understanding of course content. *vocab.*
    Good   6-7 -   Evidence of understanding of course content. *terms*
    Average   4-5 -   Evidence of partial understanding of course content. *marked.*
    Poor   0-3 -   Little evidence of understanding course content.

Sources Used   *new*
    Exemplary   (4) -   Basis of answer is from variety of sources. *3 sources used*
    Good   3 -   Basis of answer is primarily from course materials. *as documentation*
    Average   2 -   Basis of answer is from primarily one source.
    Poor   1 -   Basis of answer is from no known source.

Question Addressed
    Exemplary   4 -   Response addresses question and provides additional information.
    Good   (3) -   Response addresses question completely.
    Average   2 -   Response addresses question.
    Poor   1 -   Response is inaccurate.

English Mechanics
    Exemplary   4 -   Free of punctuation, spelling, or English mechanics errors.
    Good   (3) -   One-three punctuation, spelling, or English mechanics errors.
    Average   2 -   Four-six punctuation, spelling, or English mechanics errors.
    Poor   1 -   More than seven punctuation, spelling, or English mechanics errors.

+22 /25 **Total Points**

    Rubrics should be more than teacher-driven. The more ownership the student carries for the project, the better the performance. The student and the teacher can determine the project title, objectives, and criteria for evaluation. Together, the student and the teacher decide what the student must do to meet the objectives and determine what the final product/process will look like. The student continues to work on the project until these criteria are met or the deadline arrives.

    Rubric concerns. Rubric users hold different opinions about when to share with students the assignment rubric. Should the rubric be given to students initially? Some evaluators believe students will select the lower criteria levels and not strive for the "commendable" level. Others believe sharing the expected performance criteria with students as they begin assignments is appropriate. Generally, students welcome and appreciate the direction a rubric provides.

Exhibit 8

ACCOUNTING I & II			
Reinforcement Activity/Simulation Rubric			
Criteria	Commendable	Acceptable	Unacceptable
Neatness	Neatly handwritten; Ruler is used	Neatly Handwritten; No ruler is used	Scrawled; No ruler is used
Completeness	All work completed; No abbreviations used	All work completed; Some abbreviations are used	Work is incomplete; Strewn with abbreviations
Mathematical Correctness	All information is correct, no mathematical or transpositional errors have occurred	An early mathematical or transposition error forces later figures to be off that would otherwise be correct	Information is way off, numerous math and/or tranpositional errors have occurred
Procedural Correctness	All work is set up and done in correct order	Work is set up correctly but done out of order	Numerous arrow lines and cross outs are used
Deadline	Submitted early	Submitted on time	Submitted late
Resourcefulness	Accesses book or previous work as reference	Tries to find answer in book or previous work but doesn't and then asks for help	Seeks help only from fellow students and/or teacher, does not try to do on own
Work Ethic	Begins promptly; maintains clean work area; stays on task; brings needed materials	Once or twice needs push to begin, forgets material or becomes distracted; maintains neat work area	Several times must be prompted to begin or continue working, return to locker for supplies; unorganized

A+	= 21 points	B+	= 18 points	C+	= 15 points	D+	= 11 points
A	= 20 points	B	= 17 points	C	= 13-14 points	D	= 9-10 points
A-	= 19 points	B-	= 16 points	C-	= 12 points	D-	= 8 points

Student's Name ___Laura Franklin___

Class ___Accounting I___ Period ___2nd___ Date ___10/25/94___

Reinforcement/Simulation Title ___Reinforcement Activity 1A___

Exhibit 9

Peer Evaluation of Team Members*

Please complete the following rubric for each member of your team. The frustrations and joys some of the groups shared with me about team members should be noted here in a professional yet honest manner. You need not identify yourself. All evaluations will be given to the individual team members.

Team __*Intl Etiquette*__   __Chris__ Team Member Name

CRITERIA	COMMENDABLE	ACCEPTABLE	UNACCEPTABLE
Works toward achievement of group goals	Helps group identify group goals and works hard to meet them. Contributes equally to group output and work. (4 pts)	Carries commitment to group goals but does not carry out assigned nor equal share of output and work. (2 pts)	Does not work toward group goals or actively works against them. Did not perform equal share of output and work. (0 pts)
Demonstrates effective interpersonal skills	Actively promotes effective group interaction and the expression of ideas and opinions that are sensitive to feelings and knowledge base of others. (4 pts)	Participates in group interaction with prompting. Expresses ideas and opinions without considering the feelings and knowledge base of others. (2 pts)	Does not participate in group interaction, even with prompting. Expresses ideas and opinions that are insensitive to the feelings or knowledge base of others. (0 pts)
Attendance at all group meetings	Attends all meetings of groups in and outside of class. (2 pts)	Attends all but one of group meetings in and outside of class. (1 pt)	Missed more than one of group meetings in and outside of class. (0 pts)

Comments:
Chris gave good ideas!

__+9__ total points by peer

(10 pts total possible)

*Adapted from Marzano, R. J., Pickering, D., & McTighe, J. (1993). Assessing student outcomes: Performance assessment using the dimensions of learning model. Aurora: Co: McRel Institute, 2550 S. Parker Rd., Suite 500. Telephone (303)337-0990. Reproduced with permission. Copyright © 1993 by McRel Institute. All rights reserved.

Another concern is the time required for developing and refining rubrics. Rubrics take time to develop, and few examples exist for the business curriculum. Instructors must determine criteria, descriptors, and formatting. If the assignment is new or being revised, the instructor must take time to design the lesson and its rubric. When creating the rubric, additional time may be needed if students' ideas are solicited. Even more time is necessary if an instructor tests the rubric or requests peer review.

Providing the rubric initially may not be enough. If possible, the instructor should create an assignment sample that includes a completed rubric. The sample can serve as a model for the student who still has trouble reading the road signs. Collected copies of student work can be laminated and kept for student reference.

Rubric endorsements. Students enjoy the amount of feedback a rubric offers. The descriptive criteria tell the student how well the assignment was completed. Students may still receive written comments, though not as many are necessary due to the detail in the rubric's criteria.

Student ownership in the learning process increases with the use of authentic assessment. With the use of checklists and rubrics, students become more self-evaluative. Students refer to rubrics when completing assignments, ensuring criteria are met before submitting the assignments. Authenticity in student learning serves as a motivator. Students see the purpose and real-world connectiveness of assignments and are more willing to take on the role of self-directed learners.

Instructors enjoy the ease of grading. Written comments can be kept to a minimum. The instructor need only search for the stated rubric criteria and circle the appropriate performance level. Rubrics also reduce grading subjectivity. Because the criteria are specifically stated, students seldom question the evaluator's grading decision. Use of the rubric eliminates potential student-teacher confrontations.

Rubrics resemble job performance evaluations used by human resource departments. When used with portfolios, rubrics offer students exposure to performance-based work evaluations and provide experience in developing employment-seeking skills.

SUMMARY

Authentic assessment offers both the learner and the assessor opportunities not readily available with traditional assessment strategies. With authentic assessment, the learner has the opportunity to become more self-reflective about past learning and set goals for future work. Student self-evaluation is possible due to clearly defined criteria on checklists and rubrics.

Higher validity and reliability are possible with authentic assessment. Authentic and performance-assessment strategies are more valid than objective assessments. As stated before, the use of rubrics increases reliability. Educators using authentic assessment will discover that one can measure or "count" affective attributes, assess student learning from a beginning to an ending point, and add authenticity to learning. Authentic assessment allows one to "count everything that needs to be counted" and assess students' attitudes, skills, and knowledge with more validity and reliability.

REFERENCES

Bergen, D. (1993-94, Winter). Authentic performance assessments. *Childhood Education, 70*(2), pp. 99, 102.

Borthwick, A. (1995, March). Body of evidence. *Vocational Education Journal, 70*(3), pp. 24-26, 48.

Herman, J. J., Aschbacher, P. R., & Winters, L. (1992). *A practical guide to alternative assessment.* Alexandria, VA: Association for Supervision and Curriculum Development.

Marzano, R. J., Pickering D., & McTighe, J. (1993). *Assessing student outcomes: Performance assessment using the dimensions of learning model.* Aurora, CO: McRel Institute.

McRel Institute. *Guidelines for writing rubrics.* Aurora, CO: McRel Institute.

McRel Institute. *Verb list.* Aurora, CO: McRel Institute.

Meyer, C. A. (1992, May). What's the difference between *authentic* and *performance* assessment? *Educational Leadership, 49*(8), pp. 39-40.

Murname, Y. (1993). Good grading: Student portfolios—a primer. *The National Teaching & Learning Forum, 3*(2), pp. 1-4.

O'Neil, S. L. & Schmidt, B. J. (1992). The teacher as facilitator of the hidden curriculum. In A. M. Burford & V. Arnold (Eds.), *NBEA yearbook no. 30: The hidden curriculum* (pp. 21-30). Reston, VA: National Business Education Association.

Reynolds, J. (1992, September). A portfolio for portfolio assessment. *Project escape.* Workshop conducted at Central Decatur High School, Leon, IA.

Sugarman, J., Allen, J., & Keller-Cogan, M. (1993, July/August). How to make authentic assessment work for you. *Instructor, 103*(1), pp. 66-68.

CHAPTER 10

Technology as an Instructional Strategy

IVAN G. WALLACE

East Carolina University, Greensville, North Carolina

As a result of the development of the microcomputer and new office technologies, business educators are not strangers to technology. In fact, in most educational settings business education teachers are known for being the "experts" in the area of computers and technology. While business educators have an established record of being experts in teaching technology as it relates to computer literacy and business applications, using technology as an instructional tool in the classroom presents a new challenge. This is primarily because the role of instructional technology has emerged more recently with the advent and proliferation of graphical user interfaces (GUIs), multimedia applications, and network connections made through the Internet or other commercial network services. Since the use of technology has been so heavily entrenched in the business education curriculum, it is sometimes difficult to distinguish whether teachers are actually teaching technology or using technology as a teaching tool. In many cases, they do both. The focus of this chapter will consist of an in-depth discussion of instructional technologies as they relate to: (1) traditional technology resources, (2) presentation software, (3) multimedia, (4) telecommunications, and (4) educational uses of virtual reality.

TRADITIONAL TECHNOLOGY RESOURCES

Traditional technology resources include media components and computer software that are quite common to the classroom teacher. They include audio recordings, audio tapes, video tapes, video disks, and a variety of software packages that can assist the classroom teacher. The software packages include a wide variety of tutorials as well as specialized packages that are designed for classroom management, instructional management, and performance assessment.

Traditional audio-video materials are available from publishers and courseware vendors and can serve the business education classroom well when the facilitator would like to enhance the regular classroom routine. While videos are available on a variety of topics and subjects, a new category of video materials that can be especially helpful to a computer applications teacher include video titles for introduction, intermediate, and advanced uses of the various software packages that are being taught in the business education classroom. These videos can be particularly beneficial when used as an overview for introducing a student to a new software package.

Computer Tutorials and Built-In Software Instructional Features. Computer tutorials are very effective for many subjects from the standpoint that they can provide the student will unlimited drill and practice on a variety of subjects. Because the computer never tires and has unlimited patience, tutorials are extremely effective in situations where material must be repeated in order for learning to take place. Tutorials should be welcomed in situations that require individualized instruction or that can be individually paced. Keyboarding is one area of the business education curriculum that has experienced a great deal of success in using tutorials. A wide variety of keyboarding tutorials are available to introduce the keyboard to students, provide unlimited drill and practice, mark errors, set goals, and provide immediate feedback to both the student and instructor. The tutorials are effective in developing skills and monitoring progress for the student. Their ability to administer and evaluate timed writings frees the instructor from the time-consuming activity of grading the writings, thus providing the instructor with more time to plan instruction.

In addition to accommodating drill and practice for skill activities, tutorials are also available to provide overviews to software packages in much the same way that a video can. Many are designed so that an instructor can use an LCD projection system to overview the material with an entire class, or each student can use the software independently at a computer. Many vendors provide lab packs or site licenses that make these materials affordable.

Perhaps one of the most beneficial instructional facilitators for teachers of computer applications is the wide array of tools that are being designed into the software itself such as Help, Demos, and Wizards.

Most software packages contain context-sensitive Help, which can assist the user in many ways. Most GUI software packages contain hyper features that allow the user to immediately find solutions to a problem. By simply clicking on the "Help" icon, reviewing a list of contents, and clicking on the appropriate selection or keying in a selection, help is immediately available on practically any topic or foreseeable problem for which a user may need assistance. When teaching any software package, the instructor should teach the students how to access "Help" immediately upon introducing the student to the software. As an example of how advanced help features can be, the "Help" feature in Windows '95 actually assists the user in installing printers, monitors, cards, and other hardware devices. In many cases, books and other instructional materials are no longer necessary once teachers and students discover the vast amount of information that is built into the program to assist with its use.

Students need to adapt to being less reliant upon printed materials and begin taking advantage of the wealth of information that is often at their fingertips. If students access the built-in information, they will find that usually more than enough information is available electronically to answer their questions. Users have to reprogram themselves to rely upon extracting information from the computer system instead of a 5-pound book that is much more costly to update and reprint every time a small error is detected or information changes.

Many software programs also have other built-in features that assist the user in navigating through a software program. For example, Microsoft uses a feature called "Cue Cards" that guides the user through options and provides instruction as to what the next step might be in a process involved in using the software. Another feature that Microsoft uses is called "Wizards," which actually performs tasks for the user. The Wizards provide a preview of the outcome that one prefers and then constructs the final product. As a result of relying on Wizards, for example, a student using desktop publishing software can design and create flyers, business cards, letterheads, newsletters, and a wealth of other publications with just a few clicks of the mouse button. A speed control will slow down or speed up the construction process to allow one to view the step-by-step process involved in putting the elements together to complete the publication.

As newer versions of existing software packages are released, one can expect a variety of features available to assist in the use of the product. For example, Microsoft Word has a feature called "Demo," and WordPerfect has a feature called "Coach." Both work in the same way. They will actually demonstrate to the user many word processing functions by automatically dropping down menus, moving the cursor to appropriate selections, making a selection, and guiding the user through the exact procedure necessary to perform the desired outcome. With careful observation of the process, the student or operator can then emulate the procedure to obtain actual results.

While the previous illustrations are specific to the mentioned software packages, it is important for business teachers to be aware of all the instructional features that are being included in many other software packages as well. Once students are made aware of these features, instruction can be greatly facilitated by simply relying upon these features that have been incorporated into the products.

Instructional Management Tools. In addition to tutorials and instructional features that are built into applications software, specialized software is available for classroom management, instructional management, and performance assessment. These features may be built into one comprehensive integrated system or they might be available individually or in combinations with other programs.

Typically, classroom management software consists of tools to assist in the record-keeping and grade reporting functions of a classroom. In most business education classrooms, these require little attention since many school systems are utilizing a mandated grade reporting system or the teacher is well versed in the use of spreadsheets and has already created a template to serve this purpose in lieu of purchasing a proprietary grade-book software program.

Instructional management software is somewhat more comprehensive than just keeping up with student grade data. Instructional management software is usually rather complex in that it is designed to serve as a comprehensive electronic curriculum guide, test bank, and instructional management tool. These systems provide a blueprint for instruction which outlines the curriculum competencies and objectives and then measures the individual progress of each student. North Carolina's statewide Vocational Assessment Tracking System (VoCats) has proven to be one of the most effective systems in the country and is now being modeled throughout the nation as a competency-based instructional management model.

Performance assessment tools can be included as part of an instructional management system or they can be used independently. Many publishers provide electronic test banks that generate customized tests and answer keys for the teachers. In many cases, tests can be administered interactively at computers by software packages. Of concern to the teacher when using such performance assessment tools is that test items should be easily selected or modified to ensure that only those competencies that are taught are being tested. While objective-type tests were once the only type of assessment that was made possible by these systems, much progress has been made in this area. Today it is possible to acquire performance assessment tools that will grade timed writings, check formatting and content in word processing documents, and even score accounting documents or written compositions.

PRESENTATION SOFTWARE

Although it has been around since the mid 1980s, presentation software has become extremely popular in recent years primarily because of the acceptance of GUIs, faster computers, and object-oriented languages that are designed to manage large files, complex graphics, and sound. Presentation software is a combination of features found in word processors, drawing programs, desktop publishers, spreadsheets, and more powerful multimedia environments. As the term "presentation" implies, the purpose of presentation packages is to create presentations in a variety of ways. Two established programs are Aldus Persuasion and Microsoft Powerpoint. As their titles imply, their original intent was to develop powerful sales presentations. However, their design allows their use for any environment where it is necessary to present ideas or information and then elaborate on the points. Consequently, they are a natural for educational environments where information is disseminated in various ways.

In many cases, presentation software is very similar to multimedia authoring software from the standpoint that it can incorporate the use of text, graphics, sound, animation, and even full-motion video. While it is becoming increasingly difficult to distinguish whether a package is in fact a presentation package or a full-fledged multimedia authoring package, presentation packages tend to be more sequential or linear in presentation style whereas the multimedia packages provide for more interactive use through hyper capabilities. In most cases, a presentation package is perceived as being like an electronic slide show and is treated as such.

Currently, popular presentation packages include Lotus Freelance, Harvard Graphics, Microsoft Powerpoint, Aldus Persuasion, Corel Draw, and WordPerfect Presentations. They all provide environments for creating electronic slide shows, formatting capabilities for 35mm slide or paper output, and note capabilities which allow the user to print a sheet of notes to accompany each slide for the speaker to follow during the presentation. The packages provide a sorter feature that allows the presentation to be reordered or resequenced and importing capabilities so that data, graphics, and other content can easily be imported from other applications. Most contain a clip art library, drawing tools, writing tools, and graphing tools as standard features.

Some presentation packages contain an outlining feature which allows the presenter to key in an outline or import an outline from a word processor, which is then automatically translated into individual slides with various levels of details. Then the user simply adds clip art, photographs, charts or graphs, sound, videos, or other graphic elements resulting in a professional-looking presentation. All presentation software packages provide a variety of background templates, a variety of transitions that add interest to the presentation, and fly-ins that provide emphasis on the points the speaker is talking about. Many presentation programs provide for packaging the presentation for use on computers that don't have the actual presentation software, as well.

Presentation packages require very little keyboarding skills or knowledge of applications programs. Students, as well as instructors, can use the packages to create interesting presentations. Presentations can be incorporated into any course where students are required to make reports. A quick introduction to the software by a computer applications teacher is often all that is necessary to get students and faculty using presentation software packages. Then the creative juices take over and students and teachers alike can bring interesting presentations into the classroom. Once teachers begin creating their own presentations, they can easily modify the content, copy structures, and build libraries of exciting presentations to bring into the classroom in much the same manner that a test created in a word processor can easily be updated and improved with usage.

MULTIMEDIA

During the late 1980s and early 1990s, laser printers and graphical user interfaces such as Microsoft Windows have heralded new uses for micro-computers in the business world. Soon after desktop publishing and presentation software emerged, object-oriented programming gained acceptance as the programming tool of the future. As a result of all this phenomenal development with computer hardware and software, new peripheral devices such as CD-ROMs, sound cards, video capture cards, and color graphics processors have entered the microcomputer market to create a new application for microcomputers called multimedia. Multimedia is used to describe applications that add sound, animation, and support for both analog and digital video.

While the audio and visuals are certainly vital to multimedia, it is the ability to manipulate or navigate the multi-sensory content that really makes it effective. According to Computer Technology Research, (Multimedia Source Guide, 1995) comprehension is raised to 80 percent when one sees, hears, and interacts with instructional material. This comprehension rate is very high compared to 20 to 30 percent for just sight and just sound, respectively.

Multimedia for business education can entail two separate and distinct roles. One role involves using multimedia to assist instruction for business education, and the second involves preparing students to develop multimedia materials using authoring software packages. Multimedia hardware and software requirements will be very different depending on the role multimedia plays in the business education classroom.

Multimedia Hardware. If the primary role for multimedia is to become a teaching facilitator or instruction enhancement tool, basic microcomputer (PC) configurations would include a 486- or Pentium-based processor, 8-16 MB of RAM, 350 MB hard disk, color VGA monitor, CD-ROM drive, and a 16-bit sound card. A color projection device or LCD active matrix projection palette is necessary for projecting images to an entire classroom. For some applications a laser disk player may be required.

For authoring multimedia software applications, hardware should include a 50 MHz or better 486 DX- or Pentium-based processor, 16+ MB of RAM, 500 MB (or greater) hard disk, a 16-bit sound card, a super VGA (SVGA) display, and a CD-ROM drive. For capturing color graphics pictures into the system, a color hand- or flatbed-scanner is essential. A digital camera is extremely useful for capturing photographic images into the computer system while a video capture card is required if the goal is to include video film clips.

Apple Macintosh (Mac) Quadra and PowerMac computers are also ideal for multimedia applications since they have most of the necessary features built into the systems. Multimedia really started with the Mac in the mid 1980s with the introduction of Hypercard software. Therefore, the Mac is a natural platform for multimedia. MS-DOS systems can be acquired with all of the necessary multimedia components built in. However, multimedia devices can be easily added to any existing microcomputer system.

Multimedia Software for Facilitating Instruction. If the primary role for multimedia is to become an instructional facilitator in the classroom, software may include multimedia encyclopedias and business education tutorials for the various subjects taught in the classroom. Just as educational materials have been traditionally distributed on films, videos, and slides, more and more topics are becoming available on CD-ROM for multimedia delivery. Some software titles such as Microsoft's Works are available on CD ROM with tutorials that teach the use of the software.

Random House, Grolier, Compton, and Microsoft's Encarta encyclopedias are available for most computers. Features of multimedia encyclopedias include sound clips, video clips, animation, extensive pictorial collections, and atlas collections. All include searching features that make them ideal for teaching electronic data retrieval. Furthermore, files can be incorporated into word processing, presentation, and other common business applications, which is perfect for teaching integration concepts. For example, on a unit dealing with the world market economy or world industrial trade, the atlas could be accessed to locate various countries or regions around the world. Then photos, video clips, and animations that are related to the country could be accessed and presented to the class. Finally, text can be located in related articles through a search feature. Students as well as instructors can easily access the information and integrate it into a presentation or written report, complete with visuals.

Software for Authoring Multimedia Materials. Software for authoring multimedia materials includes the actual presentation software program plus other supporting software for editing graphics, sound, and video files. Clip art, sound byte, and video libraries make it extremely easy to incorporate multimedia objects into the multimedia presentation. Many of these programs and supporting clip art libraries are distributed on CD-ROM to facilitate the bulky file space required for the huge files.

Full multimedia packages provide for interactive activity through the use of buttons and hypertext while supporting a full range of multimedia devices to include sound, CD-ROM, laser disks, and integration of full motion video. As these software packages are revised each year, more and more features are added to them. Popular full-scale multimedia software packages include IBM Linkway Live, Authorware, Compel, Hyper Studio, and Toolbook, to name a few.

Supporting software includes many different clip art, video, and sound byte libraries. Affordable clip art libraries include Publisher's Paradise, Presentation Task Force, Masterclips, Lotus Smart Pics, Graphics Works for Windows, and Corel Draw. New packages are being introduced each day to fill the market that multimedia applications have created. Consequently, this list is never ending.

Teachers and students can author customized multimedia presentations. One Georgia computer applications teacher started using Linkway Live several years ago in her classroom. She reported that by having students develop multimedia projects, two valuable outcomes were realized. First, students learned the mechanics on how to create a multimedia presentation; secondly, and more importantly, the multimedia presentation reinforced the students' knowledge on the subject that was chosen.

Multimedia applications have opened a whole new world for the educational, entertainment, and business community as more and more people rely on its powerful resources of sound and motion to "dazzle" today's MTV generation. Most experts agree that because it does touch the user's senses of sight and sound, it is an instructional medium that is here to stay. Multimedia technology has impacted the way students will learn information, the way teachers will impart that information, and the media by which that information is transmitted. (Christopher, 1995)

TELECOMPUTING FOR TEACHING AND LEARNING

An area of technology that has experienced a colossal amount of growth in recent months has been the area of telecomputing, particularly telecomputing through the Internet and other network services such as Prodigy, Compuserve, and America Online. As more and more schools come on line and educators discover the vast wealth of knowledge and experiences that are accessible through network connections to the outside, it quickly becomes apparent that, indeed, the world is the boundary of a new educational environment.

For those who use or wish to use networked computers as a medium for teaching interactive groups of students, there are three choices for bringing information into the classroom: (1) electronic mail (e-mail), (2) bulletin board services (BBS), and (3) desktop conferencing. As the Internet, high-speed modems, and local area networks have become dramatically more accessible in recent years, teachers increasingly adapt these technologies for teaching. Educators and students like this network medium, especially under conditions where traditional classroom instruction is not feasible because students and teachers are geographically separated or have schedule conflicts (Klemm, 1994).

Many teachers are finding that students using e-mail are improving their grammar and language skills. Since written communication is the only way people can convey themselves when using e-mail, students tend to write better because their writing style is being used to affect (or impress) the reader in much the same way that people dress to impress other people in our society. E-mail can be used by students in one school to communicate with students at another school, or even with a business. As business educators focus more on the global economy, uses of the Internet and other pathways make it possible for students in the United States to interact with students in Russia or for students to interact on a collaborative project with students in another state. Teachers in schools in different regions can develop many cooperative efforts that allow students from one school to send e-mail or carry on a dialogue with students at another school through a "chat" feature that is interactive. Users who have video cameras can send video images from one location to another. For example, users who have video capabilities on their computers can use interactive video and audio with any other user around the world who has the same capabilities and Internet access, which creates endless possibilities for expanding classroom experiences.

Bob Strandquist, an English teacher, sees the Internet as a global classroom—where kids are interacting with the real world. "The Internet is an ocean and we don't know yet where in that ocean all those islands of learning are for teachers and students" (Wilson and Utecht, 1995). The Internet has become the most widely used tool of technology in recent years. As users discover the World Wide Web (WWW) and make use of navigational/browsing tools such as Netscape and Mosaic, the same resources that one would find in a multimedia encyclopedia, such as video clips, sound, photographs, graphics, and text, can be brought into the classroom at the click of the button. The knowledge base is endless as these graphical interfaces allow users to click on hypertext and immediately be linked to a server at any point on the globe. Consequently, the limits of a classroom can literally be expanded to any geographical area of the world.

EDUCATIONAL USES OF VIRTUAL REALITY

Another technology that is beginning to find its way into the classroom is virtual reality (VR). By definition, virtual reality is a highly interactive, computer-based environment in which the user participates with a computer in a "virtually real" world. Highly sophisticated immersion virtual reality involves 3-D computer simulations in which the user becomes engrossed so fully that artificial reality appears to be reality. Artificial reality is sometimes used interchangeably with virtual reality.

While virtual reality is perceived as a relatively new technology, its beginnings can be traced back more than 60 years to Link Trainers, which were designed to duplicate airplane cockpits for training purposes in the late 1920s. Like many technologies, VR has taken on several manifestations. However, it can be classified into three primary categories: (1) desktop VR, (2) telepresence VR, and (3) immersion VR.

Desktop VR is perhaps the most simplistic version and has the most application for the business curriculum. Desktop VR consists primarily of a basic computer system that is capable of generating high resolution color 3-D graphics and some sound capabilities. It is used primarily for 3-D modeling and visualization.

Telepresence VR is related very closely to robotics and involves the use of sensory equipment to sense movement of live beings and persons so that the biological actions of living things can be replicated in robots and even graphic images for cartoons and video games. The Nintendo "Mario" game character is a good example of using telepresence VR. Although Mario is only an animated character, his facial expressions and body actions are actually created by sensors that are attached to a real person.

The third type of virtual reality, immersion VR, is the most sophisticated type of virtual reality. Immersion VR requires several pieces of additional equipment. This equipment includes a head movement tracker, a head-mounted display (HMD); 3-D glasses; a hand-tracker such as a glove with sensors; a partial or full body sensor; biosensors (e.g., to detect muscle activity and eye movement); 3-D mice; a force ball (for manipulation or control); wands; optional navigational devices, and a 3-D sound processor. The goal of immersion VR is that the user will be stimulated so greatly by all the sensory devices and engrossed so intensely with the interactive nature of immersion VR that the virtual world becomes more real to the participant than real reality (the natural world itself).

Uses of Virtual Reality. Virtual reality, like other computer applications, has found its niche in practically every industry. Architects use VR to "walk through" their designs; the aircraft and auto industry uses it to design and test car and airplane designs; Hollywood uses it to design movie sets; the medical industry uses it to simulate radiation treatment; urban planners use VR with renovation plans and proposed building projects; and the entertainment industry has destined VR to be its next conquest.

While used to some extent in every industry, perhaps VR offers the longest list of possible uses to education and training. These include exploration of existing places and things otherwise inaccessible; creation of places and objects with different qualities from real ones; interaction with other people with common interests who are in remote locations; creation and manipulation of abstract models; and creation of any type of 3-D object. These objects can be drawn and studied from outside, inside, back, front, bottom, and sides. They can include natural structures such as molecular structures, cells, chromosomes, and geographical features like caves and volcanoes, or they can include man-made structures such as castles, forts, ships, homes, rooms, buildings, and even entire cities.

Virtual Reality for the Business Education Curriculum. Desktop virtual reality lends itself to being integrated very easily in business classrooms. Minimal hardware would include a 486 DX-2 processor or Pentium, 8-16 MB of RAM, 350 MB hard disk, CD-ROM, and a 16-bit sound card. Macintosh Quadra or PowerMac computers are also ideal for desktop VR. Software requirements include Microsoft Windows or other graphical user interface and the VR software.

As more and more teachers find out about virtual reality, it is being used more frequently in the classroom. For example, in marketing classes, one teacher uses Virtus Walkthrough for teaching traffic flow for retail businesses. Hence, the old shadow box models that students have used in the past for this purpose have given way to computer generated models. In the same respect, another instructor uses Virtus Walkthrough for students to design and lay out office settings for an office procedures class. In a recent project at a middle school, students scanned paintings that were created by art students and then assembled them into a virtual art gallery that "visitors" could then "walk through" within the computer system.

As computer systems become more sophisticated, teachers can expect virtual reality to be used more and more in business education classrooms. The gaming industry has brought the technology into homes with the new 32-bit processor and CD game systems. Consequently, educators can be expected to bring the same technology into the educational environment.

Virtual reality has opened a whole new world for the educational, entertainment, and business community as users rely on its powerful resources of sound, motion, sensory devices, and high resolution graphics to capture the interest of students, customers, and business leaders. In one sense, virtual reality is just another step beyond multimedia, but its applications aren't considered frivolous since it provides the abilities for users to experience a simulated environment in situations where the real thing is just not feasible because of cost, accessibility, or an element of danger.

SUMMARY

In conclusion, business educators have a solid foundation in the use of technology when compared to teachers in other disciplines. Consequently, using technology as an instructional tool is a matter of using technology in all courses that are taught within the business curriculum by all teachers, regardless of the course content. Through use of traditional technology resources, presentation software, multimedia, telecommunications, and virtual reality, business educators can rely on the powerful resources of vision, sound, and motion to recapture the attention of the MTV generation as business education moves into the next century. By making use of this technology, classrooms can be extended beyond the physical limitations of traditional classrooms into the vast expanse of the world.

REFERENCES

Christopher, D. A. (1995, March). Designing a computerized presentation center. *Technological Horizons in Education Journal. 22 No. 8,* 56-59.

Dyrli, O. E., and Kinnaman, O. E. (1995, February). Developing a technology-powered curriculum. *Technology and Learning. 15 No. 5,* 46-51.

Flatley, M. E., and Hunter, J. (1995). Electronic mail, bulletin board systems, conferences: Connections for the electronic teaching/learning age. *Technology in the*

Classroom. Yearbook No. 33 (pp. 73-85). Reston, Virginia: National Business Education Association.

Graves, P. R. (1995). Desktop presentation software—What is it and how can it be used? *Technology in the Classroom.* Yearbook No. 33 (pp. 50-61). Reston, Virginia: National Business Education Association.

Kizzier, D. L. (1995). Teaching technology vs. technology as a teaching tool. *Technology in the Classroom.* Yearbook No. 33 (pp. 10-24). Reston, Virginia: National Business Education Association.

Klemm, W. R., and Snell, J. R. (1994, October). Teaching via networked PCs: What's the best medium? *Technological Horizons in Education Journal.* 22 No. 3, 95-98.

Multimedia Source Guide. (1995-96). *Technological Horizons in Education Journal* 4.

Perreault, H. R. (1995). Multimedia: An educational tool. *Technology in the Classroom.* Yearbook No. 33 (pp. 62-72). Reston, Virginia: National Business Education Association.

Tuttle, H. G. (1995, March/April). From productivity to collaboration. *Multimedia Schools.* 2, 31-35.

Wilson, T. F., and Utecht, G. (1995, April). The Internet at Eagan High School. *Technological Horizons in Education Journal.* 22 No. 9, 75-79.

CHAPTER 11

Extending the Use of Cooperative Learning

JOYCE J. CATON

Curriculum and Instruction Consultant, Florissant, Missouri

A great deal of emphasis was placed on collaborative learning in the K-12 classrooms during the 1980s. The students in secondary and postsecondary schools today should have developed collaborative skills during that time. Instructors can build upon these skills and extend them to working in the areas of problem solving and assessing student understanding. If students have not had exposure to collaborative skills, instructors should help students develop these valued lifelong skills.

The purpose of this chapter is to review the development of cooperative learning, to suggest ways to extend these skills to solving problems and assessing learning, and to suggest strategies to deal with problem behaviors that manifest themselves when students are assigned to group activities.

REVIEWING THE COOPERATIVE LEARNING MOVEMENT

A sizable amount of research has been conducted since the 1920s on the relative effects of cooperative, competitive, and individualistic efforts of students on achievement and productivity. When students work in the individualistic mode, they work alone with their own materials, which are evaluated on a criterion-referenced basis. They are concerned only about their own achievement with little regard for what others are doing. When students work in the competitive mode, they compete with others for grades—there is a "winner" and a "loser." Evaluation in the competitive mode is norm-referenced, or may be related to a bell-shaped curve. Cooperative learning places students in learning groups that seek outcomes beneficial not only to themselves but also to other members of the group. Evaluation is based upon all members of the group reaching a predetermined goal. An ideal classroom situation includes all three modes of learning, whereby students learn to work independently, learn to compete appropriately, and learn to work collaboratively.

Models of collaborative learning approaches developed during the 1970s and 1980s followed five approaches: (1) conceptual approach model by Johnson & Johnson, (2) curriculum packages model by Slavin, (3) structures approach model by Kagan, (4) group investigation model by Sharan & Sharan, and (5) the cognitive approach model by Bellanca & Fogarty (Bellanca and Fogarty, 1992). Listed below is a sampling of specific programs that contained a mixture of learning modes:

Teams-Games-Tournament (TGT). This curriculum model, developed by DeVries and Edwards, enabled students to validate their learning through group participation in tournaments instead of taking conventional quizzes (cooperation and competition).

Student-Team-Achievement Divisions (STAD). This curriculum model, developed by Slavin, modified TGT by blending team study and individual testing with rewards for team improvement (cooperation and competition). Slavin also modified Computer-Assisted Instruction (CAI) into Team-Assisted Instruction (TAI) to include elements of cooperation and individualistic learning in a mathematics program designed for grades three to six (cooperation and competition).

Co-Op Co-Op. This structural approach, developed by Kagan, divided a main topic into mini-topics to be assigned to members of a group for individual research. Ultimately, the mini-topics were compiled into a group presentation that is shared with the class (cooperative and individualistic).

Jigsaw. This structural approach, developed by Aronson, combined resource interdependence with individualistic rewards. For example, materials to be learned are divided among students in an original group. Then each group member works within a second expert group to learn the information and prepare to teach it to the original group members (cooperative and individualistic).

In the 1980s the research of David and Roger Johnson indicated that cooperative learning, compared with competitive or individualistic efforts, tends to result in higher-level reasoning, more frequent creation of new ideas and solutions, and greater transfer of what is learned within one situation to another (Johnson and Johnson 1989). Therefore, the Johnson and Johnson model concentrated on developing students' ability to work cooperatively by including the essential components of positive interdependence ("we" instead of "me"), face-to-face promotive interaction (students facilitating each others' success), individual accountability/personal responsibility (results of the assessment of an individual student are shared with the group, which holds each person responsible for contributing his/her fair share to the group process), interpersonal and small-group skills (teamwork skills), and group processing (reflection on what went well in the group and what needs to be changed or modified). To complement some of the cooperative learning models being developed at this time, "how-to" training opportunities and resources for classroom teachers were in great demand throughout the decade. Some writers and trainers to note included the Johnson brothers with their sister Edythe Johnson Holubec, Dee Dishon, Pat Wilson O'Leary, Teresa L. Cantlon, and James Bellanca. All of these trainers and writers helped teachers translate the research into practice in the classroom. Selected publications from these trainers and writers are listed in the reference section at the end of this chapter.

Coinciding with the cooperative learning movement in education, leaders in business and industry were implementing the use of quality circles, which later evolved into self-directed teams requiring many of the same skills developed by cooperative methods in the classroom. The demand for employees who could work well in teams provided additional motivation for teachers to develop cooperative classroom methodologies.

To successfully utilize cooperative learning in the classroom, a shift in the paradigm of the role of the teacher had to be made. Teachers had to become facilitators of learning rather than providers of information (Johnson, Johnson, Holubec, 1994). Preparation time was best spent in structuring cooperative learning classroom activities supported by appropriate grouping of students and the identification and/or development of needed resources and supplies. Many teachers found this new role to be confusing as well as challenging and reported that some parents objected to group activities that did not include individual assessment, fearing that their "bright" student might be required to teach the "slow" student. However, the essential elements of the Johnson and Johnson model provided the ways and means of solving many of the problems and concerns encountered by classroom teachers. At the same time, teachers needed support for developing a proper mix of individualistic, competitive, and cooperative classroom activities.

USING COOPERATIVE LEARNING TO LEARN OR REVIEW MATERIAL

Classroom observations of teachers who developed cooperative learning activities revealed that these activities not only contributed to learning, but also contributed to developing teamwork skills that employers were demanding. Initial activities emphasized learning new material or reviewing previously learned material. Teachers often found that short, easy-to-perform activities paved the way for success. For example, some abbreviated cooperative activities recommended by trainers that began to prepare students for more extensive cooperative learning activities included:

Turn to your neighbor and...(say/write/draw): e.g., definitions from any text or lecture, steps in posting to a ledger, parts of a business letter, steps in installing a piece of software.

Pair of pairs: Students work in pairs to come up with as many ideas on a given topic as they can for three minutes; e.g., questions to ask a guest speaker, review material for a test, what to look for on a field trip, fund raising options for their student vocational organization.

Learning buddies: Students form base groups of three to four, who meet frequently to clarify or process information, ask questions, or to translate information to practical situations (should always stand when meeting).

Dynamic discussions: After an event like an assembly, a movie, or a field trip, students in groups of two to five write or draw (one paper, one pencil) *one* of the following after group reaches consensus: three most exciting parts, something that surprised the group, how they can use the information, what else could have happened, group's favorite part, or a new ending.

Pairs and homework: Students do homework individually and then meet with one other student to compare answers. When answers differ, they discuss why and attempt to find one solution. Or they compare answers with another pair and discuss which answer is correct and why. This work is followed by a quiz or check of individual students so that the emphasis is on learning rather than just having the right answer.

Groups and homework: Students sit in learning groups which review homework daily. The group encourages individuals to complete their homework assignments and bring them in on time, since the group receives a group reward or recognition when all members do so. Group members compare answers on the homework in pairs, then each pair shares their agreed-upon answers with the whole team of four to five members. The team comes to a consensus on what each answer should be. The group submits to the teacher *one* answer sheet with the consensus answers on it, which all group members sign, indicating understanding and agreement. All individual homework sheets are stapled to the back of the group answer sheet. Each group member receives his/her own grade for the homework *plus* five bonus points if all group members turned in homework, and five bonus points if the group answer sheet is 100 percent correct. Points can be applied toward learning group rewards and/or whole class rewards.

Building upon short cooperative activities, teachers began to develop full-blown cooperative learning activities that incorporated all of the following essential elements of the Johnson, Johnson, and Holubec model (Johnson, Johnson, Holubec, 1994):

Positive interdependence: Interdependence can be based upon goal interdependence (one product), reward interdependence (everyone in the group is rewarded or no one is rewarded), resource interdependence (limited resources for the group— one handout, one book, one marker, one map, etc.), role interdependence (each student is assigned a role that is complementary and interconnected—recorder, checker, time keeper, reader, etc.), and task interdependence (actions of one group member have to be completed in order for the next team member to complete his/her responsibilities).

Face-to-face promotive interaction: Promotive interaction enables students to encourage and facilitate each other's efforts to achieve, complete tasks, and work toward achievement of common goals.

Individual accountability/personal responsibility: After participating in a cooperative lesson, each student should be prepared to individually complete similar tasks. Teachers need to monitor group behavior and provide feedback to individuals and the group as a whole. "Social loafing" is when group members find they can "hitchhike" on the work of others and get a "free ride." Carefully structuring interdependence along with individual assessment can solve undesirable group behavior. The pattern of learning together and then performing alone ensures individual accountability and allows each student to benefit as a result of working in a group.

Interpersonal and small group skills: The more highly developed the teamwork skills, the higher the quality and quantity of the work of the group. Students need to be able to know and trust other group members, to be able to communicate with others, to be able to accept and support each other, and to be able to resolve conflicts. When groups are not functioning properly, these skills may need to be isolated, taught, emphasized, and evaluated. For example, if students need to learn how to encourage each other to participate, the class, or group, might be asked to brainstorm what encouragement "sounds like" or "looks like." The teacher may then require that each group exhibit at least six examples of encouragement while participating in a group activity that will be observed, documented, and evaluated. Another technique that supports the development of teamwork skills is to keep the group small (three to five) to provide more opportunities for participation.

Group processing: Groups need to be given the time to reflect on how well they functioned as a group. They should identify member actions that helped or hindered the group process and make decisions about what actions to continue or change. Group processing can be done in small groups or within the class as a whole.

An illustration of putting together all of the essential components of cooperative learning for a Jigsaw designed to develop specialized vocabulary in any business class follows:

Positive interdependence: Form groups of four to learn 20 vocabulary words. Provide each member (Member A, B, C, and D) of the group with five of the 20 words and definitions to study. Allow all of the A's to get together (as well as the B's, C's, D's) to become experts in the five words they have been assigned—they can practice with each other, develop memory strategies, and clarify any misunderstandings they may have about their assigned words. Then have all students return to their original groups of an A, B, C, and D member. At this time they "teach" the other group members their five words until all 20 have been presented. They can then engage in appropriate drill and practice to assure that all members of the group know all 20 words.

Individual accountability/personal responsibility: The teacher administers a quiz on the vocabulary words, which is taken individually by all students for a grade. Once the quiz is administered and scored, members return to their original groups (A, B, C, D). If all members of the group reach a predetermined goal (e.g., 90 percent), each member of the group is rewarded (may play a computer game, bonus points, "classroom cash" that accumulates for an auction at the end of the term, etc.).

Interpersonal and small group skills: The teacher may assign a social skill that will be observed during the group activity (e.g., eye contact, encouragement, acknowledgement of contributions, expressing appreciation, disagreeing in an agreeable way, practicing active listening). Feedback is then provided for each group by specific written examples observed during the group activity.

Group processing: Groups should be provided time to discuss how they functioned, identify positives and negatives, and commit to changing unproductive behaviors.

Support for conducting cooperative learning activities can be found in research conducted by Yager (Yager, Johnson, and Johnson, 1985). Yager examined the impact on achievement of cooperative learning with or without group processing and individualistic learning. He found that students achieved the highest with cooperative learning with group processing and that achievement was also higher in cooperative groups without group processing than when engaged in individualistic learning. A follow-up study (Johnson, Johnson, Garibaldi, 1990) added the dimension of teacher processing. Their findings supported Yager in that all cooperative conditions resulted in higher performances than individualistic activities.

USING COOPERATIVE LEARNING STRATEGIES TO CHECK FOR UNDERSTANDING

Once students have learned to work cooperatively in highly structured activities, they should be more comfortable with working in less structured groups to assess their learning. Some specific classroom methods for such activities include "Blast Off" and carousel brainstorming.

Blast Off in this application is based upon the concept of a countdown of 3-2-1 prior to "taking off" on their own to complete a test on information previously studied. For example, students in groups of two to three may be asked to generate three things they know about the topic to be tested, two areas of confusion, and one question they want to have answered prior to taking the test. Each group should note these three categories of information on a piece of chart paper using a colored marker. The teacher directs the groups in sharing their information with the class as a whole. After all groups have shared, the teacher facilitates finding the answers to unanswered questions.

Brainstorming is a useful training tool for generating and synthesizing ideas for drawing on group expertise, for getting the group moving and actively involved, and for providing content input in a way other than video or lecture. Brainstorming involves: (1) gathering as many ideas as possible without judging, (2) piggybacking on the ideas of others, (3) exhausting all possible ideas, and (4) maintaining a freewheeling attitude throughout the process.

Carousel brainstorming is an exciting group activity that expands the familiar brainstorming technique by applying the steps of the brainstorming process to *multiple topics simultaneously.* Directions for carousel brainstorming are as follows:

1. Form groups (the number of groups is determined by the number of topics you want to brainstorm or the number of concepts you want to review).

2. Post the same number of sheets of newsprint on the wall, 5 to 7 feet apart.

3. Write a topic or question related to the lesson on each sheet of newsprint. For example, "What are some ways we can apply what we learned today to a workplace setting?" "How can we apply today's lesson to our work in the classroom?" "Who are some people who might be interested in hearing about what we learned today?" "What are some 'muddy' points about today's topic?" Topics need not be stated in a question format. If more appropriate, note major concepts. For example, following a lesson on active listening, the topics listed on the charts might include paraphrasing, body matching, eye contact, etc.

4. Ask a group of three to five people to stand at each sheet of newsprint. This group will remain together throughout the activity and is assigned a color of marker that they carry with them from chart to chart. One person records and the remaining brainstorm ideas on the topic for two minutes.

5. You now have several groups all brainstorming at a different sheet on a different topic at the same time with each group recording information in an assigned color.

6. At a signal at the end of two minutes every group moves one sheet to the right and takes the colored marker. Groups then brainstorm at this new sheet for two minutes. Movement continues until all groups in the room have brainstormed on all sheets of newsprint.

7. At the end of the activity (15-20 minutes), there is a "gallery walk" where participants may circulate and read what all groups have recorded on the charts. A specific group's input can be identified by the marker color.

Carousel brainstorming is also an excellent technique to use to review for a test by placing the main topics to be covered on each sheet and asking each group to list major points to remember.

These two fast-paced activities require all students to be involved in checking their understanding of classroom concepts, which can be far more effective than one teacher randomly selecting one student to answer a question. Students also appreciate an opportunity to physically move around as opposed to always sitting still during classroom activities.

UTILIZING COOPERATIVE SKILLS TO SOLVE PROBLEMS

Students' lack of confidence in their ability to solve problems can often be reduced by having them participate in group problem-solving activities where they can not only improve their skills, but can build their confidence as well. Edward De Bono's *Six Thinking Hats* provides a technique that can be used for group problem solving (De Bono, 1985). The effective use of "thinking hats" can focus thinking more clearly, lead to more creative thinking, and improve communication and decision-making. Participants in the process are asked to think in six different modes identified with six colored "thinking hats." Having students practice the following ways of thinking will enhance the success of this approach in a problem-solving activity:

White (facts, figures, and objective information—neutral and objective): For example, have students practice wearing the white hat where they can only make factual statements—no interpretation allowed. When wearing the white hat, students may want to study the difference between a fact and a likelihood or a fact and a belief.

Red (emotions and feelings): Practice in wearing the red hat enables students to express hunches, intuitions, or impressions with no need to give reasons or justification. A group member may also practice soliciting a red hat viewpoint from another group member to test an idea.

Black (logical negative thoughts—why it can't be done): Practice in wearing the black hat can often be easier than some of the other hats, but students should develop the ability to be negative, but not emotional. Wearing the black hat also carries the responsibility to be logical—black hat reasons must stand on their own and must be usable by everyone. Black hat thinking presents the logical-negative: why something will not work. Black hat thinking is not argument—it is an objective attempt to put the negative elements onto the map.

Yellow (positive constructive thoughts—maybe this would work): When students practice wearing the yellow hat, they are thinking in the exact opposite way than when wearing the black hat. They have the responsibility of moving the hopeful to the logical by providing the basis for optimism coupled with concrete proposals and suggestions.

Green (creativity and new ideas—abundant, fertile growth): Practicing wearing the green hat can be fun as well as productive. Students need to be able to deliberately generate new ideas, alternatives, and more alternatives. They should concentrate on new approaches. However, they should also practice shaping and tailoring some of these ideas to bring them from the absurd to the possible.

Blue (control of the other hats and thinking steps): Practice in wearing the blue hat is to practice being in control of the group. Students may practice having one person in the group who wears the blue hat and moves the process along or they may practice allowing any group member to don the blue hat as needed—a leaderless group approach.

A classroom application of "thinking hats" could be structured to solve a textbook problem, a case study, or a human relations problem in the classroom or in the workplace. Throughout the problem-solving activity, the teacher may choose to wear the blue hat to control the use of the other hats and the steps in thinking. With practice, student members of groups could choose to don the blue hat when necessary to move the process along.

Once presented the problem, members of the groups would be asked to put on the white hat, whereby they can only note facts, figures, and objective information on a piece of chart paper provided to each group—nothing can be recorded that cannot be backed up with factual information. The next step would be to ask students to take off their white hats and put on their green hats.

With the green hats on they should brainstorm solutions to the problem, which should be recorded on the chart paper as well. They should do this in a rapid-fire manner and may include "off-the-wall," creative ideas. The wilder, the better! When there is evidence that the groups are running out of ideas, the students should be asked to take off their green hats and have their yellow and black hats available to don as needed. This step becomes a sorting process for the solutions generated while wearing the green hat. They may wear the black hat to identify ideas that have no chance of success or wear the yellow hat to identify ideas they feel have promise for further development. At this point in time, the group continues to work only with the yellow-hat selections.

The last hat to wear is the red hat; while wearing the red hat students should relate how they feel about the alternative solutions selected with yellow-hat thinking. Do they feel they can support the development and implementation of selected alternatives or do they feel negatively about some of the alternatives and would not be willing to pursue them any further? The solutions remaining for which group members show enthusiasm are the ones that should be developed to solve the problem! Selected solutions should be shared with the class as a whole to provide evidence that there is no one right answer to resolving problems. The emphasis should be placed on the process, not the solution.

Another group process that can be used to analyze the cause of a problem is known as "storyboarding." This technique embraces many of the concepts of cooperative learning. For example, there is role interdependence—one group member serves as the leader who guides the discussion, provides idea-generating questions, and breaks ties. Another group member serves as the "pinner" who places cards on the wall. The remaining group members serve as "writers" who generate ideas and write them on cards.

The procedure for storyboarding is as follows:

1. The teacher should place a piece of chart paper on the wall that contains a problem statement.

2. The teacher asks the class as a whole to agree on the major categories of variables that might contribute to the problem (e.g., manpower, materials, methods, machinery, time, people, practices, procedures, policies, paperwork, philosophies, etc.) and writes each of the categories on a separate piece of paper that is placed in a row on the wall—try to limit the variables to no more than four or five if possible; to buy classroom time to utilize this technique, the teacher may want to choose the variables ahead of time.

3. Members of the group are then asked to write possible problem causes on 3-by-5-inch cards (one idea per card).

4. The leader then facilitates group discussion of each major category; as the discussion progresses from category to category, group members are allowed to have the pinner post their cards under the appropriate category; the category with the most cards deserves the most attention in the problem-solving process.

Storyboarding could be used, for example, to determine the probable cause for students being tardy to class. Class members would be divided into groups of six to eight for this activity. Roles would be assigned within the group (leader, pinner, writers). The teacher would develop and write the problem statement on the board or on a piece of chart paper—"on most days, 3 to 5 students in this class are tardy."

The class as a whole (or the teacher in advance) might determine that the major categories of variables include "policies," "student behaviors," "classroom teacher behaviors," and "physical facilities." Each group would write these categories on a piece of 8 1/2 x 11" paper and post them on the wall.

At this time members of each group would be asked to write possible causes of the problem on 3 x 5" cards (one idea per card). For example some may write "the teacher never starts anything until five minutes after the class is supposed to start;" "I have to walk all the way from the gymnasium to this class, which is impossible in the time allotted between class periods;" "nothing ever happens to me when I am tardy so I don't worry about it;" etc.

The group leader would then lead a discussion about each category of variables. During this discussion members of the group would ask the "pinner" to post card(s) under the appropriate category. Each group would then be asked to generate a solution based upon the category having the most cards. The category having the most cards may vary from group to group. The group leader can then summarize the solution generated within the group to the class as a whole.

Emphasis should be on identifying the cause of the problem when using storyboarding, not on the solution to the problem. Problem-solving techniques should be employed once the group agrees upon the probable reason for the problem.

USING COOPERATIVE LEARNING SKILLS TO ASSESS GROUP BEHAVIOR

Students benefit from having an opportunity to assess group behavior. Once students have practiced appropriate social skills in highly structured cooperative learning activities, they may be interested in moving a step further to understand needs that all individuals have to varying degrees (Stech and Ratliffe, 1977):

The need to belong. The need to belong manifests itself in loners and joiners. Loners are a potential problem to a group as they may have little motivation to participate or may feel put upon by being asked to participate in a group, resulting in a sullen attitude or withdrawal behavior. Joiners can also present problems to a group by overcommiting themselves to the point they cannot deliver what they have promised or may have a greater concern about the social aspects of the group than completion of the group task.

The need to control. The need to control produces behaviors that range from authoritarian to conformist. The authoritarian is capable of becoming the self-appointed leader who controls the group's behavior, whereas the conformist goes along with whatever is happening. The authoritarians tend to set off strong emotions in others; the conformists seldom contribute to the group process and willingly go along with the majority.

The need to be liked. The need to be liked creates behaviors that range from distant to intimate. The distant individual may be difficult to understand or may be seen as a threat to others. The intimate individual can become overly concerned with friendly, affectionate, and warm actions, which interferes with accomplishing the group task.

One way of assessing group behavior is to structure a cooperative learning activity that is videotaped. Members of the group are given two copies of the following assessment sheet and asked to label their own behaviors in each category and the behaviors of one other person while viewing the videotape. The evaluation sheets are then given to all group members—they should have one of their own and at least one from another person.

Need to belong:	Need to control:	Need to be liked:
Joiner	**Authoritarian**	**Intimate**

Member of the group
Socializes with other
  group members
Knows the group
  members by name
	Talks a lot
	Interrupts
	Overrides others
	Talks loudly
		Smiles a lot
		Conforms easily
		Agrees with everyone
		Checks what others think
		  before taking a position

Loner	**Conformist**	**Distant, Hostile**

Works along quietly
Little or no involvement
  in social groups
Relates to limited number
  of people
	Nervous
	Does not talk much
	Hesitant
	Withdraws from
	  involvement
		Very critical
		Blunt, direct
		Argumentative
		Defensive

Name of Person: _____ **Check one in each category.**		
____ Joiner ____ Loner	____ Authoritarian ____ Conformist	____ Intimate, friendly ____ Distant, hostile

After completing this evaluation of group behavior, the class as a whole should brainstorm specific ways to improve all categories of behavior—joiner, loner, authoritarian, conformist, intimate, distant. An example of one method that may be used for generating ideas is to have the class brainstorm what they might say to a loner to get her/him to join in the group activity. Then the class would brainstorm some actions they might take to encourage participation. During the next group activity, the teacher would ask all groups to demonstrate examples of how they might encourage participation and would collect data (examples actually used). At the end of the group activity, this experience should be processed by the class as a whole to review what techniques worked in order to repeat their use in the future.

"Group-Work Evaluations," a technique used to assess group behavior, can also be very effective in assessing how groups are functioning (Angelo and Cross, 1993). The teacher determines what he/she wants to know about the group work and develops no more than four or five questions for collecting the feedback from students. Students should identify the group in which they were working, but should not provide their name or names of other individuals in the group. Some sample questions might include, "How many of the group's members participated actively?" "What is one thing you learned from other members of the group that you might not have learned working independently?" "What is one thing you feel your group members learned from you that they might not have otherwise learned?" and "Suggest one change that might make the group work better." The questions can be tailored to the instructor's need for information.

USING COOPERATIVE LEARNING SKILLS TO ASSESS LEARNERS' REACTIONS TO CLASSROOM STRATEGIES

Two strategies for assessing learner reactions to instruction include "Electronic Mail Feedback" and "Classroom Assessment Quality Circles" (Angelo and Cross, 1993).

Electronic Mail Feedback. Electronic mail, if available to students and if they know how to use it, can be an effective technique for soliciting students' reactions to some aspect of classroom instruction. The teacher should develop one or two questions about teaching behaviors that they can—and are willing to—change if necessary. These questions are posed in an e-mail message to students with clear instructions on the length and type of response being sought as well as a deadline for responding. This request may be sent to their individual mailboxes or posted on a class bulletin board. If students' comments can be accessed and read by others, make sure to let them know this ahead of time.

Classroom Assessment Quality Circles. A teacher determines that she/he wants to meet regularly with one or more small groups of students to get feedback on the course. The teacher asks for volunteers or appoints five to eight students to serve in Classroom Assessment Quality Circles. Students may be granted credit for one or more assignments or given bonus points for their participation. An agenda should be developed for the first meeting along with some guidelines for working effectively in a Quality Circle group (e.g., everyone is heard and everyone listens actively). The teacher should be clear with the students about which aspects of the course are open to discussion and which are not. The Quality Circles should meet on a regular basis and the instructor should respond appropriately to their suggestions. The members of the Quality Circles should be introduced to the class as a whole so that other class members have an opportunity to seek them out to share their feelings as well. This provides a wonderful opportunity for students to practice their assessment and group-work skills.

The techniques identified in this section provide opportunities for students to extend their ability to work in groups that are less structured than formal cooperative learning situations. Should the teacher find that students do not function well in such activities, he/she should return to more structured group work to provide students an opportunity to hone their skills. In addition to providing opportunities for utilizing group-work skills, these techniques also develop in students responsibility for their learning.

SOME TRICKS OF THE TRADE

Based upon personal experience in utilizing cooperative learning with adult learners and many classrooms observations of teachers ranging from K-14, some tried-and-true rules that have met with repeated success include:

1. Groups should be kept small—groups with three to five members appear to work best.

2. The makeup of the groups should be changed frequently—heterogeneous groups are usually more productive.

3. One or two problem students should not be allowed to sabotage your efforts— the problem behaviors should be labeled and the whole class should be involved in determining ways to change them to productive behaviors. The use of various forms of interdependence may be effective in resolving behavioral problems.

4. Overly aggressive students should be grouped together; quiet students who prefer to work alone should also be placed in the same group. Mixing these two extremes can be counterproductive.

5. Group grades should be avoided; when students learn cooperatively, they should be evaluated individually. Individual grades coupled with group rewards are recommended. Kagan feels especially strong about group grades and even suggests that they may be challenged in court (Kagan, 1995).

6. The key to a good reward system is to provide group rewards that are appropriate and desired by the students—group rewards work as well with adults as they do with younger students.

7. The classroom should be rearranged to accommodate the group needs. (Neighbors and administrators should be advised that the increased noise level in the classroom is productive noise!)

8. Cooperative learning activities may take more time than direct teaching methods, but also usually result in increased learning and interest.

9. One way to measure the success of a cooperative learning activity is to compare grades earned on a unit of study with a traditional individualistic method with those earned on a unit of study where students learned cooperatively.

10. Cooperative learning lessons should be developed one at a time and used sparingly until you become experienced in monitoring and facilitating student groups.

TRANSFERRING COOPERATIVE LEARNING SKILLS TO THE WORKPLACE

In the last few years, a number of reports have been issued regarding the skills needed in the workplace. All of these reports indicate the need for communication skills (reading, writing, speaking, and listening) as well as teamwork skills. Cooperative learning in the classroom setting provides a practical method for developing both communication and teamwork skills.

Empowering employees in the workplace has been evolving over time starting with employee suggestions, moving to task forces and quality circles, and finally evolving into self-directed work teams. A self-directed work team is defined as a group of employees who have day-to-day responsibility for managing themselves and the work they do with a minimum of direct supervision

(Fisher, 1993). Members of self-directed teams typically handle job assignments, plan and schedule work, make production and/or service-related decisions, and take action on problems. The use of self-directed work teams in the workplace is not likely to go away when one looks at the results—lower manufacturing costs, higher productivity, decrease in absenteeism, higher quality product or service, and a marked increase in profits (Fisher, 1993).

Classrooms that incorporate collaborative learning concepts to facilitate students' ability to learn new material, solve problems, and produce classroom projects are providing the opportunity for students to practice skills needed to function in task forces, quality circles, and self-directed work teams. To facilitate the transference of these skills to the workplace, students need to practice the application of these skills in realistic projects and assignments.

SUMMARY

Since the 1980s, a great deal of emphasis has been placed upon collaborative learning techniques. These techniques may be applied to activities designed to learn or review new material, assess student understanding, solve problems, develop and assess group behavior, and assess learners' reactions to classroom strategies. Classroom techniques that empower students in the classroom to be responsible for their learning and for their behavior support the development of skills required to be successful in the workplace.

Development of teamwork skills should start with the use of highly formalized cooperative learning techniques designed for learning or reviewing new material. These skills should then be transferred to less structured group activities. Behaviors that prevent a group from being successful should be labeled, and strategies should be developed to change these behaviors. However, instructors should also continue to incorporate individualistic and competitive activities when planning instruction to capitalize on the benefits of all three modes of learning.

REFERENCES

Angelo, T. A., and Cross, P. K. (1993). *Classroom assessment techniques: A handbook for college teachers,* pp. 327-329 and pp. 339-342. San Francisco: Jossey-Bass, Inc.

Bard, T. B. (1992). Cooperative learning with adult learners. *If mind matters, 2,* pp. 251-260. Palatine, Illinois: Skylight Publishing Company.

Bellanca, James and Fogarty, R. (1992). Building a synthesis research. *If mind matters, 2,* pp. 189-200. Palatine, Illinois: Skylight Publishing Company.

Cantlon, T. L. (1991). *Structuring the classroom successfully for cooperative team learning.* Portland, Oregon: Prestige Publishers.

Crosby, M. E, and Howard, D. L. (1992). Lessons learned in a cooperative college classroom. *If mind matters, 2,* pp. 243-250. Palatine, Illinois: Skylight Publishing Company.

De Bono, E. (1985). *Six thinking hats.* Boston: Little, Brown and Company.

Fisher, K. (1993). *Leading self-directed work teams,* p. 15 and pp. 23-25. New York: McGraw-Hill, Inc.

Johnson, D. W., and Johnson, R. T., and Holubec, E. J. (1988). *Cooperation in the classroom, revised.* Edina, Minnesota: Interaction Book Company.

Johnson, D. W., and Johnson, R. (1989). *Cooperation and competition: Theory and research.* Edina, Minnesota: Interaction Book Company.

Johnson, D. W., Johnson, R., Stanne, M., and Garibaldi, A. (1990). The impact of leader and member group processing on achievement in cooperative groups. *The Journal of Personality and Social Psychology 130:* 507-516.

Johnson, D. W., and Johnson, R. T., and Holubec, E. J. (1994). *The new circles of learning: Cooperation in the classroom and the school,* pp. 25-35, 101. Alexandria, Virginia: Association for Supervision and Curriculum.

Johnson, D. W., and Johnson, R.T., and Holubec, E. J. (1994). *Cooperative learning in the classroom,* pp. 18-23. Alexandria, Virginia: Association for Supervision and Curriculum.

Kagan, S. (1995, May). Group grades miss the mark, pp. 68-71. *Educational Leadership 52,* Number 8.

Stech, E., and Ratliffe, S. (1977). *Working in groups: a Communication manual for leaders and participants in task-oriented groups,* pp. 114-119. Skokie, Illinois: National Textbook Company.

Yager, S., Johnson, D.W., and Johnson, R. (1985). Oral discussion, group-to-individual transfer, and achievement in cooperative learning groups. *Journal of Educational Psychology 77:* 60-66.

CHAPTER 12

Innovative Teaching Strategies Motivate Students

KENNETH J. KASER

Lincoln Northeast High School, Lincoln, Nebraska

When students are involved in the learning process, they are more likely to retain the subject matter and to enjoy the learning process. A wide variety of learning activities can be incorporated into business classes. Good teachers are risk takers. They are willing to try new teaching techniques to provide students with the concepts, attitudes, and skills they need to be successful in the workplace. While some innovative teaching methods may be very success-ful, others may need revision, and yet others should be discarded altogether.

This chapter focuses on innovative teaching techniques developed by the author to motivate students. A wise person once said, "The world is moving so fast these days that the person who says it can't be done is generally inter-rupted by someone doing it." Creativity, enthusiasm, and sincere interest in stu-dents equal an exciting learning environment for both students and teachers.

INTERNATIONAL ACTIVITIES

International business is a relatively new course for high school students. Many unique activities can contribute to student motivation in an inter-national business course. Some activities that have been used with success follow.

Business Meetings. Organizations involved in international trade can provide opportunities for students to attend luncheons or meetings involv-ing international trading partners. Students observe and take notes on the issues discussed. An example of such a meeting took place at a cheesecake manufacturer in Lincoln, Nebraska, that trades internationally. During the visit, students were thrilled when they were allowed to share ideas in an American/Japanese business session devoted to making Sugar Spoon cheese-cakes more to the liking of the Japanese consumer by decreasing the sugar content. Also discussed was the problem of shipping a highly perishable item. The students thoroughly enjoyed the experience.

Field Trips. Students often are surprised to find out how many of their local businesses participate in international trade. Students can acquire an appreciation of international issues by touring businesses. For example, students visiting the Bison Corporation were intrigued by the manufacturing process that produces basketball hoops and backboards to the varying speci-fications of different countries. Another example of how students gain more information about international business through field trips is illustrated by the visit to a cut-flower wholesaler, Sunwest Farms, which buys flowers from all over the world. During the visit, the tour guide informed students of all the countries from which Sunwest Farms bought flowers and of interesting information concerning social status and political stability in many of the countries. Students were interested in learning that Sunwest would not trade with certain countries due to poor labor practices and undercutting of the U.S. market.

Interdisciplinary Projects. Interdisciplinary projects require coordination between the teachers of the participating classes but the results of such projects are well worth the effort. An example of an interdisciplinary project that has been very successful is an exchange of classes for at least three days between an international foods/etiquette teacher and a business teacher. Students in the International Business course learn about international etiquette and expectations concerning gift giving. The learning experience is enhanced by cooking an international meal of stir-fry vegetables. An added touch is eating the meal with chopsticks. Students in the International Foods/ Etiquette course learn about international trading do's and taboos, franchises (McDonalds and Kentucky Fried Chicken) in other countries, and international trade in the state.

The Advanced Spanish class and the International Business class also exchanged learning experiences for two days. Menus from an American restaurant were translated from English into Spanish by students in the Advanced Spanish course, while the International Business students changed dollars to pesos. A fun activity was the demonstration in Spanish of the preparation of a Mexican dish, guacamole. Both classes enjoyed the meal.

Interdisciplinary activities strengthen relationships among departments in a school and serve as great recruitment devices for future students. Inviting classes from other disciplines to hear some of the International Business guest speakers is a good way to begin a cooperative learning environment.

International Speakers. A number of exceptional speakers are available. The International Students Association from a local college or university, foreign exchange students at your school, airline representatives who have worked for airports in other countries, and business people who deal in international trade are great motivators for successful learning.

Informational Bulletin Boards. Bulletin boards are great for displaying reports and information students obtain about other countries. Two excellent sources for international information are Culturegrams, which can be purchased from Brigham Young University, and the *Do's and Taboos* series, available through NBEA. The easy access to information leads to good quality reports and bulletin boards about international trade practices. Students can give oral reports on the information they learn about other countries. Another interesting activity is to challenge students to find items at home that were made in other countries and to develop a bulletin board including the items and the country of origination.

PICTIONARY

Pictionary works great for a unit on trademarks, franchises, product labels, or aspects of government. To play the game, students are split into teams of 8 to 10 members. A student from each team is designated as the "drawer."

The drawers are given the same item to draw. The item can be a picture of a trademark, franchise, product label, or an aspect of government. The other members of the team try to guess the answer as the three drawers create the item on the chalkboard/white board. The first person who stands and states the correct answer earns a point for his or her team. Drawers are rotated for each new picture to keep all students actively involved.

PYRAMID POINTS

Another game that works well for review purposes and current events is Pyramid Points, which is very similar to Jeopardy. Six to eight categories are put on the board, and students are given an answer sheet. Each student takes a turn by choosing a category worth a stated number of points and then is asked questions from that category (the larger the number, the tougher the question). All students attempt to answer the question on their answer forms. A category cannot be selected consecutively. At the end of the activity, students exchange papers and assign points to questions answered correctly. Students with the highest scores receive prizes.

FOOD STAMPS

High school students often need an extra incentive to participate actively in class. Food stamps is an idea that can be implemented into any business course. As students participate positively in class discussions or answer questions correctly, they receive a rubber stamp imprint in their notebooks. Once a week an inflation rate (the number of stamps necessary to buy a small piece of candy) is announced. Factors that influence inflation such as bad weather for the sugar crop and competition from international markets are discussed. At the end of the class period, students can use their stamps to purchase candy or other treats. This activity also is good for organizational skills because students must keep their notebooks in order, and they must bring the notebook to class.

SECRET OF MY SUCCESS

An activity that helps students develop writing and computer skills and assists them in discovering characteristics for successful leadership is the Secret of My Success. At the computer, students compose letters to successful people. The purpose of the letter is to find out what characteristics are necessary for leadership or success. An addressed, stamped envelope is included with the letter to encourage a response. All responses received are photocopied and displayed with the student's original letter at a prominent location in the high school. This activity is a marvelous recruitment device.

FILMING TV COMMERCIALS

An excellent activity for a marketing or business management class is creating commercials for a product, service, or special promotion. Evaluations of the commercials are based on creativity, script, quality of sound, and preparation. Students have the option of taping at school or at home. The final copies of student commercials are put on one tape for interested parents, administrators, and other students to review.

BILLBOARDS

Students in a marketing or business management class can make billboards that advertise existing products, services, or an upcoming event. Students can be given the option of promoting their own products, services, or special events. The billboards are displayed for a set period of time in the classroom or other areas in the school. Evaluation of the billboards is based upon creativity, timeliness, and customer appeal.

BANKING BUSINESS

An activity that works well in a general business or accounting course is called banking business. Job titles typically associated with banking are put into a hat. Students draw one position from the hat and research the job responsibilities and the expected salary associated with the job selected. Students are given time cards that they use each time they attend class. At the end of a two-week period, each student calculates the gross pay, deductions, and net pay of another student in the class and prepares the corresponding paycheck. After the paycheck is given to the appropriate student, that individual completes a deposit ticket and records the transaction in his or her check register. Students learn about careers, payroll calculations, and banking transactions.

PIZZA BUSINESS

An interdisciplinary project that has been very successful at the high school level is an imaginary pizza business. Students serve on the board of directors and make all business decisions. Some examples of the interdisciplinary participation that can be included follow: (a) business management/ marketing classes design the advertising; (b) business law classes research law cases related to the pizza business; (c) business management classes develop a customer survey; (d) sociology classes distribute and collect the surveys; (e) math classes calculate the survey responses; (f) art classes design a logo or billboard; (g) computer applications classes design a menu and business cards; (h) composition classes write a restaurant review; (i) industrial arts classes design the building; (j) accounting classes set up a payroll system; (k) family and consumer science classes develop the menu and design the interior of the restaurant; and (l) foreign language classes write menus and restaurant themes in different languages.

The possibilities are endless in this project. The business community can play a supportive role in the project by providing guest speakers and sponsoring field trips. A kickoff pizza buffet/rally for participating students and teachers is a good way to begin the project, and a pizza banquet at the end of the school year provides an opportunity to recognize students for their accomplishments. This project is possible only through the cooperation of many teachers and the administration.

BINGO

Bingo is a fun activity to familiarize students with new terms and definitions. Students are given 24 terms for their blank bingo cards. When definitions of the terms are called, students mark boxes like a regular Bingo game. This activity reinforces learning definitions. It takes the typically boring lesson of reviewing terms and turns it into a fun activity.

INVITED SPEAKERS

Most students have some kind of work experience. Students can be given the opportunity to invite a business person as a guest speaker. The student helps the speaker identify an appropriate topic and makes all arrangements for the visit. The student introduces the speaker and sends a thank-you note immediately after the presentation. The activity encourages the student to take an active role in class activities, and it provides the entire class with an opportunity to hear about actual business practices.

FIELD TRIPS

Field trips can be very beneficial learning experiences. For example, a trip to a local car dealership allowed high school students to talk with representatives from customer service, the body shop, and new and used car departments. Students took notes during the field trip, and the next day in class they completed a work sheet about the field trip. Their notes were available to them as they completed the work sheet. A field trip is a great way to strengthen ties with the business community. It does require advance planning by the teacher, and students must be made aware of behavior expectations.

BUSINESS PARTNERSHIPS

Business management classes can make good use of a high school's business partners. The partners give students many opportunities to learn more about operating a business, satisfying customers, and working with employees. Learning experiences may be gained through speakers, interviews, and field trips. Dedicated business partners are exceptional role models for community involvement.

SUMMARY

Numerous creative teaching ideas are available to make business classes more exciting. The activities shared in this chapter can be modified to fit a specific subject area, class level, or time allowance. Students become more engaged in their coursework when they see the relevance of the information and when they enjoy their classroom experiences. Incorporating motivational activities is one way to make the classroom a more productive and enjoyable place for students and teachers alike.

PART III

INVIGORATING THE BUSINESS CURRICULUM

CHAPTER 13

Workplace Readiness Skills

MARCIA A. ANDERSON-YATES
Southern Illinois University, Carbondale, Illinois

For several decades, employee nontechnical competency has been an area of concern to employers. Lack of competency in the affective areas of workplace skills is constantly reiterated by employers who seek competent employees in all aspects of work, not just technical skills. Ability to perform effectively in every aspect of employment determines job success. The continuing challenge for educators is determining how to incorporate instruction in these nebulous nontechnical skills. This article provides a background on workplace skills with issues regarding curriculum for teaching such skills. Specific strategies and student activities for use in various courses are suggested.

DEFINING WORKPLACE SKILLS

Workplace skills, according to the Vocational-Technical Education Consortium of States (1994), are "the generic essential employment skills related to seeking, obtaining, keeping, and advancing in any job" (p. xix). The Commission on the Skills of the American Workforce (1990) found that the primary concern of more than 80 percent of employers was finding workers with a good work ethic and appropriate social behavior—"reliable, a good attitude, a pleasant appearance, and a good personality" (p. 24). *Workplace Basics: The Skills Employers Want,* according to Carnevale, Gainer, and Meltzer (1990), include problem-solving, personal management, and interpersonal skills. Employees in command of these skills, particularly with innovative solutions to problems, will be in great demand.

Need for competence in workplace skills is further emphasized in the SCANS Report (U. S. Department of Labor, 1991), which identified competencies and a foundation of skills and personal qualities that constitute job performance. The report said that "these requirements are essential preparation for all students, both those going directly to work and those planning further education. Thus, the competencies and the foundation should be taught and understood in an integrated fashion that reflects the workplace contexts in which they are applied" (p. xv). Different aspects of "tomorrow's workplace" as described in the SCANS Report are: (a) flexible production, (b) on-line quality control, (c) decentralized control, (d) flexible automation, (e) customized production, (f) work teams, (g) multiskilled workers, (h) authority delegated to workers, (i) labor-management cooperation, (j) screening for basic skills abilities, and (k) workers as an investment.

Predicted changes in America's workplace clearly focus on giving more authority and more freedom to decide to the individual worker while expecting both more responsibility and more accountability. To the extent that these predicted workplace changes happen, individual workers will (a) better understand the importance of their specific job in the total work organization, (b) be more motivated for high quality job performance, and (c) develop greater pride in themselves and in their job assignment. These qualities should serve to increase worker productivity.

Workplace skill competence represents a critical component reflecting the degree to which students will be successful in their chosen careers. In the educational reform movement, emphasis is being placed on the need to develop specific skills businesses are demanding. Reformers have also concluded that if education changes to meet this need, a positive "ripple-effect" will occur in the improvement of not only worker employment success and market productivity, but also in global competitiveness (Schlichting & Echternacht, 1994).

PREPARATION FOR TEACHING WORKPLACE SKILLS

Wentling (1987) stated that failure to include employability skills in classroom teaching is due many times not to lack of recognition of importance but more often to educators not knowing which factors to stress or how to instill the needed personal qualities in students. In a research study involving Illinois business instructors, Anderson-Yates, Coffman, and Baker (1992) found that a majority of instructors felt very prepared to teach "work behavior/ work ethics" and "maintain working relationships" competencies. They were not prepared or were uncomfortable teaching such competencies as "channel emotional reaction constructively," "identify and react to sexual intimidation/ harassment," "direct co-workers when necessary," "identify leadership style required for effective teamwork," and "be creative to meet changing needs." Business instructors reported they used their own personal experiences to teach workplace skills and that their college course work was of minimal assistance in preparing them to teach such skills.

To develop their expertise in teaching the affective workplace skills, instructors can attend professional development activities or enroll in courses that emphasize methods of teaching workplace skills. They can also assemble available resources designed to develop students' workplace skills. A comprehensive resource is the V-TECS Product Elements for Workplace Skills (1994), which includes duty and task lists, performance objectives, enabling competencies and related academic skills, instructional activities, instructional resources, instructional materials, and instructional worksheets.

CURRICULAR ISSUES

Curriculum at secondary and postsecondary levels is already overextended with expanding program requirements; however, careful planning will achieve desired emphasis on workplace skills in the curriculum. Best results seem to be achieved when workplace skills are integrated with academic and vocational skills training. In this way, relevance of all required skills is interrelated and taught as basic to job market success—something in which the learner has a level of interest. Alternate methods for infusing workplace skills into the curriculum include the following:

Units of Instruction. Units reflecting specific categories of workplace skills can be included in business instruction. For example, a specific unit on oral communications and on body language could form part of a business communication course.

Special Topics. A workplace skill can be used as a topic in different units of instruction. For example, "practice time management" might be taught in an office systems course in organization of work, stress management, and productivity standards. Time management, initiative, and decision making could also be taught in keyboarding.

Ongoing In-Class Activities. Instructors, while developing technical skills, should select activities that will also assist students in developing workplace skills. For example, in a computer course, instructors might emphasize the workplace skill, "following oral and written directions." Instructors should present information on the need for such skills with techniques for listening and following oral/written directions. Instructors would then explain to students that periodically they will give assignments using either oral or written directions. They would be expected to complete assignments without questioning students or the instructor. At other times, students could be encouraged to ask questions for clarification. Grades should be given for how well directions were followed.

Continuing Emphasis. Instructors should emphasize workplace skills in all classes whenever the opportunity presents itself. Hoyt (1993) suggested ongoing classroom behaviors that consider both students and teachers as workers. The worker (student) must be shown the importance of work tasks. When students ask "why should I learn this?" many teachers have no good answers to provide that will really motivate students to learn. Students must be able to relate how the academic/technical skill they are learning is needed and valuable in occupational success.

Student work must be rewarded when it occurs. Instructors should find some way of providing each student who honestly tries to complete a given assignment some kind of credit for having done so. If instructors expect students to perform work tomorrow, they should provide the student with some form of credit/recognition/appreciation/reward for the work the student does today. Students are typically reminded of when they don't accomplish tasks but are seldom recognized when they really try to do what is asked.

Workplace (classroom) activities should require a variety of behaviors. If workers are asked to do exactly the same things in the same ways day after day, soon worker boredom increases—and worker productivity decreases. Instructors should insert both experiential and cognitive activities in the teaching/learning process.

Workers (students) need to develop a sense of "ownership" in their work. Students should be allowed to determine what they consider to be the best way of reaching specified goals. A way to reward effort is for instructors to give students ownership of their ideas through comments such as "Remember

Joe's idea on how to best accomplish this procedure?" A sense of "owner-ship"can, by emphasizing the concept of accountability for both teachers and students, be a very effective way of increasing educational productivity.

Good work habits must be recognized and rewarded. Since the classroom is a workplace and students are workers, students will acquire/practice certain work habits during their school years. "Habits" are ways of behaving that, when done often enough over a long period of time, become almost automatic for the person. Habits typically held by highly productive workers have been well known for many years. The instructor's priority goal should be to engage in vigorous efforts to expect students, beginning in the early elementary school years, to abide by such productive work habit rules as:

Come to work (to school) on time.

Do your best to carry out each assignment you are given.

Complete your assignments by the time they are due.

Follow directions.

Cooperate with your fellow workers.

Set up and use a schedule for getting your work done.

Keep your workplace as neat and clean as possible.

Organize work plans every day allowing you to do things in priority order.

Be considerate of your fellow workers—don't make things difficult for them.

Be responsible and accountable for what you do on your job each day.

Be dependable—make sure others can count on you to do your job.

Be polite to those with whom you work. (Hoyt, 1993, p. 8)

If students are to develop and practice good work habits, recognition and/or reward for doing so is essential. One way of emphasizing the importance of developing such habits would be for instructors to make periodic reports to students and their parents on the extent to which students are practicing good work habits. What is important is a plan for developing good work habits. Until and unless such a plan exists, problems with development and use of productive work habits by both students and employed adult workers will continue to exist. Good work habits cannot be expected to develop in either an incidental or in an accidental manner. They are characteristics to be developed—not something the individual possesses at birth.

Studies conducted to define workplace skills needed for job success typically identify similar types of characteristics but often use different words and systems of organization to define them. While no one "correct" system to use exists, some organizational system must be used to facilitate the integration of this important content area into the curriculum (Poole & Zahn, 1993).

Koffel (1994) identified one such system for instructors to consider. She suggested that to redesign a course infusing workplace skills, instructors should begin with the content blocks that are currently used for the course and set course objectives for each content block. These content blocks are then matched with appropriate teaching strategies for developing workplace skills that parallel the content in the block. Koffel developed the Workplace Skills System to upgrade students' skills in the seven workplace-skill areas of critical thinking, basic skills, communication, teamwork, leadership, motivation, and career development. Using the Workplace Skills System will require the instructor to plan strategically each segment or content block of information for the course so that students learn both the subject matter of the course and learn from the workplace-skills experiences developed through the system.

INSTRUCTIONAL STRATEGIES

Since workplace skills are infused into existing courses according to a plan, business instructors must be creative with general teaching methods to develop positive student behaviors. Lectures should be used only to introduce a topic. Then the key is to get students involved in displaying appropriate behaviors. Strategies emphasizing student involvement (McEwen, McEwen, Sheets, & Anderson-Yates, 1992) to consider are:

Role playing. Probably the most effective strategy to use for developing workplace skills is role play—effective for developing such skills as conflict resolution, human relations, and professional characteristics. During role playing, students experience positive and negative attitudes. As a result, they know the effect of different behaviors on others. They learn, in a concrete way, what is and what is not desirable behavior.

Case Studies. Case studies are especially useful in situations where no right answer exists. The case may be written by the instructor, selected from textbooks, or developed from a business situation. Case problems can be presented in narrative form or on video tape or other multimedia. Davies (1981) discussed three types of case studies that could be considered for teaching workplace skills: (a) The critical incident case gives a detailed account of events leading up to a problem solution. Students could be asked what further information is required before a solution can be identified; (b) The next-stage case provides facts leading up to a problem, and students are asked what is then likely to happen; (c) Live cases remind students of well-publicized news items in the media and require students to ponder what will happen next. Case studies are most effective if the situations are based on realistic problems.

Discussion and Cooperative Learning. Class discussions and small cooperative learning group discussions, are excellent ways to involve students in exploring problems. Instructors must have specific goals in mind for the discussion, asking thought-provoking questions that stimulate higher-order thinking and encourage application of knowledge. For small groups, instructors must explain what each student is to do and what is to be learned through the discussion.

Discussion topic ideas can be obtained from newspaper articles, videos, and local businesses. Each class member should contribute to achieving the group's goals by playing different roles—facilitator, recorder, praiser, or summarizer. Through these roles, students can learn responsibility, interdependence, problem solving, and team work. Because group members must face one another during the discussion, students also practice eye contact and active listening.

Brainstorming is another skill that students should practice. The group lists any and all ideas with no judgments. After brainstorming, the group discusses all input and narrows the list to the most appropriate ideas (e.g., for problem solving or decision making). Also, the entire class can brainstorm with the instructor or a student facilitating this process.

Personal Journal. Keeping a journal is usually a fun activity for students. They can observe and record positive work habits of classmates and family members or other role models. Students could also record personal activities that demonstrate positive work habits. The instructor should provide examples for journal entries.

Debates. Debates allow students to explore issues in the workplace, such as business appearance standards. This strategy helps students to examine issues from two sides as each team represents a point of view. Debates require a great deal of preparation. Students should select judges, a moderator, and a timer as well as decide on criteria for judging. Debates help students develop team work and encourage respect and tolerance for views of others.

Student Organizations. Student organizations represent the ideal environment for developing workplace skills. Through regular meetings, students learn to express ideas clearly and to appreciate different points of view. Working with committees and projects helps students develop leadership skills, communication skills, and self-confidence.

Another important activity can be an organization's award program. An award may be given for "Student of the Month" based on contribution to the organization, professional behavior, and outstanding school work. Such activities encourage positive attitudes and develop interpersonal skills.

Resource People. Guest speakers link the classroom with the community and depict reality of the workplace for students. Local business persons can speak about their successes and failures and the importance of appropriate behavior for job success. Personnel officers can discuss problems they have had with employees who have exhibited poor work attitudes and qualities employers seek in potential employees. Instructors should prepare students for the presentation by discussing the general topic and having students formulate questions they will ask the speaker.

Alumni Scrapbook. Stories about successful graduates can be assembled in an alumni scrapbook. Scenarios might emphasize the importance of positive workplace skills in career success. Students are then encouraged to emulate graduates who have been successful in their careers. These graduates also make excellent guest speakers. Letters from graduates can also be read and posted on display boards.

SPECIFIC ACTIVITIES

Teaching suggestions that might be used to teach competencies in identified workplace skill areas include the following:

Solving Problems and Critical Thinking

1. No other strategy for motivating students to appreciate the importance of individual thought and critical thinking can have as much impact as an instructor who models critical thinking for students. Instructors who demon-

strate aloud their thinking provide a role model for thinking that students will emulate and remember long after the text material. To become a model for critical thinking, instructors will need to become conscious of their own critical thinking process and practice step-by-step reasoning by writing down their reasoning processes for some of the problems or issues. The critical point is to develop a systematic method of writing down steps of reasoning involved in major problems and working through those steps for student benefits (Koffel, 1994).

2. In getting students to employ reasoning skills, instructors should present a lecture on reasoning skills and how such skills can affect the people involved with a problem situation. Students can be assigned a simple problem with several solutions with instructions to use reasoning skills to determine who would be affected by each solution and to decide which option/solution would be best for solving the problem.

3. Students often have not been shown how to make distinctions among pure fact, inference of fact, and opinion, or the importance of being able to make such distinctions. Assignments can be developed using already prepared case studies. Students can analyze the "facts" presented in the case study to determine which of the ideas are facts, inference, or judgment. They can then use this determination to argue for or against a particular solution. Once students are provided with a framework for this kind of reasoning, they can analyze cases more objectively, and they are able to analyze information they may read or hear as part of their everyday life.

4. Student thinking can be enhanced if students are paired while solving a problem or case study and then advised to observe and comment on the critical thinking of their partners. Students essentially take on a role of coach —giving ideas, criticizing, and reviewing carefully the thinking skills of another student while trying to help the student by identifying ideas their partners may have overlooked. Ground rules would include the following: (a) Students in the roles of mentors/helpers should strive to improve their partners' ability; (b) participants should not be criticized but coached; (c) both coach and participant need to take turns listening and talking (Koffel, 1994).

Demonstrating Work Ethics and Behavior. To emphasize the competency "demonstrate a willingness to learn," instructors might organize the game "Just-in-Time Learning." Periodically, class members can be assigned to learn a specific task that relates to content being addressed; then they teach it to the rest of the class when that content is definitely needed. Basic training principles should be reviewed prior to the assignment.

To focus on "exhibiting pride," students can be asked to identify several businesses of interest (ones they routinely visit outside of school). They will need instruction on identifying what constitutes pride in the workplace and how to observe ways that employees in those businesses demonstrate pride in their workplace.

When addressing "display initiative," instructors should explain different workplace opportunities that would provide employees a chance to display initiative. This explanation can be followed with a class discussion on the connection between displaying workplace initiative and assuming responsibility for their own decisions and actions. Students might then choose a job position of interest and brainstorm situations in which the employee could display initiative.

Maintaining Interpersonal Relationships. To emphasize "resolve conflicts," students could list three conflict situations in which they have been recently involved. For each situation, students would write a paragraph describing how they resolved the conflicts; or, situations involving differences of opinion among workers might be dramatized with students discussing how they would resolve differences. Students could answer individually followed by groups deciding the best way to resolve the conflicts.

To "value individual diversity," business representatives from different fields could be invited to discuss diversity skills needed to be successful in that occupation. Students would be asked to develop six questions about diversity in the workplace to ask each guest speaker. After questioning speakers, a discussion follows on how and at what levels individual diversity can be an asset via bringing a new outlook/perspective, cultural values, and experiences, etc., to a given situation. Or, as follow-up activity, students could identify several factors about themselves that make them individually diverse and discuss how their diversity might benefit the workplace.

When teaching "display a positive attitude," discussion should include how a positive work attitude makes the workplace more pleasant for the worker and everyone else involved, while a negative work attitude can have the exact opposite effect. Then an example of how one person's work attitude affects multiple people should be provided; or students might be told that the following day the instructor will be conducting the class using primarily negative attitudes. Students will be asked to take notes about the instructor's negative attitude and how it made them feel and want to react. Time should be allowed to discuss student notes and reactions. The instructor would end the class with at least 10 minutes of positive attitude and with a brief discussion on how students felt.

Demonstrating Team Work. Workers (students) need to be taught how to work in teams. Increasingly, most tasks to be performed by information society workers are being viewed as team efforts where each individual team member has specific kinds of authority, responsibility, and accountability. Team work is not something most people do naturally—it is a learned behavior. Collaborative learning groups will require some explanation of the collaborative process at the outset because the traditional classroom norms require that students do not work together but rather work independently in competition with one another. To change this paradigm and to get students to accept a different norm for collaborative learning requires some training in group process and, at the very least, some explanation giving students permission to talk with one another, to help one another, and to collaborate.

To foster collaborative learning, the instructor can set up permanent learning teams, taking care to place "high status" or gifted students evenly throughout the groups and to avoid concentrating problem students in any one group. The instructor should give problems to the learning group throughout the course and require group members to help one another in solving the problems. In some cases, individual problems are assigned, but the students are instructed to get assistance from their learning group when necessary. Learning group members make certain that each group member can work out each problem. Evaluation of a collaborative effort should be a group evaluation as any success or failure is due to the group process and not individual members (Koffel, 1994).

A group test strategy conducted in much the same way as an individual test might be considered. Students are each given essay exams to complete within a class period, but they are assigned to three- or four-person groups. They are allowed to discuss the answers to the examination without using any notes or books. Each student formulates and writes an answer to each question. While students are allowed to talk about the topics of the examination, the final responsibility for the answer lies with the individual student. They are allowed to discuss answers, to listen, and to evaluate the worth of the answers of their fellow students; but, ultimately, they must choose the answers they believe to be the most correct. This test strategy requires as much preparation as an individual examination, perhaps more. Students not only need to know the content, but also they must exercise good judgment in what to accept and what not to accept based on their classmates' answers (Koffel, 1994).

In assisting students to "identify style of leadership used in team work," instructors should discuss and demonstrate three styles of leaders—autocratic, democratic, and laissez-faire. Role playing situations using each style provide realistic examples. Analysis of situations in which each leadership style is appropriate should be provided. Discussion on how different leadership styles have varying effects on individuals is useful.

EVALUATION STRATEGIES

Feedback and assessment are critical elements in developing workplace skills. Instructors must provide frequent and immediate feedback assuring that students are aware of their progress as well as their failures. Feedback must be consistent after a workplace skill is addressed so correct performance is reinforced. To prevent student embarrassment, Buck and Barrick (1987) suggested use of a "secret signal" (nonverbal) to alert the student to unwanted behavior. An example would be when the instructor makes eye contact with the student and shakes the head to indicate "no." Other specific strategies include the following:

Observational Checklists. A variety of affective behavior observational checklists, such as DaSalva's (1990) School Store Student Evaluation Form, exist. Such instruments can be adapted to fit specific situations.

The process of constructing observational checklists involves determining the workplace skills to be evaluated, specifying the items to be observed, and identifying criteria for acceptable performance of each item. Items on the instrument should be constructed so as to describe the environment in which the behavior is to be exhibited and specifics about the behavior expected. A four-point scale could be used to note students as exceptional, above average, average, or below average in each of the identified workplace skills. This evaluation should remain as part of student files and used in their portfolios. Students should be taught to use the checklist, both for self-evaluation and for peer evaluation. Observational checklists are ideal for use with role plays and simulations but are best used for daily monitoring of student progress.

Critical Incidents. Often instructors notice when students "slip-up." A more effective strategy is to catch them demonstrating professional behavior in any one of the workplace skills. In such cases, the instructor should take two critical actions: (a) Compliment the student, publicly and privately, and (b) make a note of the incident in the student's record to be used for summative evaluation. Critical incidents have been successfully used in business.

Self-Evaluation. Students should be expected to monitor their own progress. After role play or simulation exercises, students involved should be given the first opportunity to critique themselves regarding what they did correctly and what should be improved. Students could also be requested to keep weekly records—maybe on a simple checklist—of their strengths and weaknesses. They can identify which weaknesses they will work to improve and how.

Peer Evaluation. Peer evaluation should be used prevalently in workplace skill development. In addition to observational checklists discussed earlier, students can also review one another's written assignments. For example, they can work in groups of three or four to evaluate one another's case solutions. They should be encouraged to identify errors and to make comments on strengths and weaknesses of their peers' written work.

Students also should be encouraged to accept praise and corrections from their peers. Perhaps a "Praise Day" could be established when a special effort is made by all students and instructors to praise one another for some accomplishment. As Buck and Barrick (1987) noted, this action will "help students to improve their on-the-job social skills as well as their relations with supervisors" (p. 30).

Portfolio Development. Stemmer, Brown, and Smith (1992) described a portfolio approach used by Michigan schools to enable students to discover, document, and develop their workplace skills. The Employability Skills Portfolio (ESP) contains evidence of students' attainment of employability skills in academics, personal management, and team work. A completed portfolio might hold numerous school records, personal journals, school awards and honors, sample school work, and student-made resumes. Evidence of the academic skill of "writing in the language in which business in conducted," for instance, might include a letter from a past or present employer. To show that students can "work without supervision," they might include a personal career plan or a letter of recommendation from a teacher. As an example of team work skills such as "actively participating in a group," a student could include documentation of membership in one or more organizations.

The basic premise is that learning is a lifelong process. Students upgrade their portfolios as they gain new or more advanced skills. Such portfolio development encourages students to recognize successes, seek opportunities to fill gaps in skills, and gain confidence in preparing for work.

SUMMARY

If business educators are to prepare students for and about business, then what businesses want should be a major influence on what students are taught (Bartholome, 1991). Business educators must work with businesses in identifying workplace skill curricula. Such curricula must be planned systematically so instruction can be successfully integrated into a majority of student experiences. Variety in classroom activities, feedback, and evaluation will provide meaningful practice for students in preparation for workplace realities. Students should be expected to display behaviors similar to those expected in the workplace so productive habits are developed.

Much work and creative effort lie ahead for all educators in attempting to educate and train members of the labor force so they can work to their fullest capacity. Such investment in human capital is imperative if this nation plans to stay economically competitive. Educators must tackle this tremendous challenge—and help rebuild part of the basic foundation of this country.

REFERENCES

Anderson-Yates, M. A. (1991). Preparing students for the high performance work organization: Balancing business training and education. *Business Education Observer, LXIII,* 75-79.

Anderson-Yates, M. A., Coffman, M. J., & Baker, C. M. (1992). *Nontechnical competency instruction in Illinois secondary and postsecondary business education.* Paper presented at the Delta Pi Epsilon National Research Conference, Los Angeles.

Bartholome, L. W. (1991). Preparing business education for the 21st Century. *Business Education Forum, 46*(2), 15-18.

Buck, L. L., & Barrick, R. K. (1987). They are trained but are they employable? *Vocational Education Journal, 62*(5), 29-31.

Carnevale, A. P., Gainer, L. J., & Meltzer, A. S. (1990). *Workplace basics: The skills employers want.* San Francisco: Jossey-Bass.

Commission on the Skills of the American Workforce. (1990, June). *America's choice: High skills or low wages!* Rochester, NY: National Center on Education and the Economy.

DaSalva, S. (1990, April). Designing and using school store evaluation forms. *Business Education Forum.*

Davies, I. K. (1981). *Instruction technique.* New York: McGraw-Hill.

Goree, K. (1992). Integrating ethics into business education. *Business Education Forum, 46*(3), 19-21.

Greathouse, L. (1986). More than technical skills needed for career success. *Business Education Forum, 41*(2), 9-10, 12.

Hoyt, K. B. (1993). *Career education and transition from schooling to employment.* (ERIC Document Reproduction Service No. ED 371 242).

Koffel, L. (1994). *Teaching workplace skills: Creative ways to teach students the skills employers want.* Houston: Gulf Publishing.

Mason, G. (1986). A message to business educators from a businessman. *Business Education Forum, 41*(1), 10-11.

McEwen, T., McEwen, B. C., Sheets, J. L., & Anderson-Yates, M. A. (1992, July). Teaching and evaluating nontechnical skills. *Delta Pi Epsilon Instructional Strategies: An Applied Research Series, 8*(4), 1-4.

Nellermore, D. A. (1992). Preparing students for employment—or, what managers really want. *Business Education Forum, 46*(3), 11-13.

Poole, V. A. (1985). Work experience programs can help develop human relations skills. *Business Education Forum, 39*(4), 9-10.

Poole, V. A., and Zahn, D. K. (1993). Define and teach employability skills to guarantee student success. *The Clearing House, 67*(1), 55-59.

Schlichting, D., & Echternacht, L. (1994, December). *Educator concerns about affective work competency.* Paper presented at the meeting of the Business Education Research Sessions of the American Vocational Association, Dallas, TX.

The Secretary's Commission on Achieving Necessary Skills. (1991, June). *What work requires of schools: A SCANS report for America 2000.* Washington, DC: U.S. Department of Labor.

Smith, M., & Boyd, D. (1986). Training students for complete career success. *Business Education Forum, 40*(9), 32-33.

Stemmer, P., Brown, B., & Smith, C. (1992, March). The employability skills portfolio. *Educational Leadership,* 32-35.

Wentling, R. (1987). Teaching employability skills in vocational education. *Journal of Studies in Technical Careers, IX*(4), 351-359.

Vocational-Technical Education Consortium of States (V-TECS). (1994). *Workplace skills (Occupation #601).* Decatur, GA: Commission on Occupational Education Institutions.

CHAPTER 14

Applied Academics: Relevant Education

E. REBECCA LIMBACK
Central Missouri State University, Warrensburg, Missouri

BIBIANO ROSA
Hostos Community College, Bronx, New York

"What will I ever do with this?" Students often have been heard wondering what relevance a course or topic has for their lives. At the same time, employers desire employees who can apply what they have learned in the classroom to work situations. Educators seek to make the connection of academics (theoretical principles) to real-world relevance (concrete applications) through applied academics by providing a context of work-relevant examples. The intent is to "show the work relevance of subjects such as physics, mathematics, and language arts" (Wang, 1994, p. 2).

As defined by Walter (1992), applied academics simply means the use of certain types of teaching methodologies that result in students reaching higher standards because of a more relevant, "hands-on, approach to learning" (p. 3). The purpose of this chapter is to provide resources and examples of successful applications to those considering an applied academics program.

TECH PREP AND APPLIED ACADEMICS

Federal statutory basis exists for an applied academics program within the Tech Prep provisions of the Perkins Act (Carl D. Perkins Vocational and Applied Technology Act of 1990), which defines Tech Prep as "a combined secondary and postsecondary program which . . . provides technical preparation in at least one field of engineering technology, applied science, mechanical, industrial, or practical art or trade, or agriculture, health, or business; and . . . builds student competence in mathematics, science, and communications (including through applied academics) through a sequential course of study; and . . . leads to placement in employment." State funding for an applied academics program to implement Tech Prep exists within Section 343 and other provisions of the Perkins Act (1990). Public funding, however, is not the only source. Major corporations are often willing and eager to participate in joint ventures involving applied academics and Tech Prep.

According to Walter (1992), most of the Tech Prep programs in the country

. . . involve-three major components: 1) implementation of applied academics and the integration of academic and occupational content; 2) the blending of academic and occupational coursework into focused pathways that meet occupational associate degree programs; and 3) the articulation of secondary and postsecondary curricula to eliminate redundancy and to provide qualified students with advanced standing associate degree programs (p. 1).

Walter (1992) indicates that of the three components, applied academics is "probably the greatest reform-oriented aspect of the Tech Prep initiative, (p. 1).

The use of applied academics in Tech Prep programs has been seen as a way to motivate students who might not take the usual college preparatory courses to attain higher academic standards. More relevant academic content is motivational. Also, the applied formats are a better match for the learning styles of many students who are not successful with a traditional (lecture) classroom format (Walter, 1992).

APPLIED ACADEMICS OPTIONS

Applied academics can be included in a school's curriculum in a variety of ways. Specific applied academics courses may be offered such as Applied Mathematics, Applied Communications, Applied Science, or Applied Technology. The courses can be taught by an individual teacher from the discipline involved or may be team taught by two or more persons. Applied academics may be incorporated into existing courses, bringing in "real world" examples and applications to use within the class. The applied academics curriculum might utilize a partnership with a business where students are given practical experience using knowledge and skill from the area of study. Teaching techniques discussed in other chapters of this *Yearbook* are appropriate and useful in incorporating applied academics.

GETTING STARTED

When the decision has been made to incorporate applied academics into a school's curriculum, the next step is to form teams (or a team) to work out the details and implement the curriculum. Fortunately, materials and resources are available, and schools do not have to "start from scratch."

A good way to begin is to visit one or more schools where applied academics is being used in some form. Observe some classes. Visit with students, teachers, administrators, and human resource directors in businesses that hire from those schools. Ask lots of questions! What works? What doesn't work? What did they do to get the program off the ground? What would they do differently?

In addition, several studies have been completed regarding applied academics. The National Center for Research in Vocational Education at the University of California, Berkeley, sought answers to how cooperation and teamwork could be enhanced in developing applied academics or integration of vocational and academic education (Schmidt, 1995). Ten school sites that were considered "exemplary" for their integration efforts were studied. (The complete report and resulting case studies, which can be used as a tool in building cross-discipline teams, can be obtained by calling (800) 637-7652. The NCRVE integration report is MDS-275, and the case studies are MDS-780.)

Applied academics in Illinois was studied by Illinois State University and the University of Illinois (Haynes, 1991). A focus of the study was the interaction/collaboration of the academic/vocational teachers. This study found that—

- The applied academics materials were effective.
- Academic/vocational collaborations were promoted by the use of the materials.
- Use of the materials had a positive impact on the interest of students in the content.
- Barriers to collaboration were time constraints and lack of a clear mission. (Haynes, 1991)

A result of the study was the development of a flowchart for strategic planning for integrating curriculum and the content outlines for a guidebook for integration of activities for teachers and administrators. The report includes a list of recommendations specifically for business educators.

MATERIALS AND INFORMATION

Through federal grants, nine national demonstration centers for Tech Prep were established. These centers disseminate Tech Prep information such as course guidelines and applied-academics packets for various areas to high schools. One center is Mt. Hood Community College where applied-academics packets for mathematics, English, and economics have been developed (National Tech Prep Demonstration Center Annual Performance Report, 1994). The address for the center is National Tech Prep Demonstration Center, Mt. Hood Community College, 26000 SE Stark Street, Gresham, OR 97030, and the telephone number is (503) 667-7313.

The Partnership for Academic and Career Education (PACE) in South Carolina developed a handbook, *Developing Real-World Applications for Academic Concepts . . . A Teacher's Guide,* intended to give practical tips for developing real-world applications to teach academic concepts (Walter, 1992). Materials from the handbook can be copied for educational use. The handbook is available from PACE, P.O. Box 587, Pendleton, South Carolina 29670, (803) 646-8361 Extension 2107 or from ERIC as listed in the References section of this chapter.

Applied academics teaching materials have been developed through multistate consortium efforts. The following materials are available from Agency for Instructional Technology (AIT), Customer Services Department, Box A, Bloomington, IN 46402-0120, 800-457-4509:

Applied Communication. Contains 15 activity-oriented instructional modules each containing 10 lessons. The lessons can be infused into the existing curriculum or form the core of a year-long course taught by English/communications, business, or vocational educators.

Economics at Work. Contains five modules on topics of producing, exchanging, consuming, saving, and investing. Good for infusion into existing classes.

Principles of Technology. Described by the American Association for the Advancement of Science as the "best technical physics curriculum available"

(Wang, 1994, p. 3). It covers 14 units over a two-year period. The materials are being used nationwide by science teachers, vocational teachers, and teams from both areas.

Workplace Readiness. Contains modules on problem solving, teamwork, self-management. It includes videos and instructors and learners guides.

Applied-mathematics materials that use hands-on activities and work-based applications to transform abstract concepts into concrete experiences are available from CORD Communications, Attention Customer Relations, P.O. Box 21206, Waco, TX 76702-1206, 800-231-3015.

After reviewing a variety of applied-academics materials, Wang (1994) indicates that the materials provide the following features:

- Use modularized student units

- Incorporate teacher-empowering guides

- Include competency-based objectives

- Are enhanced by instructional videos

- Are written at an estimated eighth-grade reading level

- Target secondary vocational students as the primary audience; also useful in postsecondary adult learning settings

- Emphasize holistic learning

- Can be infused into vocational courses or taught alone as a credit course by either vocational or academic instructors—or a team that includes both

- Are not meant to replace "traditional" academic courses for the top 25 percent of the student population

- Emphasize developing teamwork skills in students. (p. 4)

Textbook publishers provide a variety of materials specifically designed for applied academics. Resources also may be available from the state vocational resource center if your state provides one. The American Vocational Association sells materials related to Tech Prep and applied academics.

PRACTICAL APPLICATIONS IN BUSINESS CLASSES

The prepared materials listed are a starting point for the team of teachers who are planning the applied academics curriculum. They include activities from which schools can select and adapt to fit the local situation. Some of the suggested activities may stimulate inspiration for the creation of unique activities designed for a particular school/class, perhaps involving one or more local businesses.

In addition to collaborating with other educators in planning for and implementing applied academics in a school, business educators also may find many opportunities to infuse these practical applications into existing business courses. At Nichols Career Center in Jefferson City, Missouri, business students have many opportunities to see the business applications of what they are learning in class.

Student teams representing three programs in the vocational school— Office Technology, Marketing, and Graphic Arts/Printing—work together to develop brochures that are distributed to subscribers of TCI Cablevision. A portion of the proceeds resulting from the promotion is donated to the YMCA summer camp program. Individuals from the cable company and the YMCA present information about the program, and students must ask appropriate questions in order to develop the materials. The students work cooperatively to develop the brochures and meet the specified requirements. Representatives of both the cable company and YMCA evaluate the completed projects and select the brochure to be used. This is an example of a project developed by instructors specifically for their school. The cooperative learning exercise is excellent preparation for a team-oriented business world.

Prepared applied academics materials also are utilized at Nichols Career Center. Applied Communications (AIT) materials are used for a variety of activities involving job interview skills, written communications, use of graphics, and gathering and using information. Two of the modules are incorporated in a lesson where students locate, gather, review, and synthesize information about Phi Beta Lambda. Students plan and organize a persuasive message about the organization and develop a flyer using a desktop publishing program.

In another activity, Office Technology students visit a Jefferson City business and tour the various departments to learn about the skills and training requirement for jobs in those departments. Students are instructed to ask appropriate questions to determine company policy regarding defective merchandise. In the next class session, students work cooperatively in groups using information from an Applied Communications module—Presenting Your Point of View—to compose an appropriate letter to return a defective product to the company. Letters are exchanged between groups. The group considers the point of view presented in the letter and writes a response consistent with company policy.

These are just a few examples of how materials can be adapted and incorporated into business or applied academic courses. More ideas can be obtained from reviewing some of the studies mentioned or by visiting with teachers in schools currently using the materials.

SUMMARY

Applied academics provides realistic applications of academic material/knowledge/skills to real-life (work-related) situations. It helps students understand what they will do with what they are learning in the classroom.

The key to successfully incorporating applied academics is a team-building process involving those who want to make it work and who can be excited about it! Using applied academics provides many opportunities to use a variety of teaching methodologies and to reach students with different learning styles. Business educators should take the lead in their schools in working on applied academics teams as well as in seeking ways to incorporate activities within existing classes.

REFERENCES

Carl D. Perkins Vocational and Applied Technology Education Act of 1990, 20 U.S.C. 2301 (2), PL 101-392, sec. 1, 104 Stat 753.

Haynes, T. S., Law, D., & Pepple, J. Integrating academic content into business education: Results from research in Illinois. 1991. (ERIC Reproduction Service No. ED 335 520.)

Schmidt, B. J. (1995, February). Case by case. *Vocational Education Journal*, 34-36.

Walter, D. M. (1992). *Developing "real world" applications for academic concepts . . . a teacher's guide.* Partnership for Academic and Career Education, Pendleton, SC. (ERIC Document Reproduction Service No. ED 362 638.)

Wang, C., & Owens, T. (1994). Multiple approach to evaluating applied academics. Paper presented at the Annual Meeting of the American Educational Research Association, New Orleans, 1994. (ERIC Document Reproduction Service No. ED 378 199.)

Business education applications provided by Arlene Broeker, Nichols Career Center, Jefferson City, Missouri.

CHAPTER 15
Dealing with Change

BONNIE J. WHITE
Auburn University, Auburn, Alabama

As a society, we no longer have the luxury of gradual readjustment to technological advances. If we take too long to make changes, someone else has already made the change and is reaping the benefits of being first in a global market. Rapid changes are forcing us into response roles that require us not only to know how to respond quickly but also how to learn quickly.

Students cannot rely on a body of learned knowledge to sustain them throughout most, or even a small portion, of their careers. What students learn today must be transferable to a variety of job situations. To be successful in a changing work environment, students need to know how to meet and master the challenge of rapid and constant change. Knowing how to plan for change is now considered an essential lifeskill.

Strategies that students need to know and apply to master change effectively will be identified in this chapter. The fundamentals of planned change, for example, provide the basis for coping with both personal and job-related changes. Not all changes, however, are planned. Responding successfully to unplanned changes requires different strategies. Ultimately, students can successfully address personal change throughout their lifetimes by applying self-management strategies. Likewise, students who are taught to identify and apply positive career management strategies can more effectively cope with changes on the job. The purpose of this chapter, therefore, is to provide an overview of strategies for dealing with change.

MANAGING PLANNED CHANGE

Change has been defined as a planned or an unplanned response to pressure (Dalziel and Schoonover, 1988). The nature of change covers a broad range of responses. Some changes happen suddenly, almost without warning. Other changes can be the result of deliberate, careful planning. Whereas an unplanned response to pressure can result in chaos, planned change typically results in a more orderly response. Wherever possible, people prefer to plan for change. The steps to planning for change, whether personal or organizational, typically follow a logical sequence:

Define the change needed. Change involves not only knowing where you want to go and how you will get there but also involves knowing where you are now and where you have been. There must be a starting point. Business leaders often introduce change by developing and clarifying goals for the organization. Likewise, individuals who want to make changes in their personal lives will clarify the changes they want to make by setting goals.

Goals that specify what is to be changed and how the change will occur are important to reducing false starts. Goals that specify expected outcomes provide a clear direction for change. Knowing how to identify and state goals clearly has become a foundational skill for managing change.

Gather information. Gathering information is basically the act of creating an inventory of available resources. Information gathering can verify areas of strength as well as determine areas of deficiency that need to be openly addressed.

Gathering information can take different forms. Businesses rely on information-gathering techniques such as end-user surveys, employee input, and attitude-assessment techniques. Individuals seeking change in their personal lives gather information by such techniques as feedback from friends and relatives, exploration of alternatives, and professional assistance. The act of gathering information often provides active suggestions for accomplishing goals.

Diagnose the situation. Once information has been gathered, it is time to diagnose the situation. In diagnosing organizational changes, business leaders need to know what the barriers are to change. What people problems will they likely encounter? Not all barriers to change, however, need to be eliminated for planning to continue. Rather, concentrated effort should be placed on solving these problems that have a significant cost or impact on the desired outcome. Whether diagnosing a situation for business change or for personal change, determine which problems should be dealt with first. Assign priorities for dealing with those problems.

Resolve problems. The problem-solving phase begins once barriers to change have been identified. The focus of resolving problems is to determine how to confront these barriers and to identify the best means available for dealing with the problems. Resolving problems continues throughout the entire change process. At this stage, individuals as well as business leaders look for solutions that bridge the gap between the "ideal" and the "actual."

Implement strategies. Although the process of change begins with identifying desired changes (goals), the change process can easily fail without an action plan that focuses on how to make the change. Once the desired business or personal outcomes are known and goals are set, the action plan or steps to reach the goals can be determined. Well-defined goals are relevant, specific, attainable, and measurable. An action plan for implementing strategies can be developed from such goals. It is at this point that the details and steps of completing the change become focused. Tasks are defined and time frames are determined. In business, people are given specific assignments. Personal, organizational, and technical factors must be clarified to assure that change can proceed smoothly.

Evaluate strategies. Evaluation and revision of strategies help assure continued progress. For example, what specific progress has been made toward achieving the goals? Further, are the change strategies actually moving you toward the goals? Only by evaluating these strategies can one determine what progress has been made.

MANAGING UNPLANNED CHANGE

Not all changes can be planned. Unexpected changes can occur quickly on the job—added job responsibilities, company merger, rapid downsizing, new technology, forced retirement. Unexpected personal changes occur just as quickly—destruction of one's home, a child's illness, death of a loved one.

No matter how carefully people plan their careers and personal lives, changes will happen that are beyond their control. During unplanned change, people may have only limited control over what is happening to them. They have, however, control over how they react to sudden change. If they can be constructive in their reactions, they better their chances of dealing effectively with critical situations.

Some personal and job changes may have strong negative impacts. In those instances, a person's control of the situation is limited. Yet, how an individual responds can influence the outcome:

1. It is important that the individual not panic. People need all their mental and physical resources to help get them through a crisis. Special care must be taken to control emotional responses and interactions with others. During a time of crisis, people should take precautions to keep physically healthy.

2. If time permits, writing down thoughts and perceptions is useful. By identifying the worst-case and the best-case scenarios, a person can begin developing strategies for dealing with these scenarios.

3. If the change has not yet occurred, information about what will happen can be gathered. The more information the better.

4. The amount of influence that can be exerted over a pending change should be determined. A person not directly involved in the change may be able to make practical suggestions and offer alternatives that otherwise may not be considered.

5. Asking for help is wise. People have an important source of help in the network of personal friends and professional colleagues they have developed.

6. People should consider successful past strategies when determining how to respond to pending change. If a person had to deal with unplanned change in the past, how was it handled? What strategies from past situations apply to the present?

7. People's attitudes affect not only themselves but those around them. Whether the crisis is personal or professional, keeping a positive attitude will actually help a person identify alternatives that would never be considered with a negative attitude.

People may not be able to control all changes that occur, but they can control how they think and respond to changes. Unexpected or unwelcomed change can be threatening. People, if they are not alert, can miss the opportunity in a change if they are mired in the threat of the situation.

RESPONDING TO CHANGE

People often have difficulty responding to change whether the change is planned or unplanned. Change requires that we leave the familiar and move into the unfamiliar. Individuals generally experience the same following stages when making transitions linked to change:

Deny existence of change. People are often shocked by the first news of change and may refuse to accept it. At some point, however, the reality of the change must be accepted.

Resist movement to change. Resistance is basically a mourning of the loss of the past. At this stage in the transition to change, people may attempt to attach blame or even to sideline the pending change. Complaining is a common behavioral characteristic during this phase. During this time, individuals may have personal doubts as to their ability to survive the change.

Explore alternatives. This stage represents the beginnings of moving from a negative to a positive approach about the change. People realize they are going to survive the change and begin to explore the new alternatives associated with the change. Energy levels and creativity are often high.

Commit to change. In this stage, the individual has worked through the problems associated with the change. The individual selects a new course of action from the alternatives that change has brought and commits to it. This phase is often characterized by growth and adaptation to the change.

Not all individuals move through these phases at the same rate or with the same intensity. Unfortunately, some individuals may get bogged down in one of the early stages and not work their way successfully through the change. They no longer seem to fit within the organization; they seem at odds with people and goals.

Other individuals may move too fast through the initial phases and find themselves doubting or questioning the change later. If questions and concerns are not resolved adequately when moving through the change transition stages, they will resurface later. Thus, while other employees are fully in gear and working toward the new goals, some employees may be plagued with concerns they have not fully resolved. These employees may begin to lose their leadership roles and fall behind in the organization.

MANAGING PERSONAL CHANGE

Personal changes involve both predictable and unpredictable transitions. Scott and Jaffee (1989) report that how people prepare for the changes in their lives has much to do with how difficult or easy the event will be for them. Predictable transitions, for example, can be made more easily by using the strategies for managing planned change discussed previously.

In addition to using strategies for planning change, those who know and practice personal change-management skills are better able to cope with the effects of change. Change-management skills include the following:

Recognize stress. People respond differently to change. Change affects one's body, mind, and emotions. Yet, individuals may only be aware of the effect of change in one area. One of the first steps in dealing effectively with change is to learn the signals from the body, mind, and emotions that serve as warnings to individuals that they are being affected by change. A person's body, for example, may signal stress through headaches, stomach aches, exhaustion, or increased illnesses. The mind may signal stress by lack of concentration, sleeplessness, forgetfulness, or negative thoughts. The emotions may signal a range of feelings from anger to exhilaration, anxiety to excitement, or fear to over-confidence.

Once individuals recognize they are under stress, they can use stress reduction techniques to reduce stress levels. Become familiar with several stress reduction techniques such as biofeedback, short mental breaks, and exercise. Practice two or three of these techniques during periods of non-stress so that they become familiar. By being familiar with the procedures used in these techniques, a person will be better prepared to use them effectively when stress occurs.

Maintain self-care. Change requires physical self-care. Long hours and demanding schedules can drain a person's energy. During times of change, particularly those that stem from a crisis, individuals are tempted to cut back on their self-care. They look for ways to save time and are willing to put themselves in physical jeopardy to meet schedules. This approach, however, is short-sighted. For example, consuming fast foods on the run over a period of time will increase one's propensity to illness. Safeguarding one's personal self-care is a necessary foundation to managing change. Diet, rest, exercise, and relaxation are key elements of self-care. Positive self-talk can help keep a person's spirits up.

Enhance personal growth. Creativity is the key to continued personal growth. Self-doubt, poor habits, and preconceived ideas are all barriers to creativity that stifle personal growth. People often hide behind barriers such as these because they have been programmed throughout their lives to conform. Yet, the ability to handle change often involves creative problem solving. Creative problem solving requires innovation. People can develop and practice innovative ways of problem solving. Goman (1992) suggest five guidelines for learning to solve problems creatively:

1. There is more than one right answer. Don't stop at the first right answer. Gather lots of ideas. Try to develop creative connections between the ideas.

2. Failure can be good. Failure in itself is not bad. Not learning from failure, however, can be disastrous. There are three steps to analyzing failure: First, carefully review what happened. What were the behaviors leading to the failure? What lessons can be learned? Second, using this information decide how the failure could have been corrected or avoided. Develop mental strategies for future reference. The basic question is: If you had to do it over again, what would you change? Third, let the failure go. Release it mentally and emotionally. People learn from their failures by studying how they can improve their performance in similar situations and by developing future strategies. By mentally releasing their failures, individuals free themselves for future personal growth.

3. Cultivate diverse perspectives. Look for insights and solutions you do not already have. Find people with different perspectives. Ask their opinions and value their ideas.

4. Challenge the rules. Blindly following rules can lead to mental laziness. Rules can quickly become an end in themselves with the purpose for the rule forgotten. Question the status quo by asking such questions as—

   What would happen if . . .? or

   How would someone who didn't know the rules do this?

5. Respect intuition. A person's intuitive feeling is often based on a more subtle logic or experience. Highly creative individuals rely not only on logical problem solving but also on their own intuition. There may not always be time for a lengthy, logical analysis of a pending charge. Keep a record of your intuitions and your responses to document how well your individual intuitive level works.

MANAGING ON-THE-JOB CHANGES

The conditions of work are changing. Traditional work groups, career paths, and employee benefits, for example, are undergoing change as organizations change. Organizations are finding they must change from their traditional work patterns to successfully meet the challenges of doing business in a technology-based global economy.

Smaller work units with shorter life spans will be commonplace. Work units will come together to handle a project or problem and disband after the project is completed, often to move to other projects. Because work units will be more fluid, the strict demarcations of today's organizational structures will change. More responsibility will be moved to lower levels. Rank-and-file employees today are making decisions mid-level managers made only a few years ago. This trend will continue. Businesses will demand employees who can make sound decisions and interpret management policies.

The work pace of future jobs will quicken. Traditionally, permission to work was granted by a supervisor. The order of work was established by the supervisor and any change from the normal had to be approved by the supervisor's superior. By eliminating layers of management, organizations are able to work at a faster pace. As the rate of change to which organizations must respond accelerates, businesses will need a workforce who can work at a faster pace. The time between the inception of ideas to their application will continue to lessen.

The working environment of the future will be one of continuous change. Effective employees will be those who can adapt easily to change and who can perform satisfactorily under conditions of continuous change. Strategies for working with changing conditions include:

Learn how to learn on the job. Individuals may not know how to negotiate all changes that occur; however, those individuals who have learned how to learn can manage change more effectively. Keys to learning how to learn on the job include:

1. Stay abreast of new technical skills. Do not wait until forced to learn. By continually updating one's skills, the individual can acquire new skills at a controlled pace.

2. Learn from people who already know or who are learning. Find out how they learn. What techniques do they use to stay up to date? How do they go about learning something new?

3. Look for better ways to do things. Major improvements in procedures, products, and relationships can result from minor changes brought about by people looking for ways to do things better. Challenge yourself to look for better ways.

4. Strengthen your human relations skills. Good rapport with one's colleagues helps make adjustments to change and to learning easier.

Develop job resiliency. Organizational needs will change quickly. Those employees who are flexible and can respond quickly to changing needs are more likely to be retained.

Organizations will rely heavily on training, using computers to bring temporary employees up to par as well as to retrain their core employees. Excellent computer skills are foundational skills for the jobs of the future.

Develop coping skills. Developing good coping skills involves learning to work smarter, not harder. Using time wisely, keeping a sense of humor, being flexible, and getting a perspective of the effects of change are all important coping skills.

The urgent and the important will always vie for our time, particularly when change is pending. Goman (1992) presents five strategies for maximizing time during periods of change and chaos:

1. Break the work-time dilemma by reducing wasted time. Improve work methods, and if necessary, work longer. Reduce expectations of the results. Ask, what level of perfection does the work need to have?

2. Set priorities and stick to them. Do not spend time on activities that will not help achieve the goals.

3. Work on one thing at a time. Schedule the number one priority when fresh or at peak performance. Stay with it until it is finished.

4. Reduce interruptions and work in blocks. Work uninterrupted during peak work times. Work on large projects in blocks of time, such as one, two, or four hours.

5. Use time more efficiently. Double up on minor tasks. Group similar tasks, and postpone nonessential tasks until the crisis has passed. Delegate work where possible.

Develop security skills. Scott and Jaffee (1989) identified four strategies individuals can use to help create personal security in a changing work world:

1. Span boundaries at work. Communicate with others in different parts of the organization. Be alert to common needs and interests in the organization. Become involved beyond one's group.

2. Go beyond the job description. Individuals should do their jobs well but be willing to go beyond their job descriptions. Learn what needs to be done and do it eagerly.

3. Be multicompetent. Learn several skills or activities. If individuals have only one skill, they become vulnerable. Be eager to learn new skills and avoid becoming complacent with what you already know.

4. Be flexible. Be willing to try something new. Let go of procedures that do not work. Be willing to try alternatives.

Apply for your own job. Periodically, reevaluate your talents in light of the job you hold. Look at yourself as though you were a candidate to be hired by your firm. By completing a periodic reevaluation, individuals can more easily review the relevancy of their job skills. They can pinpoint their strengths and weaknesses. Then, act to remedy weaknesses, such as taking additional course work or training. To keep yourself a viable candidate for your position, continue to enhance and expand your strengths. Accept new and challenging assignments. Volunteer for the challenging assignments that will further develop your strengths.

PREPARING FOR A LIFETIME OF CHANGE

Careers characterized by the traditional and predictable job promotion ladders are no longer the norm. Career management will not be judged by developing a career path toward a single, long-term goal within one company. Rather, career management will involve keeping abreast of the multiple job opportunities within a related job field. Career management will involve being flexible enough to move through the job field to secure rewarding and challenging positions.

Traditionally, workers have expected employers to chart their career progress within the company. Workers have expected to rise through the ranks and have assumed a stable career path. Today's graduates, however, will need to be able to chart their own careers. They need to know how to develop flexible career strategies. Charting one's own career requires a two-dimensional approach: self-management and career management.

Positive self-management. Timm (1993) defines self-management as "a process of maximizing our time and talents to achieve worthwhile goals based on a sound value system." Positive self-management is based on five components:

1. *Perspective.* How much control do we feel we have over our lives? Some people feel they have very little control, while others act as if they have control over all things that affect their lives. Some people focus control externally —the outside world controls them. Others focus control internally—they control what happens to them.

Self-management builds upon the focus of internal control tempered with reality. That is, for most events in life we have some control, but not ultimate control. Timm suggests a strategy for dealing with control: View life as a never-ending stream of demands on your time and efforts that is constantly fed by employers, coworkers, family, friends, and community. This stream of demands is also fed by your individual goals, dreams, and values. Thus, the cornerstone to successful self-management is to "take control by choosing to respond to those demands that best meet your true needs" (Timm, 1993). Allocate time and talents carefully.

2. *Purpose.* A strong sense of purpose adds focus to life. Purpose is clarified by one's value system or one's concept of what is desirable. Personal values are values one is willing to give significant time and energy to achieve, such as financial security, family success, or being a good team player. A person's purpose is strongest when values and goals are aligned. Goals should be specific, realistic, measurable, deadline-targeted, value-anchored, and written. If a goal is not written, it is only a wish.

3. *Personality.* Understand your personality. How assertive/receptive are you? Assertiveness refers to being pleasantly direct and should not be confused with aggressiveness. Assertiveness gives one the power to say no when the decision warrants it. Whatever your personality type, always be receptive to feedback. Guidelines for receiving good feedback include: (a) Listen, don't defend. (b) Ask for clarification or elaboration. (c) Be honest in your reaction. (d) Thank the person. The objective is to encourage useful feedback now and in the future. Receiving good feedback is a key element to positive change.

4. *Planning.* Practice daily planning. Develop daily priority task lists and use time management techniques for assigning priorities. Weekly, monthly, and yearly plans translate into long-term goals. Review long-term goals frequently in planning to assure that your daily activities are consistent with long-term goals.

5. *Productivity.* Guard your productivity. Learn to recognize and control activities that reduce productivity: interruptions, clutter and paperwork, unproductive communication, procrastination, indecision, and self-overload.

Positive career management. The world of work is changing radically. Current economic and business conditions have brought changes in both job skills and career fields. The workforce of tomorrow will be extremely flexible and cost-effective. Barner (1994), noted author in career management, suggests that in the next 10 years, the traditional organizational structure will continue to move toward a more adaptable structure. The movement from a large, permanent employee base to a more adaptable base will continue. This base will consist of three groups:

1. *Core employees*—a small, permanent group with broad skills which allow them to handle a variety of functions. This group will be expected to adapt quickly to changing conditions. They will be characterized by fast-paced learning and flexibility.

2. *Supplemental employees*—just-in-time employees who can be added or eliminated as needed. These employees typically will contract for the work to be completed or will work through temporary services.

3. *Outsourced work functions*—major functions of an organization completed by companies specializing in the needed functions. Outsourced work functions will eliminate large amounts of overhead.

Barner (1994) lists five basic strategies for career management in the changing work situations we will see in the future:

1. *Track the broader picture.* Watch carefully for trends in your profession. These trends can become either potential growth opportunities or potential roadblocks.

2. *Have a clear picture of your personal and career needs.* When changes come, they can do so rapidly leaving little time to make decisions. For example, employees may be given options during times of reorganizations and downsizing with little time to respond.

3. *Assess your skills.* If you were to leave your job today, how would you know what your skills are worth? Review salary levels and skill requirements for job openings in your field. Stay up to date and current within your field.

4. *Develop contingency plans.* Always prepare two career plans. Plan both worst-case and best-case scenarios. Plan for unexpected career moves. Keep resumes updated, maintain professional networks, and stay abreast of job opportunities in your field.

5. *Develop portable skills.* Although skills unique to the organization are important, those skills that can be transferred easily to other work situations add to your flexibility. Likewise, these portable skills add to your marketability. Skills which can transfer easily from one organization to another are usually the most up-to-date skills.

SUMMARY

Dealing with change is not easy. Traditional business structures and career pathways are disappearing, and the pace of organizational change is accelerating. Within the past 10 years, over 30 million workers have been dislocated by organizational restructuring. Within the past five years, more than 12,000 businesses have changed ownership. Since 1980, over 3.2 million jobs have been lost in Fortune 500 companies alone; and today, businesses expect to further reduce their workforces by 15 percent (Scott & Jaffee, 1995).

The impact of recent and projected changes in the job market will be enormous. Workers will be constantly challenged to remain current and be productive.

Students will need to use effective personal and career management strategies to succeed in future working environments. Students need instruction in how to plan for and to deal with change. Strategies for dealing with change, such as those presented in this chapter, provide a foundation for surviving the many personal and career changes our students will encounter.

REFERENCES

Barner, R. (1994, September-October). The new career strategist. *The Futurist*. pp. 8-14.

Burns, R. (1993). *Managing people in changing times*. St. Leonards, Australia: Allen & Unwin.

Chapman, E. L. (1993). *Plan B, converting change into career opportunity*. Menlo, CA: Crisp Publications.

Dalziel, M. M., & Schoonover, S. C. (1988). *Changing ways*. New York: AMACOM.

Felkins, P. K., Chakiris, B. J., & Chakiris, K. N. (1993). *Change management*. White Plains, NY: Quality Resources.

Gilbreath, R. D. (1991). *Save yourself*. New York: McGraw-Hill.

Goman, C. K. (1992). *Adapting to change*. Menlo, CA: Crisp Publications, p. 30.

Hyatt, C. (1990). *Shifting gears*. New York: Simon & Schuster.

Jellison, J. M. (1993). *Overcoming resistance*. New York: Simon & Schuster.

Mink, O. G., Esterhuysen, P. W., Mink, B. P., & Owen, K. Q. (1993). *Change at work*. San Francisco: Josey-Bass Publishers.

Scott, C. D., & Jaffe, D. T. (1995). *Managing change at work*. Menlo, CA: Crisp Publications, pp. 3, 7.

Scott, C. D., & Jaffe, D. T. (1989). *Managing personal change*. Menlo, CA: Crisp Publications, p. 14.

Timm, P. (1993). *Successful self-management*. Menlo Park, CA: Crisp Publications, Inc., pp. 4, 11.

CHAPTER 16

Team-Building Skills: Value-Added Education

MELODY WEBLER ALEXANDER
Ball State University, Muncie, Indiana

The concept of teamwork is based on the theory that employees at all levels in an organization have something to contribute. As reported by Ehrilch (1994), employee participation is crucial in the processes of solving problems and making decisions. Teamwork skills are in high demand in business, and the ability to work in a team has become one of the top five characteristics necessary for applicants to secure a professional position (Perrigo, 1994).

Increasingly, business managers are recognizing the need to involve employees in planning and implementation stages, especially in times of change (Friedman, 1994). Authors in business have cited numerous benefits and company successes as a result of having employees working in teams (Day, 1994; Deitz, 1995; Lienert, 1994; Runge, 1994). A study by Booth (1994) found that businesses are becoming more team orientated. Some businesses report changing their focus to include the use of teams (Cane, 1994), while others are now referring to their business as a team-based organization (Harrison, Conn, Whittaker, & Mitchell, 1994).

The benefits of team-building activities have also been investigated in education. Studies have found that participants who had team-building experiences had significantly higher levels of trust, social support, openness, and satisfaction (Bottom, 1994). The findings from another study indicate that when participating in a team project, students who had previously participated in team-building activities had better interactions with team members than those who had not (Mazany, Francis, & Sumich, 1995). In order for graduates to meet workplace demands, team-building skills must be part of a student's education (Kerr & Sutton, 1995). Business courses are the ideal place to use team assignments and teach team-building skills (Kunz, 1994; Holter, 1994).

As Smith (1995) theorizes, businesses are changing their philosophies and are focusing on new programs that incorporate employee and management teams. Educators must change accordingly. Therefore, the purpose of this chapter is to provide business teachers with materials to incorporate team-building skills in their courses. These materials include: (1) lecture materials for presenting a rationale for teaching team-building skills, (2) suggestions for teaching team-building concepts, (3) strategies for building students' skills as a team member, and (4) examples of successful team projects that can be used in business courses.

A RATIONALE FOR TEACHING TEAM-BUILDING SKILLS

As downsizing has become a trend of the nineties, many organizations have eliminated mid-management positions. Typically, the mid-manager served as a communicator between top management and employees. With the elimination of mid-management positions, top management has begun to rely on work teams to take decision-making responsibilities that were typically handled by a mid-manager. As businesses change to incorporate the use of teams, it is important to define why teams are used in business, why employees are involved, and new managerial roles.

Teams in Business. Businesses are changing and, as they change, many business leaders are using the team approach to get work done. Teams and teamwork have the potential to provide many benefits to business. They can be formed for any purpose, are responsive, and can be focused to market demands.

Employee Involvement. Managers are recognizing the advantages of involving employees in planning and decision making. Sharing responsibilities utilizes the strengths and knowledge of all employees, which is likely to result in increased productivity.

Manager's Role. The restructuring of middle management positions means that the remaining managers are working in team situations and work closely with large groups of employees. Team leadership skills, as well as group facilitation skills, are important attributes for the revised managerial positions.

TEACHING TEAM-BUILDING CONCEPTS

When students enter the workforce, it is probable that they will be required to work in a team where problem-solving and decision-making responsibilities will be shared by all members of the team. It is essential, therefore, that during their education students are given direction and practice on how to work in teams.

Effective Team Process. Effective teamwork utilizes the skills and knowledge of every person on the team. Ideally, working together produces a stronger product, leading to results that could not have been accomplished individually.

If teams are to function productively, the following requirements must be met:

1. All team members need to understand the project goals.

2. A team leader needs to be chosen, or it should be determined in which situations leadership will be shared.

3. All team members need to participate actively (talking and listening).

4. All team members need to respect other members' ideas and contributions.

5. All team members need to communicate freely, trusting that other members will respect their views and ideas, even when disagreeing.

6. All team members need to work together to make logical decisions and follow through on solutions.

7. The team needs to evaluate its process and function continuously.

STRATEGIES FOR BUILDING STUDENTS' SKILLS AS TEAM MEMBERS

As with any skill, there are tactics that can be used to enhance student learning. The following strategies will help to build students' skills as team members.

Strategy 1: Clarify Team Members' Roles. Explain the role of the student as a team member. In general, each member needs to understand the project, help to set realistic project goals, actively participate by contributing ideas, listen and respect other members' viewpoints, and stay focused and positive.

Explain the role of the team leader, who is responsible for facilitating the team process. In general, the team leader will set boundaries, evaluate the team's progress, summarize key points, intervene when necessary to keep the group focused, handle conflicts, and attain closure.

Strategy 2: Provide Information on Contents of a Good Meeting. Meetings are the foundation of a team's process and should be planned and designed well ahead of the meeting time. Members need to understand clearly why they are meeting and what they are expected to accomplish. Setting meeting objectives focuses the team and helps to direct a good meeting. After determining what is to be accomplished at a meeting, additional objectives include deciding: the purpose of the meeting; who needs to be at the meeting; when, where, and how much time is needed for the meeting; and what preparation members need before the meeting.

The team leader needs to facilitate the smooth flow of the meeting and keep team members on target. This is accomplished by setting an agenda. The leader must focus the group on the purpose of the meeting, make sure every team member is participating, motivate team members to work to the best of their ability, facilitate the group process, and guide the team to consensus and closure.

Team members have a responsibility to come to the meeting prepared to discuss the meeting's objectives. They need to actively participate in suggesting ideas and problem-solving activities. After the meeting, objectives focus on the meeting's outcomes. For example, were meeting purposes met? If the meeting did not achieve the purposes intended, how should future meetings be structured?

Strategy 3: Engage Students in Activities To Reach Closure. Brainstorming encourages creativity and promotes idea generation if guidelines are followed. Criticism is forbidden and members can say whatever they want. Emphasis is on quantity, and as one member relates an idea, other members can combine ideas or improve on them as they see fit. Ideas can then be evaluated, and the team can reach an agreement as to which ideas are best. Getting to consensus is the point where the team has reached an agreement on solutions to the given problem. After reaching this consensus, plans need to be made as to how to best implement the solutions.

Strategy 4: Provide Information for the Effective Handling of Problems. The team leader is responsible for resolving any problems that might arise. Individuals who serve in this capacity need instruction on how to handle difficult situations and difficult individuals. Difficult individuals include those who talk too much, talk about items other than the topic, will not talk at all, are misinformed and continue to make incorrect suggestions, or will not see anyone else's viewpoint but their own. Teachers need to provide guidelines for team leaders to deal with difficult individuals tactfully, such as:

1. Deal with the situation before it becomes a problem. For example, if some team members are carrying on a side conversation, the team leader could say, "Bill and Sue, we can't hear what you're saying. Please share your ideas with the rest of the team."

2. Talk to members without embarrassing them. For example, if a team member tends to dominate the conversation, the team leader could get other team members involved, saying, "That was an excellent suggestion, Sam. Karen, what do you think?"

3. Preserve all team members' self-esteem. For example, if a team member is habitually late, don't criticize him/her in front of the team, but wait until a break to discuss the problem.

4. Control the situation in a firm but positive way. If a team member tends to get off the purpose of the meeting or go off on a tangent, thank him or her for the comment and reiterate the focus of the meeting and indicate that the team needs to get back on track.

Strategy 5: Assess the Team Process. After the team project has been completed, the participants need to evaluate the team members, the team leader, and the team itself. Evaluation is critical, and areas of improvement should be identified and discussed.

When evaluating the team members, the role of a good team member needs to be reviewed. Team members should evaluate their participation, along with that of others. Team members should evaluate each member.

Did the team member:

- ask questions to clarify knowledge and understanding?
- participate in setting team goals?
- contribute ideas from personal backgrounds?
- listen to all team members?
- consider and build on others' ideas?
- think creatively and constructively?
- focus on goals and objectives?
- remain positive and enthusiastic?

However the team leader was selected (whether teacher-appointed, self-appointed, or team chosen), all members should evaluate the team leader. Some of the questions that could be included in a team leader evaluation follow.

Did the team leader:

- set boundaries?
- interpret project goals?
- provide direction?
- keep the team focused?
- listen to all members' ideas?
- display understanding of different viewpoints?
- summarize key points?
- resolve conflicts?
- facilitate the reaching of consensus?

Finally, the team should be evaluated to determine how it functioned and how effective it was. Items that could be included on this evaluation follow. Did the team:

- demonstrate an understanding of the project goals and objectives?
- utilize the talents of all team members?
- deal with differing viewpoints and ideas?
- participate fully in all aspects?
- communicate openly and with trust?
- use creativity and ingenuity in problem solving?
- arrive at decisions logically and effectively?
- produce an effective final result (project, presentation, paper, etc.)?

EXAMPLES OF SUCCESSFUL TEAM PROJECTS

Team projects can be used in virtually every business course at every level. The following examples comprise five successful team projects that have been used in business courses. The projects can be adapted to meet teacher needs at both the secondary and postsecondary level. Each of the projects differed in scope and content, but all had some important similarities. First, all teachers devoted at least one class session to a discussion of teams and teamwork elements. Second, in each example, team leaders were self-appointed or team selected. Third, all projects ended with giving the team members an opportunity to evaluate the other team members. Peer evaluations can be much more significant to a student than a teacher evaluation, and in many cases they will motivate students to look more closely at their work responsibilities.

TEAM PROJECT 1—PRINCIPLES OF MANAGEMENT

Background. One class session was allotted to prepare the groups for the project; all other teamwork activities were done outside of class. A half hour in class per group was set aside for the team project presentation and discussion.

Project Description. Teams of five to six members were formed, and group leaders were chosen on an informal basis. Each team was given information on the American Disabilities Act and a company profile at least three weeks before the scheduled class presentation. The charge for each team was to develop a plan to disseminate information on the law throughout the company. Students had to determine to whom the information is important, how it should be presented in order to be the most effective, and if employee training was needed.

The team presentation required visuals or demonstration aids that would be appropriate in a business setting. In addition, a team-written report was submitted to the teacher.

Team Evaluation. Each team member evaluated other team members on a confidential basis. The students established the criteria and weight for each item from a teacher-made evaluation form. This evaluation accounted for 50 percent of the student team project grade. The remaining 50 percent was teacher assessed. The team project accounted for 10 percent of the students' total class grade.

Teacher Comments. Students did an excellent job, with some teams producing much more than was required. Due to the confidentiality of team members' grading of one another, it was very obvious if some members did not do their share.

TEAM PROJECT 2—BUSINESS COMMUNICATION

Background. One-and-a-half class sessions were spent on team building and how to work in a team. An additional class session was spent on how to give an effective presentation. The teacher gave a sample training session, including handouts and transparencies. Forty-five minutes per team was allotted for a training session presentation and question and answer period. If the student audience did not ask questions, questions were asked by the teacher to give team members practice in thinking on their feet.

Project Description. The teacher randomly composed groups of three to four members. Each team's objective was to present a 40-minute training session, which included a 30-minute presentation with visual aids (transparencies and handouts) and a 10-minute nonlecture exercise. Teams selected a topic from a teacher-provided list of business communication topics that included: conflict management, listening skills, conducting an interview, and writing policies and procedures. Teacher presentation outlines and sample transparencies and handouts were given, and time was spent talking about effective visuals. The 10-minute nonlecture section could include videos, role playing, guest speakers, etc. Teams were given a specific audience and told the level of expertise of their audience. Approximately one month before the team training session was given, a two-page proposal outlining what the team intended to do and how much time would be spent on each area was submitted to the teacher for approval. After the team training session presentation, a team-written report was prepared and given to the teacher.

Team Evaluation. After each team presentation, other teams and the teacher evaluated the presentation on content, delivery, visual aids, and overall effect. One statement was written on the team's strong points, and one statement was written on an area in which the team could improve. After the written portion of the project, team members evaluated themselves and the other team members as to their percentage of contribution to the total team project.

Teacher Comments. Team presentations and written projects force a student to work in a team setting much like what they will encounter in business. The chances are that students will have to work with people they do not like, do not respect, or who have different values. Team projects are an important structure of every communication course.

TEAM PROJECT 3—ORGANIZATIONAL BEHAVIOR

Background. One class session was spent discussing the team project, including the expectations of the team and how the team would be evaluated.

All other team activities were performed outside of class, with one final class session for team project presentation.

Project Description. Students formed teams of four to five members. No team leaders were formally chosen, but one member soon emerged who took control of the team organization. The project consisted of a salary-and-benefit survey for a local bank. Each team was given an assignment to complete.

Team 1: Did all background work for the survey and made all initial contacts for the survey.

Team 2: Designed and administered the survey.

Team 3: Completed the data analysis.

Team 4: Wrote the summary report.

Team 5: Presented the findings to the bank vice president for human resources.

Team Evaluation. Each member of the team evaluated the other members as to their participation in team activities. Any team member who did not receive at least an average rating was required to have a personal conference with the instructor to determine problem areas or concerns.

Teacher Comments. This type of team project increases the visibility of a school program to the community. Students are working with actual job situations and have the opportunity to interact with working personnel. Presenting the final report to the vice president of human resources of the bank brought an additional realistic element to the project.

TEAM PROJECT 4—INFORMATION PROCESSING

Background. A chapter of the class text focused on teamwork in the office, and approximately two class sessions were spent discussing the importance of the team process. Students were assigned outside required readings from current periodicals in relation to the team project topic they were given.

Project Description. The teacher assigned students to teams of four to six members. Team leaders were self-appointed or team selected. Topics addressed were teacher provided and included staffing support services, evaluating peripherals, determining office automation needs, and selecting software. All project reports were to focus on office use, not personal use. Ten guidelines for each topic were given for further investigation and included many outside activities such as obtaining current research, conducting an analysis of statistics, identifying company practices/policies, interviewing, and analyzing data. The required readings completed earlier in the semester were a part of this investigation. The teams had the entire semester to complete the project, leading to a 30-minute oral presentation including handouts, graphs, demonstrations, and/or audio visuals. All members were required to participate in the oral presentation. After the oral presentation, the team submitted a written report of the findings to the teacher, who graded the report on content and format equally. Teams had to use citations and correct grammar, spelling, and word usage for full credit.

Team Evaluation. Each member of the team evaluated the other members of the team. Evaluations were confidential and were based on the team member's contribution to the team process and final report. The class as a whole evaluated each team's oral presentation. The students' final project grade was based on team member ratings, student ratings of the oral presentation, and teacher assessment of the team-written report.

Teacher Comments. Since students knew from the beginning that the ratings they gave each other would be figured into final project grades, the teams became quite competitive. Many students indicated they liked being part of the grading decision. Grading on writing mechanics provided additional incentives for accuracy.

TEAM PROJECT 5—BUSINESS POLICY

Background. The overall goal of the business policies course is that students exit the course prepared to work in teams. The first class session was spent discussing the importance of working in teams in the business world. Approximately 75 percent of the work completed in the course is through teamwork.

Project Description. The teacher formed four- to six-member teams, to ensure equal representation among the management, marketing, accounting, and finance majors. The team selected its leader. Teams were given the charge to develop a strategy that responds to a specific company situation. A variety of companies and situations were used including companies that have a bad product mix, are trying to decide whether or not to expand internationally, are facing new competitors that are entering the market, or are experiencing financial difficulties. Teams were given industry and company financial information. The assignments were to:

1. Analyze the industry.
2. Analyze the company.
3. Come to a consensus about what the company's problem was, define the problem, and develop two alternative strategies to solve the problem.
4. Project the financial consequences of both alternatives and estimate the profitability and investment; evaluate the alternatives, including profitability as a criterion.
5. Prepare a written draft of the strategic plan proposed.
6. Present the project to the class. All team members must present (using handouts and overheads as appropriate for clarification) and be prepared to address questions.
7. Using feedback obtained from the presentation, complete the written report for teacher review.

Team Evaluation. Upon project completion, team members rated each team member on participation (quantity and quality) and the ability to get along with each other. The team leader was rated on his or her organizational and motivational skills. Evaluations were confidential and were a percentage of the student's final grade.

Teacher Comments. It was a pleasure to see students mature and refine their ideas and to gain insight into their strengths and weaknesses as a team member. Students agreed that the important lessons they learn from this class were not from the book, but from the team project experience.

SUMMARY

Students with teamwork experience have a valuable skill that can help them to obtain a job. Businesses are looking for workers with interpersonal communication, leadership, and teamwork skills. Since the team facilitator can make or break a team, it is worthwhile for teachers to give training on how to lead a team. Teachers need to give students the chance to discuss problems that were encountered in other team projects and to identify how these problems could be resolved in future team projects.

Teachers must offer students the opportunity to learn and practice the team process so that they will be able to repeat it for any content area in the business work environment.

REFERENCES

Booth, P. (1994). Embracing the team concept. *Canadian Business Review, 21,* 10-14.

Bottom, W. P. (1994). A diagnostic model for team building with an illustrative application. *Human Resource Development Quarterly, 5,* 317-336.

Cane, A. (1994). Pushing back to profitability. *The Financial Times, 32524,* 1.

Day, M. (1994). Can organizations have a learning disability? *Canadian Manager, 19,* 21-25.

Deitz, D. (1995). An infrastructure for integration. *Mechanical Engineering-CIME, 117* 78-80.

Ehrilch, C. J. (1994). Creating an employer-employee relationship for the future. *Human Resource Management, 33,* 491-592.

Friedman, A. S. (1994). Full-service firm runs on teamwork. *National Underwriter Life & Health-Financial Services Edition,* 7-9.

Holter, N. C. (1994). Team assignments can be effective cooperative learning techniques. *Journal of Education for Business, 70,* 73-76.

Harrison, D. B., Conn, H.P., Whittaker, B., & Mitchell, J. (1994). Mobilizing abilities through teamwork. *Canadian Business Review, 21,* 20-24.

Kerr, D. L., & Sutton, J. C. (1995). Focus on teaching: Classroom-to-workplace bridges. *Business Communication Quarterly, 58,* 47-51.

Kunz, R. D. (1994, April). Total quality education: A concept in reality. Paper presented at the Annual Convention of the American Association of Community Colleges, Washington, DC.

Lienert, A. (1994). Forging a new partnership. *Management Review, 83,* 39-44.

Mazany, P., Francis, S., & Sumich, P. (1995). Evaluating the effectiveness of an outdoor workshop for team building in an MBA program. *Journal of Management Development, 14,* 50-69.

Perrigo, E. M. (1994, November). Business and professional communication: Where are we now? Are we teaching skills that are necessary in business today? Paper presented at the Annual Meeting of the Speech Communication Association, New Orleans, LA.

Runge, L. (1994). If I fail, you fail. *Computerworld, 28,* 77-78.

Smith, S. L. (1995). How a Baldrige winner manages safety. *Occupational Hazards, 57,* 33-36.

CHAPTER 17

Developing Problem-Solving Skills

ANN M. REMP

Eastern Michigan University, Ypsilanti, Michigan

I've seen it over and over again. Different ethnic groups have trouble working together because one group doesn't feel respected by other groups. Engineers off in their design areas make a change without any idea of how it affects other parts of the business. Students apply for a job, expecting a $45,000 salary, but are unable to tell me what they can bring that will earn that $45,000 back for the company let alone bring a profit. And managers look at me as if I'm strange when I say, "This affects our bottom line."—Anonymous, Human Resources Manager, Japanese-American Business.

The quote provides examples of problems which can be created when individuals do not see the interrelatedness of their actions within the total business. The Secretary's Commission on Achieving Necessary Skills (1991) states that competent and expert workers "understand their own work in the context of the work of those around them; they understand how parts of systems are connected, anticipate consequences, and monitor and correct their own performance . . ." (p. 13). In demonstrating an understanding of complex interrelationships, the competent worker "suggests modifications to existing systems and develops new or alternative systems to improve performance" (p. 12). Competent individuals, in other words, employ a systems perspective to prevent problems as well as to solve them.

The problem solver uses a systems perspective in a complex and comprehensive manner. Problem solving is more appropriately described as a performance than a task because the variety of problems to be solved requires flexibility in applying many skills. The overall performance ensures that the problem is addressed, not only its symptoms; that solutions are evaluated before being implemented; and that valid and complete information resources are the basis of the process. The individual "performs" problem solving readily if problem solving has been practiced regularly, just as the entertainer or musician performs in a seemingly effortless way because of many rehearsals.

This chapter discusses problem solving in order to clarify the elements which come together in the total performance, followed by achievement standards and related performance expectations for problem-solving. Instructional approaches to developing a systems perspective, working toward total problem solving performances, and creating an appropriate learning environment are presented. The chapter concludes with assessment by discussing the role of the student, the evidence on which judgments of achievement are based, and the instrument for recording observations of the performance.

Business teachers have a continuing record of developing complex performance skills successfully and using varied methods of assessment. The business teacher should apply this expertise to developing students who will exhibit high quality performance in problem solving.

DEFINING PROBLEM SOLVING

The SCANS Commission states that a competent worker is one who "recognizes problems and devises and implements [a] plan of action" (1991, p. xviii). Five other higher order abilities are related to effective problem solving: creative thinking, decision making, "seeing things in the mind's eye," self-management of learning, and reasoning (critical thinking). Marzano et al. (1993) define problem solving as one of five types of tasks that "encourage meaningful use of knowledge": "Problem solving involves developing and testing a method or product for overcoming obstacles or constraints to reach a desired outcome" (p. 79).

Developing problem solving requires a definition appropriate to teaching and learning. The definition used in this chapter is: Problem solving is a comprehensive performance during which the student applies readily available research, reasoning, and decision-making skills in an integrated fashion to improve business systems. Two operational definitions illustrate the steps involved in the problem-solving process:

MacLeod and Nelson (1993) define problem-solving performance as:

When a business problem is present and when a solution is demanded, an individual can complete the following eight steps to solve the problem:

1. Define the problem.
2. Identify the factors of the problem.
3. Determine the means of transforming and interpreting data.
4. Develop conclusion criteria.
5. Gather data.
6. Interpret data.
7. Draw conclusion(s).
8. Make recommendation(s) if requested. (p. 1)

Meyer and Allen (1994) identify a five-stage problem-solving/decision-making process as:

Identify problem or opportunity.

List solutions or options.

Evaluate alternatives.

Choose solution.

Act and get feedback. (p. 72)

Either approach, regardless of the number of steps, requires that the problem solver have research skills: Identifying problems, causes, and possible solutions depends on asking questions, locating relevant and complete resources, evaluating the quality of the available information, and sometimes generating new information. Problem solving employs reasoning strategies (analysis, synthesis, evaluation, for example): Symptoms must be separated from causes, criteria for evaluating and selecting the solution are needed, and alternatives must be weighed for their potential effectiveness and impact on the system as a whole. Decision making is required to choose among solutions and make recommendations. The student must have these component skills available for use. The effective teacher helps students develop each component skill as needed and aids students to integrate these skills in the problem solving process. The "systems perspective" provides a total context for the process.

ACHIEVEMENT STANDARDS AND PERFORMANCE EXPECTATIONS

For the business education curriculum, the achievement standard is that the business student solves problems effectively. The performance expectations are that the business student will—

1. Practice problem solving frequently in formal and informal settings.

2. Use a systematic problem-solving process appropriate to the problem.

3. Demonstrate effective research skills to locate and use comprehensive, relevant information resources and to generate new information when necessary.

4. Use a systems perspective to analyze the causes of problems and the impacts of various solutions.

5. Select and apply several reasoning strategies throughout the problem-solving process.

6. Make effective decisions about solutions and monitor solutions for improvement of the business systems.

7. Evaluate the effectiveness of his or her own problem-solving performance and plan continuous improvement.

The standard sets the overall goal of the learning process. Many schools state this standard for problem solving as a standard for all students. Performance expectations provide guidelines to describe the overall performance in terms that will be observable in some manner. As a result, the expectations lead directly to decisions about assessment: What evidence will demonstrate that the student applies reasoning strategies or uses a systems perspective? The standard and the related performance expectations permit and encourage multiple forms of assessment. The standard does not restrict the assessment of achievement to one teacher; the teacher in collaboration with other teachers, employers, counselors, parents, and others may assess achievement of the standard.

The standard leads to the use of multiple approaches to the learning activities—teacher directed, student directed, and collaborative. The standard may be achieved across several educational experiences—in one or more classrooms, in student organizations, in the workplace, or in the community. Finally, the problem-solving standard is general, and therefore applicable to problems in interpersonal or supervisory relationships, the introduction of new technology, a bottleneck in a procedure, or other types of problems.

DEVELOPING A SYSTEMS PERSPECTIVE

A systems perspective is the recognition that a system is a whole made up of parts, all of which work to achieve a goal. Each part has a role to perform, and the performance of each part influences the effectiveness of every other part and the success of the whole. A well-designed system is supposed to monitor itself and correct its performance, but whether well-designed or not, systems develop means of balancing conflicting or competing elements. Similarly, well-designed systems monitor the environment to anticipate problems, but whether well-designed or not, the environment will impact the system.

There is no such thing as a "problem" if there is not a system: Problems are conflicts about goals, inappropriate performance of parts, faulty relationships, lack of feedback and self correction, or failure to consider pressures from the environment (factors outside the boundaries of the system). Somewhere, in every problem, there is a system that is not working. If the system can be "found," solutions (or interventions) can be designed. When a student develops a systems perspective, the student is becoming a problem solver. When does the teacher know that students have developed this perspective? The perspective is developed when the student can use five basic concepts (goal, element, relationship, feedback, and environment) as part of the problem-solving process.

Two approaches that teachers can use to help the student learn to work with these basic concepts are graphical modeling and questioning strategies. The examples that follow are based on the notion that the classroom is a system in which problems in teaching and learning occur.

Graphic modeling represents the components of a system, their relationships, feedback mechanisms, and the environment of a system in a visual way. The value of graphic modeling in the learning environment can be documented in many sources. Bellanca and Fogarty (1992) advocate "maps" or graphic models as "cognitive organizers" (p. 9). They identify webs, "sequence chains, vector charts, story maps, analogy links, flow charts, matrices, Venn diagrams, and ranking ladders," among the wide variety of visual devices which help individuals learn. McTighe and Lyman (1992) illustrate "thinktrixes," matrices which "aid teachers and students in generating responses," and wheels, as well as examples of other types of maps. The business environment also relies on graphic models for many purposes. Senge (1994) includes such models extensively in illustrating the development of the systems perspective in the workplace.

Because the "classroom as system" uses the experience of all students, the teacher might begin the process of modeling with each new class by asking students to draw a graphic model of "the class." Identifying elements of teacher and students would be a start, although not a complete listing. The role of teacher and student, the relationships between and among them, and feedback mechanisms have to be drawn into the model. Students should include factors in the environment which influence teachers and students and identify the goal of the system. Such a model would not only lead to better understanding of student and teacher assumptions about the learning environment, but can be used to continue the process of learning to ask "What if . . . ?" and "If . . . then . . . ?" questions about the assumed roles and relationships.

One experience in modeling will not develop a systems perspective. Modeling must be used frequently. The teacher should have students model the business transaction to be implemented in a spreadsheet, whether it is a payroll, budget, pricing, or other application and then ask the following questions: Does the graphic model reflect all the variables important to the transaction? Are the relationships among variables (e.g., formulas) clear and correct? Are the outcomes clear?

Interpersonal systems or networks based on case studies of employee relationships or communications can be modeled as well. Comparing models of the formal communication system (organizational chart) with the actual system in use (based on observations of frequency of contacts in person, by electronic mail, by telephone conversations, etc.) can reinforce systems thinking.

Exhibit 1

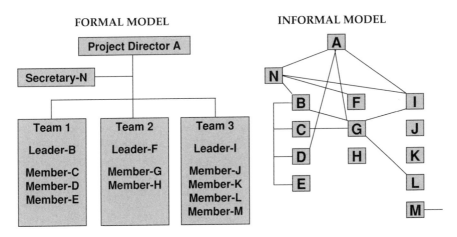

The problem solver can compare the presumed communication channels of A with A's actual channels to D and G, but not B and I, and begin to anticipate possible problems. Likewise, the role of G in the system cannot be understood from the formal model. N has a different role than A in the organizational chart, but actually seems to communicate in the same way that A does, possibly confusing team members and leaders about the authority of N's position. There may be isolated groups (J and K) or individuals communicating outside their teams or outside their system entirely (L and M). Analysis of such models aids anticipation of problems and leads to better ability to define problems from the "relationship" perspective.

Teachers can integrate graphic modeling of systems into formal problem-solving activities and use the approach in other learning activities to develop the systems perspective. One classroom teacher noticed that many students did not know why they were taking the class. She took a class period to have students prepare a graphic model of their career goal and the foundations needed to reach the career goal. Student teams developed triangles with supporting legs, interlinked circles, and other graphic models. Observations of group interaction, listening to individual contributions, seeing the models, and hearing the rationale for the model provided evidence that students were beginning to see the class as part of a career development system designed to prepare them to reach their career goals.

Graphic models provide one basis for teaching students to ask questions that the solving of problems requires. The link (line, arrow, or relationship) in the graphical model between each element allows the question to be asked: Is this the "weak link" in the chain that has led to the problem? For example, Exhibit 2 is a common graphical model of a computer system.

Exhibit 2

After the initial presentation of the model, business teachers can use the model to help students ask questions about solving problems in their work:

1. Did I know what I really wanted to get (output)?

2. Did I provide the data or the form of the data (input) in a way that leads to the outcome?

3. Did I choose the application best suited (processing) to the outcome I want?

As implied in these questions, the graphic model must include the goal of the system. Identifying the goal of the system allows students to ask other questions such as: Is the purpose to make the best product? To reduce costs? To have satisfied customers? At some point in problem solving, the teacher will help students ask the question, "Is this the 'right' goal for this system?" Such a question is not intended to raise questions of value, but to emphasize that problem solving may require that the stated goal of a system be challenged and alternative goals to be considered. For example, if a system states its goal in terms of decrease in costs and the problem is a decrease in profits, it may be necessary to ask if the stated goal is the "right" goal.

Graphically modeling the system in which a problem occurs provides evidence for the teacher and employer (via class discussion, observation, the portfolio, or other means) that the student understands the interconnectedness of the business environment.

In addition to using the graphic model as a basis for learning to ask and answer questions, brief case problems and unanticipated problems that occur in the learning environment can be used to aid students to learn to ask questions. Typically, teachers ask questions for students to answer, and students ask questions for the teacher to answer. Often the answer, not the question, is the focus of learning. Problem solving is facilitated by having students develop questioning strategies. Some strategies which emphasize the system perspective are chaining questions that begin with Why, the five W's, How, What If, and If-Then questions.

Chaining questions that begin with "Why" helps students to go back to causes of problems, rather than stopping at symptoms of problems. Teachers may want to use brief cases that relate to the focus of instruction to prompt students to ask, "Why?" For example, when dealing with a unit on communication, a class may begin with a brief incident, such as:

You are the administrative assistant to the Project SPAN Manager. One of the team leaders calls you to ask if the manager approved sending a proposal to a prospective customer. You check all messages that you have and respond that the manager has not left any information with you about this matter. Later you are quizzed thoroughly by your manager about whether you gave authorization for the proposal to be sent. The proposal was sent; it was not approved by the manager; and it contained serious errors. The team leader said he assumed he had approval because the manager would have left a message with you if the proposal should not have been sent.

Start the students off with the first "Why": Why did the team leader assume he had approval? When one student suggests a reason ("Maybe he thought . . . ."), ask another student to ask a question: "Why did he think that?" Have a third student respond with a possible reason and pose a third "Why." Lead the students back to the multiple scenarios that might explain the problem: One possible explanation is that the team leader knew perfectly well that there was no approval, but gave an explanation that he knew would take some time to sort out and divert attention from himself. If this is determined to be the cause, what is the appropriate action? Another explanation is that in previous instances, the manager has always left word of disapprovals with the administrative assistant and has created an expectation that no disapproval is the same as approval. If this is the cause of the problem, what should be done?

Senge (1994) recommends the chaining of questions as a device to eliminate the hasty "jumps to conclusions" or quick solutions that often assume the wrong cause. Further, forcing answers to the series of questions emphasizes the interrelatedness of the elements in the system in which problems occur. Teachers familiar with nondirective questioning techniques realize that such questioning could become circular, so limits are put on the number of repetitions. The purpose of the questions is to discourage the teacher from solving the problem for the student and to ask the student to initiate the search for causes.

Real-world problem solving requires students to gather information that is comprehensive. The rule of thumb used by news reporters is that stories must answer five W's and How: Who, What, Why, When, Where, and How. These questions can also be used to develop understanding of particular aspects of the system in which the problem occurs. To illustrate the questioning strategy, assume that the teacher has distributed a copy of the guidelines for appropriate use of computer resources (particularly software and proprietary information). Can the students apply knowledge of the policy to a problem? Ask them to pose several questions and to answer them. One question should start with "What," such as, "What does the policy cover?"

Another should start with "Who," such as, "Who is covered by the policy?" Students should create questions for "Why" ("Why was the policy developed?"), "When" ("When does it apply—during employment? What about after leaving the company?"), "Where" ("Does the policy affect work from home?"), and "How" ("How is the policy enforced?"). Following the questioning strategy with a case allows the teacher to observe whether the information can be applied:

> You are a new employee. Because you are working on computer software with which you are not familiar, you have mentioned to a co-worker that you wish you could practice at home. You have a computer, but you don't have the particular software. A few days later, in the lunchroom, the co-worker says that you can have a disk with the software on it and gives you the disk. Your problem is whether to take the disk or not. What questions should you ask before you decide whether to accept the disk? Are there some conditions under which you can accept the disk without violating company policy?

The case may be used for group discussion or result in a "think paper" composed on computer.

Asking "What If" requires the asker (student or teacher) to consider that a system does not have to operate the way it does. These questions challenge students (and teachers) to consider alternative scenarios. The "If-Then" question poses a cause-effect relationship. For example, in the "classroom as system" example, the teacher might pose a question: "What would happen if you (the students) decided how you are graded (system feedback)?" After the laughter dies down, students might engage in a discussion about the purpose of feedback, the form of feedback they could provide, what they need from the teacher, or other aspects of the feedback mechanism in the learning environment. The "What If" leads to considering possibilities. The "If-Then" tries to anticipate effects of particular changes: "If you (the student) were responsible for giving feedback to your partner on group discussion, then what would result?"

It is not enough for the teacher to pose the questions. To learn to ask meaningful questions and answer them is part of learning how to learn. It is also part of learning how to solve problems; it is not, however, total performance. Each illustration provides an opportunity to learn only part of what is needed to problem solve. The teacher needs to develop problem solving as a total performance.

WORKING TOWARD TOTAL PERFORMANCE

Using many opportunities to model and question throughout instruction prepares the student for the total performance. Students can now engage in the formal process. The teacher must select a process, perhaps the eight-step approach outlined by MacLeod and Nelson (1993), the five steps presented by Meyer and Allen (1994), or another. Some teachers use several approaches for solving different types of problems. The teacher also determines how the problem will be selected and how to provide multiple experiences for the student. Within the classroom, the teacher then develops understanding of the particular approach to be used and finally engages students in the process.

Selecting the approach will influence the skills students need to employ in problem solving. For example, MacLeod and Nelson (1993) emphasize the methods of gathering, transforming, and interpreting data. Meyer and Allen (1994) emphasize the decision-making, implementation, and monitoring aspects of problem solving. Each approach requires a problem situation suitable to the emphases and a time frame appropriate to performing the activities.

Other factors the teacher should address in the planning of instruction are: How many opportunities will be provided for problem solving? Should the experience provide for group interaction or will there be value if done by the individual student? Should the experience be a developmental or culminating experience? There is no right or wrong answer, but the teacher needs to remember that the opportunity to repeat key steps is needed to improve performance. Coordination with other teachers to plan problem-solving experiences across the student's curriculum is the best way to ensure that students engage in many different types of problem-solving experiences.

The introduction of the actual problem-solving approach begins with describing the steps and purposes of the steps to students. The teacher may provide an example of how the process is used to solve a particular problem. Then students should rehearse the process, while the teacher monitors the interaction. During this rehearsal, the teacher must ensure that students do not skip steps. The value of a systematic problem-solving process is its inclusion of all the necessary steps to arrive at a solution. The process allows students to ask questions, receive feedback on their rehearsal, and gain confidence in their ability to use the approach.

Engaging students in a full problem-solving experience requires selecting the problem to be solved. The teacher may select the problem or may allow the students to select the problem. Students are more interested and involved in problems they select; however, the teacher should review the problems to see that they are amenable to the problem-solving approach to be used.

As students undertake the formal problem-solving process, the teacher may observe that some students are more adept than others at "defining the problem" or "identifying constraints or obstacles." Some may be better than others at locating resources, comparing and contrasting alternatives, identifying ethical or legal consequences of certain solutions, or other "parts" of the whole performance. Communication problems may develop. The teacher needs to be prepared and willing to support the further development of these skills so that students can be successful in their problem-solving performances.

To provide this support, the teacher needs a repertoire of performance tasks which are relevant to both the particular content of a lesson and the particular skill that needs further development. There should already be many performance tasks in the teacher's "toolkit." Marzano et al. (1993) state: "The guiding principle when developing a performance task is to select the reasoning process that most strongly emphasizes the content information . . . " (1993, p. 27). The teacher needs to modify performance tasks that already exist to include an emphasis on particular research, reasoning, or decision-making skills. Including basic communication skills in these support tasks is essential.

The following are several examples of very brief performance tasks that the teacher may already include in a "telephone techniques" unit:

Identify three types of general assistance an office employee can provide during telephone calls from prospective new customers to encourage them to become customers. Identify three types of assistance that would be inappropriate to provide.

Identify three factors which you might use to decide whether to telephone or fax information to a business person. Develop a chart which employees could consult to decide which channel is best for frequently encountered situations.

Gather information from five persons who work in small businesses on the telephone features they use and do not use. Combine your information with information from other members of your team and summarize the information.

In these brief performance tasks, students are asked to classify, develop criteria, compare, analyze, gather, and summarize information. With a repertoire of such performance tasks, the teacher can strengthen skills for the next opportunity to practice the full problem-solving process.

CREATING THE ENVIRONMENT FOR PROBLEM SOLVING

Problem solving is a cognitive activity, but it is not one performed in isolation. The classroom is a system, and performance is influenced by the total learning environment. There is an affective component to problem-solving, for there must be willingness to solve problems, including taking the risks that problem solving requires. The learning environment of the problem-solving classroom is characterized by trust, confidence, resources, and flexibility. The physical environment and the communication of the teacher are important in building this learning environment.

Many elements of the physical environment may be targeted to create this atmosphere: Bulletin boards, constructed by students, may portray successful people who solved problems in spite of difficulty or hardship. These may be famous persons or, if trust has been built, success stories of the students themselves or members of their families. It is important to find examples of individuals who did not succeed the first time. The milieu must support the building of confidence that the student can succeed because others have succeeded.

The environment must also support problem-solving activities through readily available resources. These may include books, CD-ROMs, the Internet, economic resources, business persons, or other sources. If the teacher has taken a systems approach to problem solving, the resources may emphasize references to problems that have been solved in that manner.

The environment must be flexible, so that students may easily form work groups. Some teachers form "centers" or areas in the classroom for resource centers or group work. One problem that some teachers and students will want to address through problem solving is how to create flexible centers or areas for problem solving when furniture and other physical features of the room do not lend themselves to change.

Teacher communications contribute to the total environment. "Mentions" are the verbal reinforcements of themes that are threaded throughout instruction. Students "mention" to us their "attitudes" about problem solving all the time. Every teacher hears: "This is boring." "I'm not good at this." "I'll never really have to do this." "Teachers live to make life tough!" "I'm tired." "I don't have time." "Mr. X doesn't make us do this much work." "I don't like doing team projects." These "mentions" influence the teacher.

Some teachers take the assertive route. They "shape" and change the "mentions" made by students. The teacher may stop a student and ask him or her to "smile first" before "mentioning" some problem that prevents the student from doing an excellent job. Students may be required to find a way to "mention" that includes only positive words. It is especially important to re-shape "mentions" about feelings of personal failure. Students should analyze unsuccessful solutions. Lack of resources, the scope of some problems, or the need for further development of skill and knowledge may result in having to withdraw temporarily or permanently from a problem before a solution can be achieved; this is not "failure."

"Mentions" can be based on examples of students' work: "Oh, that's a great comparison. Susan, tell the class what you did." "Mei Ling, could you let other students see your model? Why did you decide to draw it this way?" "You know, Scott, you are using systems concepts. How could you use this to solve the communication problem?" "I think you think you're not getting anywhere. Take a few minutes to think about something else. Some very famous problem solvers got their best ideas when they worked on something else." "Jona, you've really thrown yourself into the case from the employee's perspective. How do you think the supervisor feels?" A repertoire of "mentions" on problem solving may help to develop not only a willingness to solve problems, but excitement about the process.

The importance of the total learning environment to actual learning of problem solving cannot be ignored. Problem solving is hard work, and an appropriate learning environment can remove distractions and obstacles that interfere with learning and help students to focus on learning in a positive way.

ASSESSING PROBLEM SOLVING

Several authorities advocate making students an integral part of assessment. Wiggins (1993) says, "An explicit aim [of the national assessment plan] was to ensure that assessment results would be empowering to the student. Thus the need for 'user friendly' feedback was deemed essential to student motivation and the raising of standards: 'Formative assessment must be in terms to which pupils can respond and which clearly indicate what has been and what remains to be achieved.' " Further, standards and instruments must be shared by students and teachers (pp. 157-8). If, for example, a journal is a reflection upon the problem-solving experiences significant to the student, the student may need to determine whether this is relevant evidence for effective problem solving.

What types of activities and products should the teacher use to assess the achievement of effective problem solving? There is no single answer, for the trend is toward multiple approaches. Whatever the teacher emphasizes should relate to performance expectations. The teacher should favor evidence that is integrative. If the student engages in problem solving regularly as a part of student organizational work and demonstrates competence in all the areas of performance, then there may be no need for other evidence.

Assuming that students are becoming problem solvers, evidence may need to document progress toward achievement. If the performance expectation is, "Evaluates the effectiveness of his or her own problem-solving performance and plans continuous improvement," the evidence may come from interviews with the student or entries in a journal or portfolio. If the performance expectation is, "Applies appropriate reasoning strategies to the problem-solving process," the evidence may be provided by other students, teacher observations, or the results of supporting activities. Ideally, teachers have involved members of the business community in the activities of the classroom and directed students to business or community resources. Reports from business or community people can provide evidence of effective research or business perspective.

A rubric can be used to evaluate problem-solving activities. For the expectation, "Uses a systems perspective to analyze causes of problems and impacts of various solutions," for example, the rating scale of 3, 2, or 1 may be defined as:

3 (Exceeds standard): Demonstrates ability to apply understanding of systems to a business problem in a thorough manner (that is, in all stages of problem solving) and develops new alternatives based on knowledge of how systems operate.

2 (Meets standard): Demonstrates ability to apply understanding of systems to stages of solving a business problem.

1 (Does not meet standard): Cannot demonstrate ability or demonstrates limited ability to apply understanding of systems to solving a business problem.

There are different formats for assessment instruments. Marzano et al. (1993) suggest a gradebook format (p. 38) which places standards as fields (columns) and student names as records (rows). Each "cell" is subdivided to permit recording judgments on several activities and an overall summary judgment for the standard. If the student can produce a graphic model of a system in a case study, a rating is provided for the individual task. If the student explains a case situation to another student or hypothesizes a cause for the problem using systems language, this is a second evidence and is recorded. If a student's journal provides evidence of understanding systems, that may be a third evidence. And so on. All the individual judgments are used in providing a summary judgment of the student's achievement of the standard.

The teacher could develop a form for each student. Each performance expectation might identify particular focal points and provide a place for both comments and a summary rating. The following is a partial example of such a form:

ASSESSMENT INSTRUMENT

Achievement Standard: The business student solves problems effectively.

Performance Expectation   Evidence   Rating

Uses a systematic approach to
solving problems: _____

    Identifies problems   _____

    Lists solutions or options   _____

    Evaluates alternatives   _____

    Chooses solutions   _____

    Acts and gets feedback   _____

Overall Comments/Evidence:

Uses a systems perspective to
analyze causes of problems and
impacts of solutions: _____

    System goals   _____

    Environment   _____

    Relationships   _____

    Feedback   _____

    Elements/Roles   _____

Overall Comments/Evidence:

The overall problem-solving performance (each stage) also should be in-cluded on a form. Whatever form is used should make communication about achievement possible.

SUMMARY

Problem solving is a life skill, not simply a school skill. Effective problem solving in any individual's life (as employer or employee, citizen, family member, etc.) is a prerequisite to success. The teaching and learning of prob-lem solving is a means by which teachers and learners address the change process and integrate cultural, international, technological, and ethical considerations as problems are identified and evaluated from a systems perspective. The development of affective dimensions (self-confidence, self-management in ambiguous situations, and the desire to move from "ade-quate" to "good" to "better" and, finally, to "best") all enter the picture.

In the cognitive domain, we want students to demonstrate the skills of the in-vestigator, driven by a need to know; the interviewer and researcher, seeking information through observing, communicating, and reading; the manager, planning and implementing; the scientist, finding patterns in information and testing understanding of those patterns; and the innovator, open to insight and able to influence the change process. In these roles, we find the highest expression of the achievement of problem-solving performances.

REFERENCES

Bellanca, J., & Fogarty, R. (1992). Cognition in practice. In A. Costa, J. Bellanca & R. Fogarty (Eds.) *If minds matter: A forward to the future.* Volume 2. Palatine, IL: Skylight Publishing, Inc.

Jones, C. S. (1995, March). Portfolios: A relevant assessment tool. *Instructional strategies: An applied research series, 11*(1), 1-6.

MacLeod, L., & Nelson, S. (1993, May). Teaching problem solving in business classes. *Instructional strategies: An applied research series, 9*(3), 1-4.

McTighe, J., & Lyman, F.T. (1992). Mind tools for matters of the mind. In A. Costa, J. Bellanca & R. Fogarty (Eds.). *If minds matter: A forward to the future.* Volume 2. Palatine, IL: Skylight Publishing, Inc.

Marzano, R., Pickering, D. & McTighe, J. (1993). *Assessing student outcomes.* Alexandria, VA: Association for Supervision and Curriculum Development.

Meyer, E. C., & Allen, C. (1994). *Entrepreneurship and small business management.* Columbus, OH: Glencoe Publishing Company.

Secretary's Commission on Achieving Necessary Skills. (1991, June). *What work requires of schools.* Washington D.C.: U.S. Department of Labor.

Senge, P., Roberts, C., Ross, R., Smith, B., & Kleiner, A. (1994). *The fifth discipline fieldbook.* New York: Doubleday.

Wiggins, G. P. (1993). *Assessing student performance.* San Francisco: Jossey-Bass, Inc.

CHAPTER 18

Incorporating Business Ethics into Course Work

JAMES A. WRIGHT

Chadron State College, Chadron, Nebraska

A friend and colleague, when learning that I was scheduled to make a presentation on business ethics, once said to me, "I thought business ethics, was an oxymoron." Unfortunately, this attitude exemplifies a common perception of today's business world. To complicate matters further, businesses are controlled by laws and regulations which are enacted by legislators who, in their own right as politicians, are oftentimes subject to low public trust levels. Can businesses be ethical if they are controlled by those who are ethically questionable? Why should one run an ethical business?

The purpose of this chapter is to provide an overview of what business ethics involves, a description of several timely ethical issues, and suggestions on how to incorporate business ethics into course work.

BASIC DEFINITIONS

Before discussing business ethics it will be helpful to review some basic definitions from which the subject of business ethics is derived. Ethics and morality are words that are often interchanged. Ethics comes from the Greek word "ethos" meaning character, whereas morality comes from the Latin word "moralis" meaning customs or manners. Ethics concerns the character of an individual or individuals, and morality considers relationships between human beings. In philosophy, "ethics" is an area of study—the study of morality concerned with human values and conduct. Ethics involves right and wrong—good and bad.

BUSINESS ETHICS

Business ethics is concerned with human values and conduct in areas of business, commerce, and trade. What is good, bad, right, or wrong is of intellectual concern to the student of business ethics but is of practical importance to successful business persons. Jacqueline Dunckel, in *Good Ethics Good Business—Your Plan For Success* (1989) states emphatically, "If you want to be successful in business on a long-term basis, you must match your operational expertise with an ethical code of conduct practiced in every phase of your business. No Exceptions!"

As in other areas of ethics, business ethics includes theories that are sometimes diametrically opposed. In a world that is fast losing national borders, people with different philosophies and ideologies come face to face. As international trade increases, humans need to concern themselves with dilemmas arising from people who wish to trade but operate under conflicting ethical systems.

Compare a system that supports high governmental control with one that supports little or no governmental control. Ethical principles derived from each of these systems may differ in many ways. Each has its own set of rules and guidelines. One system supports the idea that if the government does not control business, that which is good will become unevenly distributed. Those who "have" will continue to acquire more whereas those who "do not have" will continue to receive proportionately less. Eventually, all the wealth will be in the hands of a small elite group. On the other hand, an opposing view is that the best way to insure the most good for the greatest number of people is for the government to stay out of business. This system is known as the laissez-faire or free-enterprise system. Theoretically, the consumer will be the beneficiary of the competition generated. However, as Coen (1995) points out, this system assumes an equal playing field for buyers and sellers.

History has shown that neither system in its pure form is practical. Both systems are flawed, and therefore a middle ground is more appropriate and practical. For example, to its extreme, a free-enterprise system might be obligated to tolerate deceptive advertising practices under the assumption that the consumer will eventually realize the deception and drive the deceiver out of business. On the other hand, a governmentally controlled society will enact laws that prevent unequal wealth distribution but as a result may curtail the incentive for a person to be productive and work hard. The collapse of the Soviet Union is a prime example of a governmentally controlled society which failed.

The remainder of this chapter assumes that a modified-free-enterprise system is in effect.

HUMAN RIGHTS ISSUES

As business requires extensive human interaction, and since the consequences of this interaction reach past the theoretical and jump directly into the real world, it becomes imperative for the greatest good of everyone that businesses be protected against those who would take unfair advantage. In most societies the government has taken at least some responsibility to insure equity of opportunity. For this reason, volumes of statutes have been enacted. Major issues that have ended with government control and intervention include harassment, discrimination, the environment, humanitarian issues, fair hiring practices, price fixing, bribery, false or deceptive advertising, and monopolizing. With a little thought, many more issues could be added to this list.

Issues regarding human rights have been the concern of businesses for many years. From state to state they are often handled differently. However, some issues are so important that the federal government has enacted legislation. Many issues have their basis in the guarantees afforded by the U.S. Constitution and thus receive careful scrutiny. Harassment and discrimination are among ethical issues that involve freedom of speech, equal protection, and the right to life, liberty, and the pursuit of happiness.

Business teachers should guide students to understand that when ethical principles are broken, the victim becomes deprived of some freedom or right and justice is set off-balance. The responsible parties are not only taking unfair advantage for their own gain but often become subject to prosecution under the law. People who violate ethical principles to gain some type of advantage in turn expect others to play fairly. Often they are incensed by those who display identical unethical behavior.

OTHER ETHICAL ISSUES

Other ethical issues that should be considered are those that are more subtle and often extremely difficult to legislate. These issues include truth-telling, honesty, justice, goodness, and fair play. Many laws have been enacted to require adherence to these basic ethical principles. For example, lying is illegal when the promise is reduced to writing in the form of a contract. The idea of a contract is based upon the legal responsibility for each party to uphold the ethical principle of truthfulness. An increasing number of laws are being enacted which control businesses and how they interact with each other and the public. Although these laws and regulations attempt to curtail unethical behavior, more than legislation is required to keep businesses ethical.

Whether a business is ethical or not is reduced to the principles followed by those who participate in that business. More often than not, laws are reactive in nature. They come about to curtail unethical practices after someone has been unfairly treated and are thus intended to bring fairness and justice back into balance. Ethical businesses must first consist of ethical workers. With each new legislative action comes the probability of further reduction of personal freedoms. Furthermore, in general, the law defines minimum levels of acceptable behavior. Just because an activity is legal does not imply that it is ethical. Before students enter the world of work they need to be presented with ethical issues and given the tools to solve ethical dilemmas. They should be taught how to think through ethical dilemmas and therefore must be presented with acceptable standards of measurement. This is not to say that all standards will be consistent; but students must be trained to think logically and critically—not to blindly accept the ethical standards of those around them.

INCORPORATING BUSINESS ETHICS INTO COURSE WORK

To teach students effectively about ethics requires instructors to have a certain level of expertise in the field. Teachers need to be able to identify fundamental ethical issues and have the tools to make ethical decisions. However, they should not impose their personal ethical views on students but should help students to carefully structure their own individual codes of ethics. Ethics education requires that individuals be encouraged and assisted in understanding their own perceptions and beliefs about what ethics is and what their own values are (Toffler, 1986). Teachers, however, should guide the student to realize and understand certain basically accepted ethical principles. A well-founded personal and business code of ethics is an invaluable asset for people of all ages and occupations.

Necessary realizations. The question arises about how business teachers should incorporate the study of ethics into their course work. First, the instructor must realize that just because people are ethical on a personal level does not mean that this will extend into their business practices. "One reason that making ethical choices in business is so often troublesome is that business ethics is not simply an extension of an individual's personal ethics. Just being a good person and, in your own view, having high ethical standards may not be enough to handle the tough choices of the workplace" (Ferrell & Gardiner, 1991).

A person with high personal moral and ethical principles may find her/himself working for an organization that supports or participates in ethically questionable practices. Such practices may include environmental issues, humanitarian issues, biochemical issues, and so on. As an example, should an ethical person continue to work for a company that makes items which eventually find their way into the chemical warfare arsenal of another country?

Secondly, teachers must realize that to discuss ethical issues is important, but not without risk. Parents may wish their children not to be introduced to concepts with which they do not agree. Some students may misrepresent the presentation of controversial issues as teacher directives rather than thought-provoking scenarios. Teaching students to think critically, individualistically, and ethically may cause more than a mild upset. Plato's dialogue "Crito" tells of Socrates' discussion with his students and friends regarding his decision to ingest the poison hemlock rather than face exile or execution because of his radical beliefs. This illustrates that the discussion of certain ethical issues is still not without its hazards.

Dangers. Certain dangers can be avoided if one has knowledge of what history has afforded. Many thought-provoking issues can be presented by using the writings of philosophers and ethicists. Begin reading the works of Plato, Socrates, Kant, Rand, Einstein, Russel, Bentham, Mill, Bradley, Callahan, Husserl, Kalin, etc. An understanding of the works of these persons will help teachers to present both sides of ethical issues in an intellectual manner. One must remember that students have the right to agree and disagree—the right to accept or not accept. They must not be coerced into supporting ideas that are contrary to their belief system. Students also must be relieved from the pressures imposed by peer groups. How the stage is set for student interaction is extremely important. In courses lower than college level, it may be in the instructor's best interest to make the administrators aware of controversial issues to be discussed. With this action, one will at least gain some idea of what type of support or lack thereof can be expected. Remember, intellectually growing experiences and ethical dilemma presentations will likely be charged with emotion and controversy. And, as so many ethical values have a religious basis, a teacher must use caution when challenging students with certain controversial ethical dilemmas.

Where-To-Begin Suggestions. One might wish to begin the discussion of business ethics by the introduction of several generally accepted ethical principles. Jacques Thiroux, in his book "Ethics, Theory and Practice" outlines several of these principles by which one can begin to make decisions regarding ethical dilemmas. These principles include: The Value of Life Principle, The Principle of Goodness or Rightness, The Principle of Justice or Fairness, The Principle of Truth Telling or Honesty, and the Principle of Individual Freedom. By learning and applying these principles to business situations, one can form a logical basis for developing a general business code of ethics and solving ethical dilemmas. Also, people come from many different perspectives. Instructors should have some understanding of how an ethical egoist thinks differently from a utilitarian or the difference between consequentialism and nonconsequentialism. Upon studying the works of ethical theorists, one quickly realizes that this field is packed with lively and controversial discussions.

After students have been introduced to some generally accepted principles of ethics, they should be presented with real-life scenarios where application of the aforementioned principles must be applied to come to some personal resolution of the dilemmas. Business scenarios and case studies may be either created by the teacher or student, or they can be found in many texts. Students should be encouraged to draw their own creative solutions to the dilemmas presented. These solutions can then be discussed and debated. Do not expect agreement, as a wide variety of alternative solutions will surface. However, certain general ethical constructs should apply such as principles of justice, goodness, fair play, truth telling, and the value of life.

Presentation methods may include small group discussions; assignments where students write opinions and give suggested solutions to ethical business dilemmas; presentations by professionals such as judges, attorneys, doctors, ministers, psychologists, counselors, business persons, human resource persons, etc.; and debates staged with persons representing various sides or approaches to an ethical issue. By bringing in discussion from the community, students will soon realize that community members do not agree on the solutions of many ethical dilemmas. Times will arise when ethical principles are in conflict. A dilemma may exist where the principle of truth telling and the principles of goodness and right to life may be in conflict. As an example, consider the dilemma mentioned earlier in this chapter regarding a business which makes parts that are eventually used in the creation of chemical weapons. Assume the business enters into a legal contract with a company without the knowledge that it is supplying parts used for unethical purposes. Upon discovery, should the business break the promises made in the contract or should it continue to supply items which may be used to wreak disaster and inflict unjust pain, suffering, and death upon innocent people?

Should one break the Principle of Truth-Telling to avoid breaking of the Goodness or Right-to-Life Principle? Are certain ethical principles more important than others? These questions may end in lively discussion and provoke students to think on a higher intellectual and ethical level. To learn to think on higher intellectual and ethical levels, students need to utilize critical-thinking and reasoning skills.

One method that teachers can incorporate is to introduce procedures for analyzing ethical dilemmas. These tools include: 1) analysis and identification of ethical problems, 2) identification of which ethical principles are involved and how they are being upheld or violated, 3) examination of the problem from different perspectives including opposing views, 4) identification of alternate solutions and the ramifications thereof, and 5) selection of one of the alternatives and discussing its strengths and weaknesses.

More defined methods for helping students learn to solve ethical dilemmas are available. Maddux and Maddux (1989) present a 10-step method for solving ethical problems. This method includes some of those mentioned above but incorporates other aspects such as legality, good business practices, image, competition, and probability of success. Jennings, in her book *Case Studies in Business Ethics,* (1993) carefully spells out an 11-step series of questions derived by business ethicist and professor Laura Nash for resolving ethical dilemmas. Again, these steps include several of the above, but also include questions such as, "How did this situation occur in the first place? What is your intention in making this decision? Whom could your decision injure? Will the position be valid over a long period of time?"

SUMMARY

In summary, business teachers have a responsibility to help students develop a personal and business code of ethics that can be used to help them make decisions that will affect their lives and welfare.

Students should form their own codes of ethics but must keep in mind that certain ethical standards are generally accepted in most "free" societies. Through the use of examples and scenarios, teachers can help students learn to think through moral and ethical dilemmas in a rational and critical manner. Some techniques of critical analysis such as identification of the problem, examination of the problem from all sides, identification of which principles are upheld or violated, identification of alternate solutions and their ramifications, and, finally, selecting a choice from the alternatives are methods used to help students reach ethical decisions.

In addition to traditional lecture methods, teachers may wish to incorporate discussions, debates, guest speakers, and case studies to help students practice ethical decision making.

Finally, students must be taught that not only are businesses in existence to make a profit, they ethically must provide, in exchange for the profit, an equitable product or service that has public value. Persons who enjoy lasting business success have formulated a set of ethical guidelines which serve as their navigation system. By following these guidelines they avoid many pitfalls. Responsible executives desire to gain the respect of the general public by using the powers they have for the common good (Petit, 1967).

Unethical behavior in a business setting may not only be illegal but it tips the scale of justice unevenly. Eventually, these scales must be brought back into balance. On the other hand, ethical behavior helps provide a level "playing field" for businesses, and the scale of justice remains in balance.

REFERENCES

Coen, W. (1995). *Ethics in thought and action: Social and professional perspectives* (p. 46). New York: Ardsley House.

Dunckel, J. (1989). *Good ethics good business: Your plan for success* (p. 2). Bellingham, WA: International Self-Counsel Press.

Ferrell, O., & Gardiner, G. (1991). *Pursuit of ethics: Tough choices in the world of work* (p. 3). Springfield, IL: Smith Collins.

Jennings, M. (1993). *Case studies in business ethics* (pp. xvi-xxviii). St. Paul: West.

Maddux, R., & Maddux, D. (1989). *Ethics in business: A guide for managers* (pp. 51-53). Los Altos, CA: Crisp Publications.

Petit, T. (1967). *The moral crisis in management* (p. 9). New York: McGraw-Hill.

Thiroux, J. (1995). *Ethics: Theory and practice* (5th ed.). Englewood Cliffs: Prentice-Hall.

Toffler, B. (1986). *Tough choices: Managers talk ethics* (p. 339). New York: John Wiley & Sons.

CHAPTER 19

Providing Instruction for and About International Business

Utah State University, Logan, Utah

People live in an increasingly interdependent world, a world strongly influenced by international businesses. Without international trade, residents of countries would be unable to fulfill many of their needs and wants, and their standards of living would decline. Businesses worldwide engage in the export and import of goods and services to satisfy their customers better. Businesses headquartered in developed countries transfer technology to developing countries, allowing their economically impoverished residents to modernize and to increase their standards of living.

Businesses sometimes relocate their operations abroad for various reasons, including lower wage costs and improved access to major markets, resulting in benefits for customers, new employees, and owners. Other businesses make acquisitions in foreign countries to obtain desired know-how, technology, and highly educated and trained personnel. Businesses from around the globe unite to form joint ventures to access new markets. Businesses invest in foreign operations in Eastern European and Third-World countries, using international trade as a tool for economic, social, and political development. In return for assuming the many risks associated with conducting business in the global marketplace, business owners expect to be rewarded with profits.

Increasing global interdependence requires that people better understand international business. International business helps societies to improve the lives of their citizens by fulfilling needs and wants through better access to a wide variety of goods and services. Directly or indirectly, international business provides employment for countless citizens. International business increases demand for highly educated and trained workers, some of whom actually transact business around the world and many of whom facilitate commerce in other ways. International business also stimulates demand for more sophisticated education for and about business.

Having easy access to relevant business education contributes toward the success of business persons in the competitive marketplace. Without properly educated and trained employees, businesses cannot operate well domestically or internationally. People are the critical resource who facilitate or impede the transaction of business at home and abroad. People must receive appropriate education for and about business, instruction that prepares them for work and for life in an interdependent world with a global marketplace. Consequently, business educators must revitalize their commitment to providing relevant education for and about business that acknowledges the increasingly important international dimensions of business.

This chapter provides general guidance about how business educators at all instructional levels and with varying specializations can provide relevant instruction for and about business with strong international dimensions.

PROVIDING RELEVANT INSTRUCTION FOR AND ABOUT INTERNATIONAL BUSINESS

What constitutes relevant instruction for and about business with strong international dimensions? What are the goals of international business education? What are appropriate strategies for incorporating germane international business content into the curriculum? What are some easily implemented but relevant instructional activities that can be used to strengthen international dimensions of education for and about business in common types of business-education offerings? Answers to such questions will be found by reading this section of the chapter.

Instructional goals. International business education has a variety of general goals whose sophistication level can be adjusted to reflect the backgrounds, needs, and preferences of students; the nature and placement level of the offered instruction; and the needs and preferences of employers and of society. The general goals of international business education include the following:

1. To develop awareness of the similarities and differences among cultures and countries and the profound influences that cultural variables have on international business

2. To develop understanding of the increasingly complex economic interdependence among trading nations worldwide

3. To develop appreciation of the contributions of international business to economic development, prosperity, and stability around the globe

4. To develop understanding of the major roles that international business fulfills within the global marketplace

5. To develop awareness of the wide range of career opportunities available in international business

6. To prepare selected individuals for employment at various levels within international businesses

7. To develop understanding of the complex economic, social, and political relationships among consumer and citizen decision-making at the local, regional, national, and international levels and the global marketplace

8. To prepare citizen-consumers to make prudent, responsible international business-related decisions that consider the complex relationships among the many publics to whom international businesses are accountable.

To achieve these comprehensive general goals, business educators must devise a thorough and complete sequence of instruction consisting of a variety of courses that emphasize relevant dimensions of international business while providing education for and about business.

Curriculum strategies. Business educators can use one of three basic curriculum strategies to provide relevant international business-related instruction:

(1) the infusion approach, (2) the specialized course(s) or program(s) approach, or (3) the combination approach.

THE INFUSION APPROACH. The infusion approach adds international content to existing courses. It is easy to implement since business educators add relevant international subject matter to their courses where it seems feasible to do so. As their comfort level with international content grows, so does their willingness to infuse that content into their instruction. Use of the infusion approach avoids sometimes complicated curriculum-approval processes. Further, it requires no additional faculty. One problem with the infusion approach is that it sometimes provides insufficient, piecemeal coverage of international topics. This shortcoming can be minimized by carefully developing and implementing a comprehensive department-wide plan for adding essential international content throughout all offerings.

THE SPECIALIZED COURSE(S) OR PROGRAM(S) APPROACH. The specialized course(s) or program(s) approach adds one or more courses in international general education and/or business education to the curriculum, in some cases creating an international option, emphasis, major, or minor. Students enrolled in such courses and programs are systematically exposed to relevant internationalized content in an environment where it constitutes the focal point of instruction. When taught by knowledgeable business educators with international experience, the instruction is apt to be thorough and realistic. Although educational institutions are increasingly implementing this approach—in some cases at the secondary level, especially in metropolitan areas—doing so may be beyond the resource constraints of many. Hiring qualified faculty, retraining existing faculty, developing and implementing the complex and often interdisciplinary curriculum, and similar factors price this approach beyond the financial means of some educational institutions. Limited student enrollments in such highly specialized and costly courses and programs can make justifying their existence challenging, especially in tough economic times.

Dr. Phillips High School Center for International Studies, Orange County Public Schools, Orlando, Florida, illustrates a specialized programs approach. Its magnet-school international studies program includes a core curriculum that incorporates culture and language themes through the broad discipline areas of art and humanities, social studies, foreign languages, and business. All students complete required courses in the four discipline areas, elective courses, and a practicum.

THE COMBINATION APPROACH. The combination approach tries to capture the simplicity, ease of implementation, and low cost of the infusion approach and the more realistic and sophisticated content of the separate course(s) or program(s) approach. Some envision potential cost savings from the combination approach because of its ability to provide adequate international content without extensive international course and program offerings, in effect deriving the benefits of both approaches while averaging their costs. Ensuring that all faculty contribute appropriately to the internationalization effort and coordinating the efforts of those who infuse and those who teach specialized courses and programs to yield a satisfactory international curriculum are major challenges of the combination approach.

The Department of Business Information Systems and Education, a unit within the College of Business at Utah State University, Logan, Utah, uses the combination approach. It requires all of its majors to take one college-wide core course in international business and one departmental international course, a course about global information systems management for its information-systems majors and a course about cross-cultural and international business communication for its business and marketing education majors. In addition, its faculty and those of other college and university departments infuse internationalized content into many of their courses.

Instructional activities. Creative business educators will discover that as they learn more about international business through such means as enrollment in international business-related courses and self-directed study, there are countless ways in which they can incorporate relevant international content into the instruction they provide. The remainder of this chapter provides a diverse sampling of ideas and activities to stimulate thinking about how relevant dimensions of international business can become part of every business education offering. The descriptions of instructional activities are presented in generalizable form so that business teachers can easily adapt them to their specific teaching situations. Information about evaluating the learning activities is also provided.

ACCOUNTING-RELATED COURSES. In accounting-related courses students should be aware that business transactions can be processed in a variety of monetary units besides the U.S. dollar. Some problems should involve the use of other currencies, whose values are reported in *The Wall Street Journal,* the business sections of other major newspapers, and other sources. Foreign-exchange-rate information is also available from local banks, which might get the current data from their head offices.

A typical problem might be structured similarly to this: If ABC Company, which is headquartered in your town, purchases 5,000 units of a product from a Birmingham, England, exported at 5 pounds 30 pence each, how many U.S. dollars should it send to pay for its purchases if there is no currency-conversion fee? The formula is number of units purchased times the unit price in the seller's currency times the amount of buyer's currency needed to purchase one unit of the seller's currency. There are 100 pence in one pound, and at the time of writing, $1.5635 purchased £1. The problem translates mathematically to $5,000 \times 5.3 \times 1.5635 = \$41,432.75$.

If a British company purchased 2,000 units of a product at $8.30 each from a U.S.A.-based company, then how many pounds should the British company remit? At the time of writing, £.63959 purchased $1. This problem translates mathematically to $2,000 \times 8.3 \times .63959 = £10,617.194$.

If only one exchange rate is known, the other one can be calculated by finding the reciprocal of the known rate. For example, if $1.5635 purchased £1, then $1/1.5635 = .63959 =$ the amount in pounds required to purchase one dollar; if £.63959 purchased $1, then $1/.63959 = 1.5635 =$ the amount in dollars required to purchase one pound.

The problems can be modified by changing the countries, currencies, and exchange rates. Students can calculate the amounts, add the applicable currency-conversion fee if desired for realism, and then record the appropriate debits and credits.

Business teachers should evaluate students' understanding of the currency-conversion process, their calculating the correct amounts in various currencies, and their recording the correct debits and credits.

BASIC BUSINESS- AND ECONOMICS-RELATED COURSES. Students in basic business- and economics-related courses should clearly understand the degree to which residents of the United States depend on other countries for the goods and services they consume. International businesses contribute to this interdependency by trading for goods and services around the world.

The extent of interdependency brought about by international business transactions is likely to become clear if business educators have students carefully conduct surveys of their residences and list all imported goods and services and their countries of origin. For example, in kitchens, students might find processed foodstuffs from various countries and perhaps fresh fruits and vegetables grown abroad. Students might find imported linens, china, crystal, silverware, and light fixtures in dining rooms. In living and family rooms, students might discover foreign-made electronics, fabrics, and decorative accessories. They might find imported bedding, clothing, and shoes in bedrooms. Perhaps some students will discover that one or more of the household automobiles are assembled primarily from parts made outside of the United States.

In class, business educators can have students share their lists and discover that households rely on imported products to differing degrees. The variation might reflect different cultural ties to various parts of the world, preferences for certain types of goods and services originating there, and superior reputations of particular countries for some types of goods and services. Business educators can add further international dimensions to the instruction by having students speculate about such matters as (1) what raw materials U.S. businesses sold to their partners abroad to pay for the finished goods the students discovered in their households, (2) what raw materials U.S. businesses purchased from their partners abroad and what finished products and services they sold to pay for them, and (3) how these international business transactions contributed to economic interdependency, development, prosperity, and stability around the globe.

Business educators can evaluate several dimensions of this activity, including the apparent student effort expended in conducting the survey and in participating thoughtfully in the related discussion.

BUSINESS COMMUNICATION-RELATED COURSES. Students in business communication-related courses need to be aware that not all cultures around the world rely on direct and explicit communication to the extent that many Western cultures do. Middle Eastern and Oriental cultures, for example, generally prefer to communicate much more indirectly and implicitly than Western cultures do. Although U.S. business persons typically communicate directly for most business purposes, they often prefer to deliver bad news indirectly through implication to avoid offending others.

Business instructors can have individuals or small groups of students research the relative directness or indirectness of written and oral business communication in a variety of cultures in developed and developing countries around the world. Business instructors might ask students to find out if there are notable exceptions to the prevailing cultural preferences such as the cited use of indirect communication for written and oral bad news within a U.S. business subculture that strongly values direct communication. Also, business instructors could ask students to uncover the prevailing cultural perception of silence in oral business communication. Business instructors might formulate such questions as "Is silence viewed as positive and constructive or as negative and destructive?" and "Why?" They can also encourage students to formulate generalizations about the directness and indirectness of communication from the gathered data. Business instructors might ask, "Do the discovered communication patterns relate to the locations of cultures and countries on the globe? If so, how?"

Business instructors can evaluate this activity based on the extent of the research effort; the quality and perhaps the quantity of retrieved information, keeping in mind that acquiring information about some cultures may be challenging; the degree of active participation in the related discussion; and the quality of thought exhibited in the related discussion.

COMPUTER LITERACY-RELATED COURSES. Students should realize that not all information input at a computer is written in the English language. Since other languages have a variety of diacritical marks and other symbols that are not used in the English language, students should be exposed to how these special characters can be keyed with most word-processing packages.

After explaining that other languages have a variety of diacritical marks and other symbols that are different than those for English, business educators can discuss and demonstrate the procedures for keying selected special marks and symbols with the word processing software package available in the classroom. Then they can provide students with copies of the appropriate special character set(s) and foreign-language copy. Foreign-language copy can be found in books and magazines at libraries and bookstores, on instruction sheets for products that are sold in countries with different official languages, and in the back portions of the in-flight magazines of international air carriers.

Business educators can evaluate this activity based on the use of appropriate keyboarding techniques, the accuracy of the input foreign-language copy, and perhaps the rate at which the foreign-language copy is input if students have multiple experiences with keyboarding foreign-language copy.

KEYBOARDING-RELATED COURSES. In keyboarding-related courses students should be exposed to the formatting practices of other major trading nations. When communicating with natives of other cultures and countries, students ought to realize that it is desirable—and sometimes essential—to prepare business correspondence the way other cultures sanction that it be done, not the American way.

After identifying the formatting standards of a foreign country with whom local businesses frequently trade, business teachers can present those formatting standards to their students, being careful to point out how those standards are like and unlike American standards for the same type of document. Then business teachers can have students keyboard a document from a model that conforms to the formatting standards of the foreign country.

After confirming that the students have formatted the document appropriately for the foreign destination, business teachers can assign a similar document from the textbook to be formatted by students for the same foreign destination. The sophistication of this activity can be increased by including special characters and/or foreign-language copy.

Business teachers can evaluate this activity based on the accuracy of the keyboarding, the degree of compliance with the document specifications of the selected foreign country, and the rate at which mailable documents are produced.

MARKETING EDUCATION-RELATED COURSES. Students should understand that products must be marketed in a culturally sensitive manner. Factors that persuade a consumer to purchase a product in one country may not persuade a consumer to purchase that same product in another country. Citizens of some countries such as Germany prefer that information about products be explicit and detailed. Citizens of some countries such as the United States like comparative information about products. When selecting products, citizens of some countries such as Japan depend less on explicitly conveyed product information and more on context or stored information such as product linkages with prestigious companies and celebrities.

After developing student understanding of the dominant communication preferences and patterns in the United States, business instructors can have students design a magazine advertisement for a global or universal product of their choice targeted toward some segment of the U.S. market. Next they can have students use library resources and interviews to gather information about the dominant communication preferences and patterns in one European and one non-European country of their choice. Then business instructors can have students adapt their U.S. advertisements to make them culturally appropriate for marketing the global or universal product in the selected European and non-European countries. Finally, business instructors can have students present their three culturally sensitive advertisements before the class, explaining the dominant communication patterns and preferences in each country, identifying the cultural adaptations they made to target each of the three distinct market segments, and responding to related questions from their peers.

Whether the activity is completed on an individual or small-group basis, business instructors can evaluate it on such bases as the quality and perhaps the quantity of the gathered research information, the appropriateness of the three advertisements for their targeted market segments, and the effectiveness of the related oral presentation.

MICROCOMPUTER APPLICATIONS-RELATED COURSES. One notable deficiency of many U.S. students is their limited knowledge about world geography. Geography-related information can be incorporated into data sets that students manipulate in microcomputer applications-related courses, in the process helping them to learn about the world beyond their localities where international business is transacted.

Business educators might ask their students to create a database of information related to major cities of the world. Educators can provide students with the database-component information or have them research that necessary information at a library, perhaps utilizing CD-ROM and other multimedia sources. Business educators could require students to create such fields as name of city, name of country, name of continent, most-current population, and the like, and then enter the appropriate data for either the specified cities, a predetermined number of world-class cities of their choice, or the 25, 50, or 100 cities worldwide with the largest populations. Business educators can then have students manipulate the databases they have created using the studied database commands, in the process becoming familiar with information about major world cities.

Business educators can evaluate such microcomputer applications-related aspects of the activity as the ability of students to design an appropriate database, to enter accurate information, and to manipulate the database to create specified records. With prior warning, business educators might offer bonus credit to students who correctly respond to related geography-based questions.

OFFICE OCCUPATIONS-RELATED COURSES. Students in office occupations-related courses ought to be exposed to the basics of international telephoning since sooner or later they will need to communicate with business persons residing in other countries.

Business teachers can easily add basic information about international long-distance telephoning to their telephone-related instruction. Business teachers might include information about the structure of the international telephone system, how to access the international telephone system, the use of appropriate country codes before routing (area or city) and local numbers, the determination of local times to ensure proper timing of telephone calls, the use of appropriate international dialing procedures and etiquette, and the like. Perhaps the educational institution or the local telephone company has equipment that business teachers can use so that their students can realistically simulate the placement of international long- distance telephone calls. Business teachers might then follow up with a brief case problem such as this one: "It is nearly 5 p.m., PST, almost quitting time, and Sam Welton is very frustrated. He has been trying unsuccessfully for the past six hours to place a long-distance telephone call to a prospective client, whose office is in Bristol, England. He has verified that he is using the correct international dialing procedures and the correct international access, country, city, and local telephone numbers. Each time he dials 011-44-117-956-4037, he hears a telephone ring repeatedly, but no one ever answers it. He has placed the call 22 times. Why do you think Sam Welton has not been able to communicate via telephone with the prospective client?"

In addition to factual information about international long- distance telephoning, business teachers could evaluate the appropriateness of the manner in which students place simulated international telephone calls. Teachers could also assess the ability of students to recognize that Sam Welton has placed all of his international telephone calls after normal business hours in Bristol, England, where the local time is eight hours ahead of PST time (for most continental Western European locations, the local time is one hour ahead of that in England, Greenwich Mean Time (GMT)). Further, teachers could evaluate the manner of case-problem presentation whether an oral or written format is used.

TEACHER EDUCATION-RELATED COURSES. Since each country has its own business-education system designed to meet the needs of its citizens, business teacher educators can have prospective and practicing business educators research the business-education teacher-preparation system of a country of their choice using library and people resources. Besides encouraging students to follow up on the research suggestions of a reference librarian who specializes in business and/or education matters, business teacher educators should encourage students to telephone or fax the education section or division of the embassy of the selected country, which may have experts who can provide detailed information and sometimes copies of relevant limited-circulation documents. The gathered information can then be organized into either a written or oral report that explains the business-education teacher-preparation system of the country.

Business teacher educators can evaluate the activity based on the quality and perhaps the quantity of the gathered information and the appropriateness of the presentation whether a written or oral format is selected.

TECHNOLOGY APPLICATIONS-RELATED COURSES. People ought to develop their abilities to locate information efficiently on a worldwide basis since having access to the right information empowers them in the global marketplace. Developing Internet competencies is one way to gain access to the increasingly important global information highway.

After acquainting students with what Internet is and how to use it to access sources of information outside of the United States, business instructors might require their students to gather information via Internet from students enrolled in similar technology-related courses in one or more foreign countries. Of course, U.S. business instructors should make prior arrangements with their peers abroad to ensure that sufficient numbers of Internet pen pals who are willing to communicate with their U.S. counterparts exist in other countries. The Internet communication might focus around a series of questions designed to elicit information for a report about such diverse matters as the peer and his or her culture, the nature of the business community in the peer's country, how citizens of the peer's country hold the international business community accountable for its actions, or the use of a specific technology in the peer's country.

Business instructors can evaluate such dimensions of the activity as the ability of students to devise relevant series of questions; to formulate, send, and receive Internet communications; and to organize the gathered information into an appropriate oral or written report as specified.

TRAINING AND DEVELOPMENT-RELATED COURSES. How a culture perceives the world influences how it prepares its members for work, which impacts the educating and training of prospective and practicing members of the business community.

Business teachers can have students use library and people resources to investigate how employees in a country of their choice are educated and trained for international business, including identification of mainstream practices and their frequency of use. Business teachers might ask students to ponder how these practices are like and unlike the mainstream practices in the United States. Further, they might ask students to speculate about why these practices have evolved to meet the particular needs of the international business community of the country. Then business teachers might have students write persuasive essays that argue that the training and development practices of the studied country are highly effective, effective, neutral, ineffective, or highly ineffective, supporting their arguments with documented facts from their research.

Business teachers can evaluate the essays based on the effectiveness of the presented arguments, the quality and perhaps the quantity of supporting documentation, and the degree to which the essays conform to generally accepted writing and formatting standards.

SUMMARY

All business educators, regardless of their instructional levels or areas of specialization, should provide relevant education for and about business that acknowledges the growing importance of international business. That instruction, carefully designed to meet one or more of the goals of international business education, ought to be thoughtfully implemented through the infusion approach, the specialized course(s) or program(s) approach, or the combination approach. International business-related content can be easily incorporated into offerings by creative business educators as suggested by the presented instructional activities. If for no other reasons than to preserve and to enhance their personal economic well-being, that of their fellow citizens, and that of the United States in the global marketplace, all business educators need to intensify their commitment to providing high-quality international business-related instruction.